This

Pain in the Critically Ill

Pain in the Critically Ill

Assessment and Management

Edited by
Kathleen A. Puntillo, RN, DNSc
Associate Professor of Nursing
Sonoma State University
Rohnert Park, California

Aspen Series in Critical Care Nursing
Kathleen Dracup, Series Editor

AN ASPEN PUBLICATION®
Aspen Publishers, Inc.
Gaithersburg, Maryland
1991

Library of Congress Cataloging-in-Publication Data

Pain in the critically ill : Assessment and management /
edited by Kathleen A. Puntillo.
p. cm. — (Aspen series in critical care nursing.)
Includes bibliographical references.
Includes index.
ISBN: 0-8342-0222-0
1. Intensive care nursing. 2. Pain—Treatment.
3. Critically ill—Psychology. I. Puntillo, Kathleen A. II. Series.
[DNLM: 1. Critical Care. 2. Nursing Assessment. 3. Pain—nursing.
WY 154 P144]
RT120.I5P25 1991
610.73'61—dc20
DNLM/DLC
for Library of Congress
91-4563
CIP

Aspen Publishers, Inc., grants permission for photocopying for limited personal or
internal use. This consent does not extend to other kinds of copying, such as copying
for general distribution, for advertising or promotional purposes, for creating new
collective works, or for resale. For information, address Aspen Publishers, Inc.,
Permissions Department, 200 Orchard Ridge Drive, Gaithersburg, Maryland 20878.

The authors have made every effort to ensure the accuracy of the information herein,
particularly with regard to drug selection and dose. However, appropriate information
sources should be consulted, especially for new unfamiliar drugs or procedures. It is the
responsibility of every practitioner to evaluate the appropriateness of a particular
opinion in the context of actual clinical situations and with due consideration to new
developments. Authors, editors, and the publisher cannot be held responsible for any
typographical or other errors found in this book.

Editorial Services: Ruth Bloom

Library of Congress Catalog Card Number: 91-4563
ISBN: 0-8342-0222-0

Printed in the United States of America

1 2 3 4 5

This book is lovingly dedicated to *Richard Puntillo*, my husband, in-house editor, and friend; and to *Lisa*, *Tim*, and *Darin*, my three greatest accomplishments.

Table of Contents

Contributors

Susan B. Christoph, RN, DNSc, CCRN
Colonel, U.S. Army Nurse Corps
Chief, Army Nurse Corps Division
USAREC Headquarters
Ft. Sheridan, Illinois

Marilyn Kuhel Douglas, DNSc, RN, CCRN
Assistant Research Nurse
Department of Physiologic Nursing
School of Nursing
University of California at San Francisco
San Francisco, California
Formerly, Nursing Educational Coordinator
Coronary Care/Cardiac Surveillance Units
Stanford University Medical Center

Katherine M. Vivenzo Dyble, RN, MA
Nurse Consultant and Nursing Unit
  Supervisor
Formerly, Clinical Nurse Specialist of Acute
  Pain Management Service
Stanford University Medical Center
Stanford, California

Julia Faucett, RN, PhD
Assistant Professor
Department of Mental Health, Community
  and Administrative Nursing
School of Nursing
University of California, San Francisco
San Francisco, California

Linda Sturla Franck, RN, MS
Director of Critical Care Nursing
Children's Hospital
Oakland, California

Nancy C. Molter, RN, MN, CCRN
Colonel, U.S. Army Nurse Corps
Chief Nurse
U.S. Army Institute of Surgical Research
Ft. Sam Houston, Texas

Heidi M. Morrison, RN, MS
Director, Children's Unit
Children's Hospital of the Kings Daughters
Norfolk, Virginia

Kathleen A. Puntillo, RN, DNSc
Associate Professor, Nursing
Sonoma State University
Rohnert Park, California

Lorie Wild, RN, MN
Clinical Nurse Specialist
Teaching Associate
Acute Pain Management
University of Washington Medical Center
University of Washington School of Medicine
Seattle, Washington

Diana J. Wilkie, PhD, RN
Assistant Professor
Department of Physiological Nursing
University of Washington
Seattle, Washington

Series Foreword

The woman was young to be facing death. At the age of 28 she had been diagnosed with Hodgkin's disease. She had multiple tests to confirm the diagnosis and was in the intensive care unit (ICU) after surgery. Although her prognosis was reasonably good, all the nursing staff felt a sense of sadness when talking about her. Patients like this woman provide uncomfortable reminders of our own vulnerability and sense of mortality. She was often tearful and visibly aware of the losses she had already encountered in her illness. I liked her and found myself developing a special bond with her during her stay in the ICU.

One morning while I was caring for her, I noticed that her intravenous line had infiltrated. I discontinued it and got the material to restart another line. She was extremely thin and had had numerous "sticks." As I was looking over her arms with their collection of bruises for a potential vein candidate, she told me how much she dreaded having the intravenous line restarted. I told her that I would try and make the procedure as painless as possible. Unfortunately, the attempt did not go smoothly. I could feel the vein, but the angiocath kept moving it to the side rather than puncturing the vein wall. I looked away from her arm for a moment to see how she was doing, and she said "How could you like me and still cause me this pain?"

Pain. It's a palpable presence in any critical care unit. Some of the pain is caused by disease—the pain of myocardial ischemia, ectopic pregnancy, a localized infection, cancer. Some of the pain is caused by nurses and physicians—the pain of surgical incisions, needle sticks, suctioning, dressing changes. Some of the pain is physical, some psychological. Often physical and psychological pain overlap in the critically ill, conscious patient, one playing off the other. Always it is hard for nurses to be the cause of someone's pain. Yet, in the invasive environment of the ICU nurses often must perform procedures that cause pain. Instead of comforting and supporting the critically ill person, nurses can add to the physical burden that the patient bears. Sometimes that burden is temporary; for example, a nurse may have to take an electrocardiogram before giving morphine sulfate to a patient with chest pain. Sometimes the burden is unavoidable; for example, a nurse may have to administer an injection of local anesthetic. But always for the patient in the ICU, the burden is there.

Given the nature of the men and women drawn to nursing as a profession, I believe that we have only two choices in dealing with the reality of the pain experienced by our patients. On the one hand, we can ignore it. We can harden ourselves to the reality of this pain and learn to block out patients' expressions of pain. When we stick the patient with a needle, we can make sure that we don't look at his or her face until we've completed the task. When we suction we can focus on the catheter and not let our eyes drift upward in case there are grimaces or tears. We can minimize patients' complaints of pain, telling ourselves that they are exaggerating its severity. We all have worked with nurses who have consciously or unconsciously chosen this alternative as a way to protect themselves emotionally from the constant exposure to pain.

On the other hand, we can learn everything we can about pain and the variables that affect it. We can look for new ways to reduce patients' pain and become assertive advocates for effective pain management. This book is written for those nurses who choose the latter course.

The book represents an important landmark in the critical care nursing literature. It is the first book about pain written specifically for the critical care practitioner. Its publication represents our growing awareness that the most negative aspect of hospitalization in the ICU for the majority of patients is pain.

The authors of the chapters in Part I provide us with the most recent scientific theory about the mechanisms of pain in the critically ill. They describe the ways in which pain contributes to the psychological stress experienced by the patient in the ICU. Readers will find the chapter on assessment techniques particularly helpful, being followed as it is by a discussion of the ways in which we should vary our assessment to account for cultural differences in the expression of pain. Accompanying chapters provide a superb summary of the knowledge that critical care nurses need to assess pain appropriately in the patients for whom they care.

Part II contains chapters on pain management, which include discussions of the important epidural and intrathecal methods of analgesia; these routes of pain medication delivery have proven to be highly effective in certain populations (e.g., postoperative patients).

In Part III, the authors discuss the patient populations that are most problematic for nurses: the very young, who cannot express their pain verbally; patients with burns; and patients who are recovering from surgery. Despite pain medication, critically ill patients often experience terrible pain. The material presented in this last section of the text provides important information about the best ways to prevent and treat pain in the critically ill.

Ultimately, every critical care nurse has had experiences like the one I related. We have caused pain when we wanted to comfort; we have been oblivious when we meant to be attentive. This book will help us be more aware of how and why our patients experience pain and what we can do to prevent and relieve that pain.

Kathleen Dracup
Series Editor
and
Professor
UCLA School of Nursing

Preface

Critically ill patients with widely diverse diagnoses and treatments have certain things in common. For example, the critically ill are treated in unique, often foreign, environments. Moreover, they receive intensive, highly competent, and almost continuous nursing care. Finally, for the most part these patients experience pain.

Scientific understanding of pain has grown tremendously over the past three decades. Unfortunately this knowledge base, gained from research and practice, has not yet been effectively disseminated to professional critical care nurses in a comprehensive manner. Specifically, no nursing text exists with a specific focus on pain in the critically ill. Not surprising, pain assessment and management practices of nurses have not kept pace with the increased knowledge base. This book corrects the situation. It presents current research and clinical knowledge of pain and its application to critically ill patients. Its purpose is to serve the educational needs of critical care clinicians and clinical nurse specialists as well as nurse educators and their students.

With pain and its alleviation as the focus of this book, three nursing concepts serve as themes throughout: (1) the *person* in pain; (2) the particular *environment* in which pain in critically ill patients is experienced; and (3) *nursing issues* related to the person in pain, including nursing diagnosis and management of pain and nursing's involvement in medical pain management. It is hoped that this book will make a significant contribution to both the professional critical care community and patients in pain.

Kathleen A. Puntillo, RN, DNSc

Acknowledgments

I would like to thank Ruth Bloom, Supervising Editor, Sandy Cannon, Senior Developmental Editor, and other members of the editorial staff at Aspen Publishers for their kind and able assistance in the development of this book. The contributors and I would also like to thank the following editors, clinicians, and investigators for their time and expertise in reviewing content in specific chapters: Jay B. Brodsky, MD; Michael J. Cousins, BS, MB, MD (STD), FFARACS, FFARCS; Margaret Doherty, BS, RN; Kathleen Dracup, DNSc, RN; Sharon Lamb, RN; Carol Landis, DNSc, RN; Davis B. Lawrence, BA; Julien Lipson, PhD, RN; Orla L. Loper, AD, RN; Kate McClure, MS, RN; Afaf Meleis, PhD, RN, FAAN; Peter Morrison; Virginia Olesen, PhD; Stella Petrakas-Pawson, MS, RN; Col. Vasil A. Pruitt, Jr., MD; Connie Robinson, PhD, RN; David Sanchez, PhD; Mary Smith; and Mary Tesler, MS, RN.

Part I

The Person with Pain in the Critical Care Environment

Chapter 1

Pain and Related Stress in the Critical Care Environment

Kathleen A. Puntillo

Critically ill patients either have or are at high risk for many life-threatening problems (American Association of Critical-Care Nurses, 1986). Often the critically ill are cared for in a hospital's specially designated critical care unit (CCU) with its unique environment. In these settings, patients receive the most advanced intensive care and at the same time are subjected to significant stress.

Indeed, pain itself can be a significant source of stress to patients. Furthermore, pain is one experience that many critically ill patients in a critical care environment—regardless of age, medical condition, or event—have in common. Such pain can result from injury or illness, or it may be iatrogenically induced.

This chapter serves as a brief introduction to the many issues of pain presented in this book. Because pain is such a subjective and personal experience, the chapter begins with patients' recollections of pain in the critical care setting. These stories highlight the impact that pain has on individuals. In addition, the chapter establishes the extent to which pain is identified as a significant stressor for critically ill patients and thus emphasizes the importance of pain reduction.

PATIENT RECOLLECTIONS OF THEIR PAIN EXPERIENCES

Clinicians know that patients in critical care units undergo major perceptual, sensory, and biological disruptions. For example, the perception of pain can come as a shock to patients regaining consciousness in an intensive care unit (ICU) after undergoing surgery. One such female surgical patient recalled feeling intense pain under these circumstances:

> When you are coming out of it [the anesthetic], you are not really cognizant of what you are doing, and you will move things that are better left unmoved. You are going to give yourself pain. You are not aware

where [you are] or what to do; you just know your mouth is dry, you are foggy in your head, and you're not sure it's over. You are going to move something. I learned, "Oh, it hurts; it hurts"; and I'm sure you then tense up . . . and it makes the whole damn thing worse.

When this woman was asked how she communicated her pain to the ICU staff, she said that they should "just assume that it hurts; it's bound to hurt."

Uninterrupted sleep is virtually impossible in a CCU partly because of necessary procedures constantly being performed and the generally high activity and noise levels. Pain itself has been identified as a leading cause of disrupted sleep in critical care patients (Jones, Hoggart, Withey, Donaghue, & Ellis, 1979).

As a case in point, a physician who underwent his second mitral valve replacement recollected his personal ordeal with postoperative pain and sleep (Donald, 1976):

I would be a liar if I did not straight away admit that this [pain] defies description. For the first week after operation the sensory system is presumably swamped by the sheer magnitude of the pain. I found pain and time, especially at night, to be bad companions. (p. 53)

To make environmental and other painful assaults on patients more tolerable, hypnotics, sedatives, and analgesics are prescribed. In spite of analgesic use, however, patients experience pain from procedures that is often not well controlled. For example, a 52-year-old man who had undergone four-vessel coronary artery bypass graft surgery described his recollection of endotracheal tube suctioning (Puntillo, 1990):

I would be stretched out like a board, gagging and coughing, and the pain was intense. I felt taut and tense. The coughing is what made it so painful. It makes your whole body go rigid into the cough, and that was excruciating.

Pain experienced from chest tube manipulation or removal is also particularly disturbing to CCU patients (Paiement, Boulanger, Jones, & Roy, 1979). The following is how a 31-year-old woman with aortic valve replacement graphically described her feelings during chest tube removal (Puntillo, 1990):

When they pulled that out, I thought they were pulling all my guts out. They told me to take a deep breath during the procedure, but when you have just had heart surgery, you can't take a deep breath.

Sometimes the more capable and communicative critical care patients learn ways to exert some degree of control over their pain by intervening on their own behalf with critical care health professionals. For example, one woman explained after her thoracic surgery:

> When you are in pain, it seems like forever [to receive analgesics]. Many times you can tell a nurse that you have pain, and she'll go out to get you something and she'll get waylaid. So, I have learned—and you learn it in ICU—to tell everyone who is in your line of vision [about the pain].

PSYCHOLOGICAL STRESS OF PAIN IN CRITICALLY ILL PATIENTS

Such patient scenarios reinforce the special need for health professionals to explore in depth the dimensions, meanings, and consequences of pain in their patients. One potential consequence is psychological stress.

Surprisingly, pain in critical care patients has been the central focus of little research. Nevertheless, it has been suggested that critically ill patients in pain are more vulnerable to other critical care environmental stressors, such as ICU sensory overload (Baker, 1984), psychological discomfort (Nadelson, 1976; Noble, 1979), and even delirium (McKegney, 1966; Nadelson, 1976). Research, however, has not yet supported causative links among pain, stress, and impaired psychological responses such as disorientation, hallucinations, and paranoid delusions (Wilson, 1987). Even so, numerous investigators have explored specific factors in the critical care setting that cause patients substantial stress. Patients consistently implicate pain as a major stressor even when given a choice of numerous other potential ICU environmental stressors (Ballard, 1981; Nastasy, 1985; Wilson, 1987). In fact, the only thing causing a group of 22 surgical patients more stress than pain was being tied down by tubes (Ballard, 1981).

Sometimes patients have difficulty recalling specifics about their ICU stays, such as how long they had spent in a unit, the difference between night and day, how much sleep they got, or even being intubated (Jones et al., 1979; Paiement et al., 1979). The memory of pain is not easily erased, however. Pain has been identified by patients as both their greatest ICU worry (Jones et al., 1979) and their worst ICU memory (Paiement et al., 1979). It behooves critical care clinicians to help eliminate these worries and memories through more aggressive interventions for pain.

CONCLUSION

All that has been presented in this chapter and, in fact, most of what is known about the psychological effects of pain in critically ill patients has been learned from adult patient narratives. We know, however, that neonates and children in critical care environments are not immune to pain and its potentially negative consequences. Their special problems are presented in Chapters 9 and 10.

Nursing has a major role in pain assessment and alleviation, actions that influence the health status of patients. More than 100 years ago, Florence Nightingale advised "what nursing has to do . . . is put the patient in the best condition for nature to act on him" (Nightingale, 1969, p. 133). Greater attention to pain, and its speedy alleviation, in all critical care patient populations are essential prerequisites of the creation of such a healing environment.

REFERENCES

American Association of Critical-Care Nurses. (1986). *AACN position statement: Patient classification in critical care nursing.* Newport Beach, CA: Author.

Baker, C.F. (1984). Sensory overload and noise in the ICU: Sources of environmental stress. *Critical Care Quarterly, 6,*66–79.

Ballard, K. (1981). Identification of environmental stressors for patients in a surgical intensive care unit. *Issues in Mental Health Nursing, 3,* 89–108.

Donald, I. (1976). At the receiving end. *Scotland Medical Journal, 21,* 49–57.

Jones, J., Hoggart, B., Withey, J., Donaghue, K., & Ellis, B.W. (1979). What the patients say: A study of reactions to an intensive care unit. *Intensive Care Medicine, 5,* 89–92.

McKegney, F.P. (1966). The intensive care syndrome: The definition, treatment and prevention of a new "disease of medical progress." *Connecticut Medicine, 30,* 633–636.

Nadelson, T. (1976). The psychiatrist in the surgical intensive care unit. *Archives of Surgery, 111,* 113–117.

Nastasy, E.L. (1985). Identifying environmental stressors for cardiac surgery patients in a surgical intensive care unit. *Heart & Lung, 14,* 302–303.

Nightingale, F. (1969). *Notes on nursing.* New York: Dover.

Noble, M.A. (1979). Modifying the ICU environment. In M.A. Noble (Ed.), *The ICU environment: Directions for nursing* (pp. 303–323). Reston, VA: Reston Publishing.

Paiement, B., Boulanger, M., Jones, C.W., & Roy, M. (1979). Intubation and other experiences in cardiac surgery: The consumer's views. *Canadian Anaesthetists' Society Journal, 26,* 173–180.

Puntillo, K.A. (1990). The pain experience of intensive care unit patients. *Heart & Lung, 19,* 526–533.

Wilson, V.S. (1987). Identification of stressors related to patients' psychologic responses to the surgical intensive care unit. *Heart & Lung, 16,* 267–273.

RECOMMENDED READING

Bryan-Brown, C.W. (1986). Development of pain management in critical care. In M.J. Cousins & G.D. Phillips (Eds.), *Acute pain management* (pp. 1–19). New York: Churchill Livingstone.

Chyun, D. (1989). Patients' perceptions of stressors in intensive care and coronary care units. *Focus on Critical Care, 16,* 206–211.

Loper, K.A., Butler, S., Nessly, M., & Wild, L. (1989). Paralyzed with pain: The need for education. *Pain, 37,* 315–316.

McCaffery, M. (1984). Pain in the critical care patient. *Dimensions of Critical Care Nursing, 3,* 323–325.

Radwin, L.E. (1987). Autonomous nursing interventions for treating the patient in acute pain: A standard. *Heart & Lung, 16,* 258–265.

Chapter 2

The Physiology of Pain and Its Consequences in Critically Ill Patients

Kathleen A. Puntillo

Pain is an unpleasant and unusually complex perceptual experience that is most often associated with tissue damage and negative emotions. The perception of pain is the culmination of noxious sensory information that has been transmitted to and integrated and modulated in the central nervous system (CNS) by numerous physiological and psychological influences. As a result of these complex processes and influences, pain becomes an individualized, private experience.

This chapter synthesizes current knowledge of pain physiology and provides a physiological foundation for a better understanding of and knowledge for assessing the pain experience of critical care patients, choosing and evaluating therapeutic interventions for patients in pain, and appreciating the potential negative consequences of unrelieved pain.

INITIATION AND TRANSMISSION OF NOXIOUS INFORMATION

Pain is a perceptual process. The initiating event in the perception of pain is the stimulation of nociceptors. These are receptors sensitive to tissue-damaging or potentially tissue-damaging stimuli. Three potential peripheral sources of noxious impulses exist: cutaneous, deep somatic, and visceral tissues. For example, during a thoracotomy procedure for a lung resection, noxious impulses originate from the cutaneous surgical skin incision and from deep somatic structures such as resected thoracic muscles and the parietal pleura. Likewise, certain abdominal procedures generate similar cutaneous and deep somatic impulses as well as visceral impulses that are due to retraction and pressure applied to abdominal organs.

9

The Nature of Cutaneous Pain

Cutaneous, or superficial somatic, pain begins with activation and sensitization of skin receptors by a noxious event and leads to transmission of noxious signals to the CNS. Figure 2-1 depicts various biochemical substances that may interact with skin receptors. Hydrogen ions, bradykinins, histamine, and potassium ions (K^+)

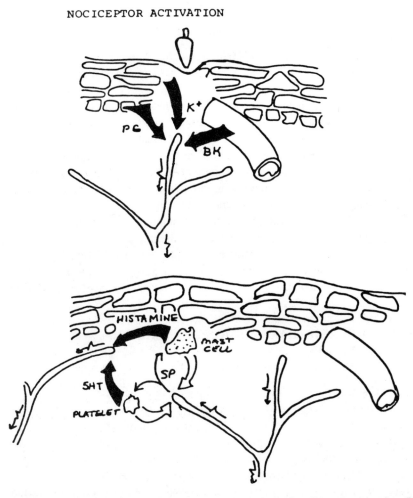

Figure 2-1 Biochemical mediators of nociception. PG = prostaglandins; K^+ = potassium ions; BK = bradykinins; 5HT = serotonin; SP = substance P. *Source*: From *Pain: Mechanisms and Management*, (p. 36), by H.L. Fields, 1987, New York, NY: McGraw-Hill, Inc., Copyright 1987 by McGraw-Hill, Inc. Modified by permission.

are specific substances that activate cutaneous nociceptors on their release from damaged cells (Levine, 1984). Prostaglandins, which are formed from arachadonic acid as a result of cell membrane injury, serotonin (5HT) released from platelets, and substance P released from peripheral nerve terminals, further sensitize nociceptors (Fields, 1987).

Impulse Generation in a Nerve

Substances such as hydrogen ions, K^+, and bradykinins bind to nerve receptors and depolarize the nerve membrane, thus generating an action potential. Depolarization is due to an increase in sodium ion (Na^+) permeability across the cell membrane and cellular influx of Na^+. Repolarization of the membrane results from closing NA^+ channels and opening K^+ channels, thereby making the cell membrane permissive to K^+ efflux. Hence the cell membrane returns to a resting potential. Depolarizations which lead to action potentials cause impulse generation along a nociceptive nerve fiber.

Local anesthetics used for pain control act on the axons of these nerve fibers. That is, local anesthetics inhibit Na^+ influx across the axonal membrane, preventing depolarization and the creation of an action potential. In short, a neural blockade is created (Mather & Cousins, 1986).

Nociceptive Nerve Fiber Types

Uninterrupted cutaneous afferent noxious impulses are transmitted through small-diameter myelinated Aδ fibers and smaller-diameter unmyelinated C fibers (Meyer, Campbell, & Raja, 1985). Pain believed to be transmitted through Aδ fibers is reported as sharp and fast in nature. In contrast, C fibers are believed to transmit pain that is described as diffuse, dull, and delayed (Torebjork, 1985).

Human studies show that cutaneous injuries lead to hyperalgesia, or an increased pain sensitivity of the skin. Hyperalgesia occurs when the threshold at which pain is sensed is lowered. There is also a greater painful response to stimuli that are usually nonpainful. This is predominantly due to Aδ fiber activity (Bonica, 1953; Lynn, 1977; Meyer et al., 1985). For example, in a postoperative patient the threshold for pain may be reduced as a result of cutaneous hyperalgesia at the wound site. Because pain receptors have been sensitized by chemical mediators, painful impulses can arise from the wound through ordinarily nonpainful stimuli such as touching and stretching.

In sum, cutaneous pain results from activation and sensitization of skin or superficial somatic receptors by chemical substances. It is transmitted by both Aδ and C fibers. Cutaneous pain is usually easy to localize. Finally, hyperalgesia frequently accompanies cutaneous pain.

The Nature of Deep Somatic Pain

Deep somatic pain is generated from noxious stimulation of subcutaneous structures such as fascia, tendons, joints, ligaments, and muscles (Bonica, 1953) and is sometimes associated with muscle ischemia (Mense & Stahnke, 1983). Deep somatic receptors in cat muscle, for example, have responded to chemicals such as bradykinin and histamine, which reportedly produce pain in humans. This noxious sensation is carried by unmyelinated C fibers (Mense & Schmidt, 1974) and is described as dull and diffuse (Torebjork, 1985).

Persistent deep somatic pain is more difficult to localize than cutaneous pain. It is also associated with autonomic nervous system (ANS) responses such as vasoconstriction, nausea, vomiting, and sweating. Somatic pain also may be accompanied by muscle spasms (Inman & Saunders, 1944). These characteristics of deep somatic pain are more similar to visceral pain than to cutaneous pain.

The Nature of Visceral Pain

Visceral pain is experienced with myocardial ischemia and infarction and also may accompany injury to internal body organs, as occurs with surgery or trauma. Less is known about visceral pain than about cutaneous pain, especially in humans, because of the difficulty in developing appropriate experimental models for study (Fields, 1987). It appears that a single visceral receptor type responds to several different types of stimuli (Leek, 1977), such as stretching, tension, pressure, chemicals, contractions, and ischemia (Cervero, 1985, 1988).

There are fewer visceral fibers (<7%) than fibers of somatic origin (>90%) terminating in the spinal cord (Cervero, 1985). Most of the visceral fibers believed to carry noxious sensation are C fibers, the type associated with dull, diffuse pain sensation. Thus a person's difficulty in localizing and describing visceral pain may be due in part to the small number and specific type of visceral fibers. Many of these visceral fibers travel to the spinal cord with sympathetic nervous system (SNS) fibers and T-1 to L-2 spinal nerves (Ganong, 1985). This may partially account for the fact that visceral pain is frequently accompanied by intense SNS and motor reflexes, indicating increased CNS excitability (Cervero, 1988).

Summary

In summary, pain can originate from various body locations, such as skin, deep somatic structures, and viscera. Current research indicates that the chemical transmitters and mediators of pain from the different locations, such as histamine, bradykinins, and prostaglandins, are the same regardless of pain site. The deeper the pain, however—that is, if the pain originates in deep somatic and visceral tissues rather than cutaneous tissues—the more diffuse will be its description regarding location and quality. This may be explained by the preponderance of unmyelinated C-fiber transmission from deep somatic and visceral areas and by the phenomenon of referral to other body parts associated with deeper pain. Finally, deep somatic and visceral pain more frequently activate the ANS than cutaneous pain. Clearly, detailed assessment practices that help identify pain sources will allow treatment interventions that are appropriate to the specific type of pain experienced.

SPINAL CORD COMMUNICATION AND INTEGRATION

Primary afferent Aδ and C fibers originating in cutaneous, deep somatic, or visceral structures terminate in the layers, or laminae, of spinal cord gray matter (Fig. 2-2). Aδ fiber terminals have been located in lamina I, and their branches also have been traced to lamina V of the spinal cord dorsal horn. Most C fibers terminate in spinal cord lamina II, the substantia gelatinosa. This is a dorsal horn site that resembles a gelatinous substance (hence its name) and contains numerous interneurons (Iggo, Steedman, & Fleetwood-Walker, 1985). The functions of interneurons allow for communication and integration of sensory information as well as modulation of that information at the spinal cord level.

Secondary neurons originate in the spinal cord and receive primary afferent (peripheral) noxious input. Some secondary neurons in the spinal cord receive only somatic noxious input. Other neurons, however, receive input from both visceral and somatic primary afferents (Fields, Meyer, & Partridge, 1970). That is, noxious input converges from different peripheral sources (Fig. 2-3). This convergence of somatic and visceral afferent fibers on the same spinal cord cells helps explain in part the phenomenon of referred pain (Fields, 1987). That is, individuals may localize pain to the somatic structure innervated by the converged neuron rather than the visceral structure, which may in fact be the source of pain. For example, under experimental conditions saline injected into rectus abdominis muscles elicits severe abdominal pain as well as slight pain in the back. In addition, intercostal injections elicit moderate pain in both the front and the back of the subject (Kellgren, 1937–38). Clinically, myocardial infarction pain originating in heart muscle is described by patients as being located in the arm, jaw, or neck. These findings underscore the need for detailed assessment of the quality and location of patient pain before treatment measures are undertaken because cursory assessments may overlook characteristics of deep somatic or visceral pain.

TRANSMISSION OF NOXIOUS INFORMATION TO HIGHER CENTERS

Willis (1985) and Fields (1987) described tract systems implicated in nociceptive transmission from spinal cord to higher centers. Three tracts contribute

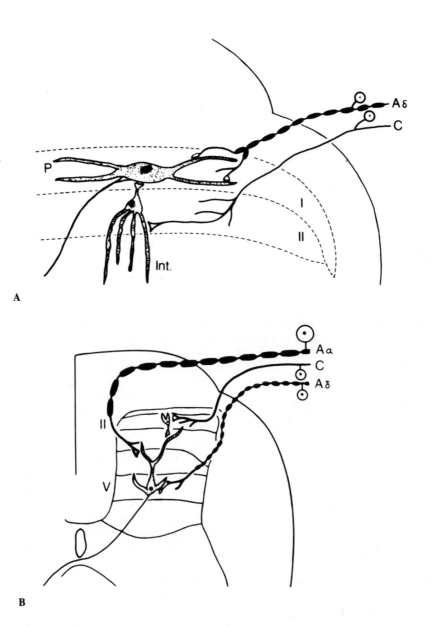

Figure 2-2 A, Nociceptive input to spinal cord lamina I is predominantly through A-delta fibers. C fibers transmit nociception to lamina II. **B,** Non-nociceptive fibers such as A-alpha as well as nociceptive A-delta and C fibers synapse with spinal cord interneurons. *Source*: From *Pain: Mechanisms and Management*, (p. 55), by H.L. Fields, 1987, New York, NY: McGraw-Hill, Inc., Copyright 1987 by McGraw-Hill, Inc. Reprinted by permission.

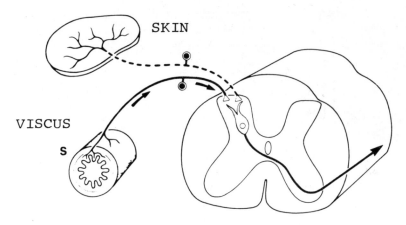

Figure 2-3 Hypothesis of referred pain. Visceral afferent nociceptors (S) converge on same pain-projection neurons as afferents from somatic structures (such as skin) in which pain is perceived. *Source*: From *Pain: Mechanisms and Management*, (p. 91), by H.L. Fields, New York, NY: McGraw-Hill, Inc., Copyright 1987 by McGraw-Hill, Inc. Reprinted by permission.

significantly to the transmission process. The first of these, the spinothalamic tract (STT, sometimes referred to as the neospinothalamic tract), has been identified as a major suprasegmental projection system. In primates, STT cells found to originate from laminae I and V have been shown to be responsive to various types of noxious stimulation of skin, muscle, and visceral structures. Input to STT cells is both direct and indirect. Direct input is from primary afferent peripheral fibers. Indirect input uses interneurons from lamina II to ascending STT neurons in lamina I (Price, Hayashi, Dubner, & Ruda, 1979; see Fig. 2-2). Finally, STT neuronal tracts ascend from the spinal cord to contralateral termination sites in the thalamus.

The spinoreticular tract (SRT) is the second major nociception tract and is sometimes referred to as the paleospinothalamic tract. The SRT has cells of origin in spinal cord laminae VII and VIII. These SRT cells project to ipsilateral or contralateral regions of brainstem reticular formation as well as other areas in the brain and subsequently project to termination sites in the thalamus. Noxious information from this area then ascends to higher centers through the next order of neurons.

The third suprasegmental projection system is the spinomesencephalic tract. This tract, like the STT, has cells of origin in laminae I and V and projects to midbrain reticular formation and midbrain periaquaductal gray (PAG). The PAG is an immensely important site of endogenous pain modulation and is discussed later in this chapter. These tracts and some of their destination sites are diagrammed in Fig. 2-4.

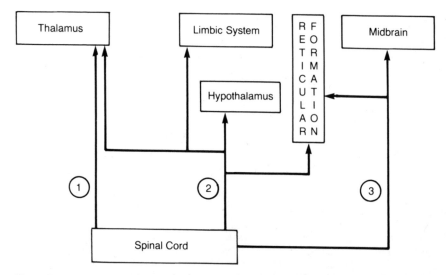

Figure 2-4 Diagram showing projection tracts from spinal cord to brain centers. Final pathways will be to cortex where pain perception occurs. *1*, Neospinothalamic tract system; *2*, Paleospinothalamic tract system; *3*, Spinomesencephalic tract system.

PERCEPTION OF PAIN

The actual perception of pain is believed to be a cortical process. The particular sites of cortical involvement have not been clearly identified, however, primarily because of the difficulty of experimentation (Andersson & Rydenhag, 1985). Nevertheless, evidence clearly suggests the involvement of many cortical areas in pain perception since introduction of a painful stimulus can lead to widespread cortical blood flow (Lassen, Ingvar, & Skinhoj, 1978). Also, even extensive cortical lesions do not consistently eliminate pain perception (Andersson & Rydenhag, 1985).

Some neurons associated with noxious stimuli have been localized in monkey brains to within and posterior to the central sulcus (Kenshalo & Isensee, 1983), a specific part of the sensory cortex. One group of these neurons had discrete, well-localized, contralateral sites of origin. Because of this finding, it was postulated that these neurons may be associated with the sensory-discriminative aspects of pain. Sensory aspects refer to identification of particular pain qualities (e.g., throbbing, burning, or sharp), whereas discriminative aspects refer to the ability specifically to localize and describe pain.

Another group of neurons terminating in the cortex has widespread sites of origin. Therefore, it is believed that neuronal stimulation from these sites may participate in general cortical arousal activities, motor adjustments, and perhaps the motivational-affective (emotional) nature of pain (Kenshalo & Isensee, 1983). Although the cortical neuronal circuitry involved with pain perception has not been well established, the importance of the cortex to pain is obviously immense. It is widely acknowledged that, functionally, the cortex plays a major role in perception and evaluation of pain (Melzack & Casey, 1968) and in influencing the psychological trauma and fear that may accompany pain (Bonica, 1953).

THE ROLE OF CONSCIOUSNESS IN PAIN PERCEPTION

Consciousness is a necessary prerequisite of the perception of pain. Consciousness is the level of awareness where thought processing and feeling occur (Vander, Sherman, & Luciano, 1990). A noxious sensation becomes pain when that sensation reaches conscious levels (Fields, 1987). Before this time, considerable processing and modifying of the sensation occurs all along the neural route (Livingston, 1978). In fact, a balancing of pain transmission and pain inhibition occurs.

It is possible that a critical care patient with altered levels of consciousness may respond reflexively to a noxious stimulus and yet not perceive pain. The reflex response to nociception can be at the spinal cord level only, as evidenced, for example, by the withdrawal of a leg in response to a pinprick stimulus. In contrast to nociception, pain requires perceptual activity. Numerous factors can alter a critical care patient's level of consciousness and, therefore, influence pain perception. These factors may include neurologic conditions, such as metabolic encephalopathy or cerebral ischemia, or the effects of numerous pharmacological agents, such as anesthetics, analgesics, hypnotics, or sedatives. Determining whether it is nociception or pain that the individual is experiencing presents a challenge in critical care patient assessment (see Chapter 4 for further discussion).

THE BODY'S ENDOGENOUS ANALGESIA SYSTEMS

In 1969, Reynolds discovered that, when a particular area of a rat's midbrain was electrically stimulated, the rat became profoundly analgesic. The analgesia was such that the scientist was able to perform abdominal surgery on the awake rat with no signs of pain to the animal. This and other studies (e.g., Mayer, Wolfle, Akil, Carder & Liebeskind, 1971) stimulated further research to locate the brain sites and substrates responsible for this endogenous analgesia, which has effects similar to those of exogenous opiate analgesia. Since that time, there has been an explosion of research in the field of endogenous analgesia systems. Two endogenous analgesia systems are categorized as opioid and nonopioid systems. The former system is mediated by endogenous opioid substances, and the latter is mediated by nonopioid substances (the monoamines).

Biochemical Substances of the Endogenous Opioid Analgesia System

Biochemical substances that mediate the endogenous opioid system are generically classified as endorphins, which are endogenous morphinelike substances. There are three major groups of endorphins: β-endorphins, enkephalins, and dynorphin. β-Endorphins are found predominantly in the hypothalamus and the midbrain's PAG (Fields, 1987; Terenius, 1984), the area of Reynolds' 1969 experiment. Axons containing β-endorphin travel from hypothalamus to the PAG in the midbrain. It is not certain how and to what extent β-endorphin contributes to pain control (Basbaum & Fields, 1984; Levine, 1984); but it appears to function like morphine (Chapman & Bonica, 1983). Some data show that β-endorphins are released as a result of acupuncture and acupuncturelike transcutaneous electrical stimulation. Other conflicting research findings exist, however (Chapman & Bonica, 1983), and further research is necessary.

The enkephalins, methionine enkephalin and leucine enkephalin, are located in neurons of PAG, medulla, spinal cord (Basbaum & Fields, 1984), vagal nuclei, hypothalamus, and limbic system (Mountcastle, 1980). Methionine enkephalin degrades rapidly and thus is a weak analgesic (Bunney, Pert, Klee, Costa, Pert, & Davis, 1979). Therefore, analgesic analogues of methionine enkephalin may not be clinically useful drugs.

Dynorphin, the third endorphin, is found in substantia nigra, PAG, medulla, and spinal cord. The analgesic activity of dynorphin is not yet clear (Fields, 1987), so that its clinical usefulness remains to be determined.

Endogenous Opioid Receptors

Opioid receptors are stereospecific. That is, they have a unique conformation that allows attachment to particular opioid molecules, or ligands (Goldstein, 1976). Attachment of an opioid to a receptor appears to lead to decreased Na^+ conductance and a blocking of neuronal transmission of pain (Goldstein, 1976). Increased K^+ conductance, leading to hyperpolarization of the cell, as well as decreased calcium conductance across the cell membrane also may block neural transmission (Jaffe & Martin, 1988).

A number of opioid receptors have been identified, including μ, δ, ϵ, σ and κ (Pasternak, 1988). Opioid receptors μ, δ, and κ have been associated with inhibition of nociception (Sabbe & Yaksh, 1990). Most opiate analgesics, such as morphine, fentanyl, alfentanil, and sufentanil, attach to μ receptors (Veselis, 1988; Zaloga, Hostinsky, & Chernow, 1984). In fact, it is believed that there are two types of μ receptors, type 1 and type 2. μ_1 receptors are associated with analgesia, and μ_2 receptors appear to mediate the respiratory depressive effects of opioids (Pasternak, 1988).

Endogenous Opioid Pathways

Basbaum and Fields' 1984 review of pain-modulating circuits is one widely accepted model of the endogenous opioid system. Figure 2-5 depicts some of the anatomical structures of this system. The first circuit involves the tract from PAG. Neural input to PAG is from cortex, hypothalamus, brainstem, and other brain sites. Efferent fibers are from PAG, nuclei in the rostroventral part of the medulla, such as the nucleus raphe magnus, and medullary reticular formation, which descend to the spinal cord.

Figure 2-6 diagrams a probable method of spinal cord endogenous opioid activity. Descending supraspinal neuron fibers from the PAG and the medulla's raphe magnus can inhibit nociceptive transmission in the spinal cord. This is due to the release of enkephalins from the descending neurons in the spinal cord. These released enkephalins then attach to opioid receptors on a nociceptive neuron and act to inhibit the release of a "pain neurotransmitter," such as substance P, from primary afferent neurons. In this way, synaptic communication between the primary afferent neuron originating in the injured tissue and the secondary neuron originating in the spinal cord is inhibited. Thus there is probably primary afferent presynaptic inhibition (see Fig. 2-6), with the inhibitor being endogenous opioids such as enkephalins (Fields, 1987).

Biochemical Substances and Pathways of the Endogenous Monoamine System

Monoamines such as serotonin and norepinephrine modulate a nonopioid form of endogenous analgesia. This second analgesia system involves medullary and pontine nuclei. These nuclei receive input from neurons originating in PAG (from above) and spinal cord fibers (from below). Descending pathways from these nuclei travel in the dorsolateral part of the spinal cord to the dorsal horn. Serotonin is believed to be a major pain-inhibiting neurotransmitter of medulla–to–spinal cord neurons. In fact, tricyclic antidepressants such as amitriptyline, which prolong the actions of serotonin by blocking its neuronal reuptake, are used to treat chronic pain (Butler, 1984).

Norepinephrine is contained in neurons that are located in the pons and project to spinal cord dorsal horn. Norepinephrine attaches to spinal cord α_2-adrenergic receptors. Application of clonidine, an α_2 agonist, leads to inhibition of nociception (Fields, 1987).

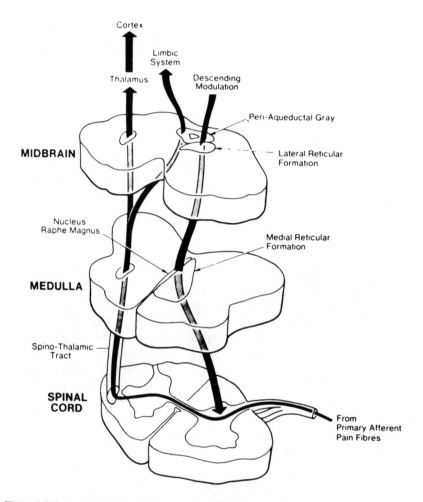

Figure 2-5 Descending pain modulation is initiated in the periaquaductal gray matter and in medullary sites such as the nucleus raphe magnus and reticular formation. *Source*: From *Acute Pain Management*, (p. 26) by M.J. Cousins and G.D. Phillips (Eds.), 1986, New York, NY: Churchill Livingstone, Inc. Copyright 1986 by Churchill Livingstone, Inc. Reprinted by permission.

Finally, a single medullary neuron can contain more than one transmitter, such as serotonin and substance P or serotonin and enkephalin. The action of a particular neuron would, therefore, vary depending on the specific transmitter released.

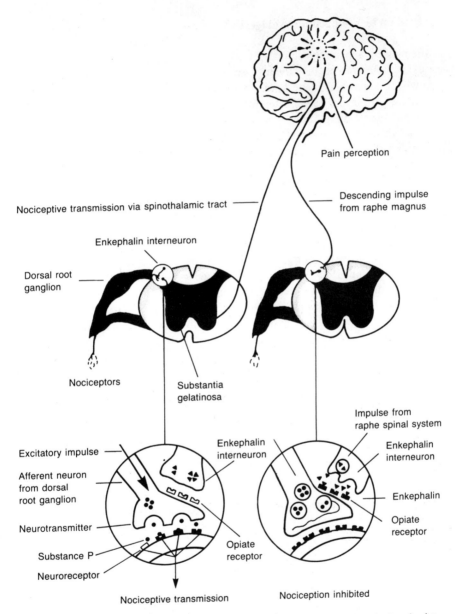

Figure 2-6 Descending impulses stimulate release of enkephalins which attach to spinal cord opiate receptors and block nociceptive transmission. *Source*: From *Acute Pain*, (p. 15) by C.R. Chapman and J.J. Bonica, 1983, Kalamazoo, MI: The Upjohn Company. Copyright 1983 by The Upjohn Company. Reprinted by permission.

Activation of Endogenous Analgesia Systems

Pain itself apparently activates endogenous analgesia systems. In addition, stress is thought to be an activator. Animal studies show that "stress analgesia" (Lewis, Cannon, & Liebeskind, 1980) or "stimulation-produced analgesia" (Watkins & Mayer, 1982) after foot-shock procedures occurs at least in part through the activation of the endogenous opioid system. Other factors that might activate this system are elevations of blood pressure (Zamir & Shuber, 1980), fear, stress, restraint, and hypoglycemia (Basbaum & Fields, 1984), factors often seen in critically ill patients.

THE GATE CONTROL THEORY AND ITS PROPOSED ROLE IN PAIN MECHANISMS

Melzack and Wall's original (1965) and reformulated gate control theory (Melzack & Wall, 1983; Wall, 1978) has added to our theoretical understanding of pain transmission and endogenous pain modulation. In fact, it is the most comprehensive pain theory to date. Anatomical units of the gate control system are presented in Fig. 2-7. The system includes both large-diameter (nonpain) and

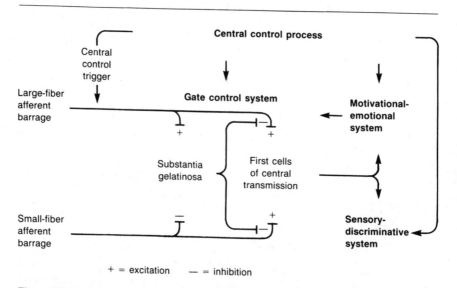

Figure 2-7 Gate control model. *Source*: From *Acute Pain*, (p. 11) by C.R. Chapman and J.J. Bonica, 1983, Kalamazoo, MI: The Upjohn Company. Copyright 1983 by The Upjohn Company. Reprinted by permission.

small-diameter (pain) fibers that project from the periphery to the substantia gelatinosa in lamina II of the spinal cord as well as to central transmission cells in other laminae. Transmission cells are excitatory fibers believed to be responsible for central transmission of the sensory and emotional aspects of pain.

Substantia gelatinosa interneurons are thought to influence the central transmission cells. In so doing, they can interrupt the balance between large (nonpain) and small (pain) fiber activity. Pain fibers are believed to inhibit substantia gelatinosa interneurons. Therefore, transmission cells are allowed to remain active. The gate to pain is opened, and there is central transmission of pain. In contrast, projections from large-diameter fibers to the substantia gelatinosa activate substantia gelatinosa cells, which in turn inhibit transmission cell activity. That is, the pain gate is closed by the inhibitory effects of substantia gelatinosa interneurons on transmission cells. Higher CNS control processes also can influence the gate control system by delivering inhibitory messages to the spinal cord. The goals of therapy, then, are to stimulate descending CNS central control processes and to stimulate large peripheral nonpain fibers, both of which are thought to close the pain gates.

The anatomical circuit originally postulated by Melzack and Wall (1965) was neither complete nor exact (Hoffert, 1986). For example, transmission cells have not yet been identified. Further, the theory does not detail the role of the endogenous opioid system. The gate control theory's major concepts are generally well accepted, however, and include the following: Small-diameter peripheral nerves transmit noxious stimuli to the central nervous system; large-diameter peripheral nerves that carry innocuous, nonpain information can inhibit nociceptor transmission in the spinal cord; and modulating descending control systems exist.

The gate control theory helps explain the effects of some current pain therapies. For example, vibration through massage or transcutaneous electrical nerve stimulation preferentially stimulates large-diameter peripheral nerves, which excite the substantia gelatinosa and thereby override and inhibit centrally transmitting pain fibers. Further research supportive of the validity of the gate control theory is needed, however (see Chapter 3 for the proposed relationship between the gate control theory and psychological aspects of pain).

POTENTIAL PHYSIOLOGICAL CONSEQUENCES OF PAIN IN CRITICALLY ILL PATIENTS

A compromised, critically ill patient can be extremely vulnerable to deleterious physiological consequences of pain. Adequate pain control can help prevent physiological consequences that occur as a result of reflex motor activity, ANS activation, and activation of an endocrine stress response.

Reflex motor activity is due to direct or indirect (through interneurons) synapsing of fibers onto lower motor neurons, whose cell bodies are in the anterior horn of the spinal cord (Kandel & Schwartz, 1984). Figure 2-8 depicts the reflex activity generated at the spinal cord level. This reflex activity may result in contraction of skeletal muscles, especially those in the abdominal wall, and may lead to abdominal wall rigidity (Ganong, 1985). As a result, reflex skeletal muscle spasms of oblique abdominal muscles can affect diaphragmatic excursion. Subsequent ineffectiveness of diaphragm and intercostal muscles can result in hypoventilation, as evidenced by elevated levels of carbon dioxide, or in hyperventilation (i.e., decreased carbon dioxide levels) if respiratory rate and pattern is rapid and shallow. Additionally, pain and spasms cause the individual voluntarily to avoid coughing, deep breathing, or moving, maneuvers that help prevent respiratory complications (Bonica & Benedetti, 1980). The voluntary nature of these avoidance activities results from suprasegmental and cortical input to the spinal cord.

In critical care patients with chest injuries, pain can lead to poor cough, shallow breathing, and subsequent decrease in lung compliance (Lloyd, Smith, & O'Connor, 1965). Low lung volumes and effort precede development of atelectasis (James, Kolberg, Iwen, & Gellatly, 1981), impaired respiratory tract clearance, and, consequently, development of pneumonia and impaired oxygenation. Atelectasis and infection, in turn, are precursors of respiratory failure. Figure 2-9 diagrams the cascade of respiratory events that may occur as a result of pain. Pain

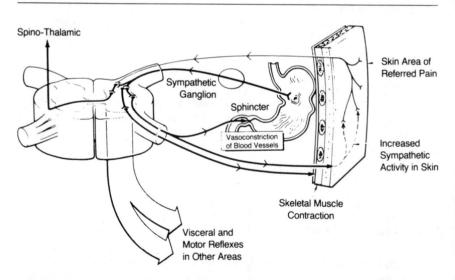

Figure 2-8 Reflex motor activity may lead to skeletal muscle contraction and sympathetic nervous system effects such as vasoconstriction. *Source*: From *Acute Pain Management*, (p. 34) by M.J. Cousins and G.D. Phillips (Eds.), 1986, New York, NY: Churchill Livingstone, Inc. Copyright by Churchill Livingstone, Inc. Reprinted by permission.

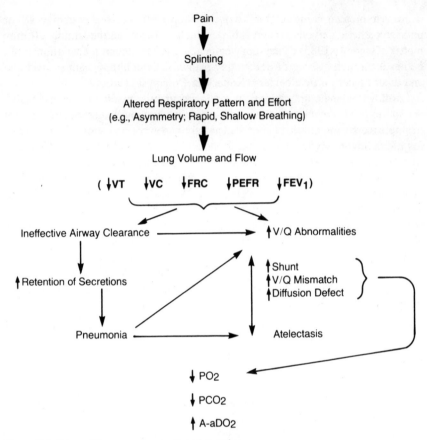

Figure 2-9 Pain and its consequences: clinical sequelae.

may cause voluntary or involuntary splinting of respiratory muscles, which interferes with normal respiratory patterns and effort. Both lung volumes and flow rates are decreased. As a result, there is ineffective clearance of secretions from the respiratory tree, creating an environment for the development of pneumonia, atelectasis, and ventilation-perfusion abnormalities.

Inadequately treated pain is likely to elicit these adverse respiratory responses (Craig, 1981; O'Gara, 1988), causing potential life-threatening complications in critically ill patients. In some patients, these complications may progress to death (Bonica, 1981).

A second physiological consequence of pain is ANS activation. ANS responses to pain occur through spinal cord reflex activity, which is under suprasegmental (brainstem) and cortical influence. That is, visceral afferents synapse with interneurons to preganglionic cell bodies of the sympathetic nervous system (SNS) or parasympathetic nervous system (PNS), which is located in the lamina VII gray matter (Ganong, 1985). The suprasegmental input to these preganglionic cell bodies is through a series of descending pathways from hypothalamus, medulla, and other higher cortical centers (Noback & Demarest, 1981).

Cardiovascular complications generally occur as a result of increased SNS activation. SNS responses can significantly alter cardiovascular parameters, for example increasing afterload and myocardial oxygen consumption while decreasing blood flow to myocardial tissue (Bouckoms, 1988; O'Gara, 1988). Critically ill patients may be particularly vulnerable to these responses.

Finally, severe pain may lead to the development of reflex physiological endocrine stress responses (Kehlet, 1986; Wilmore, Long, Mason, & Pruitt, 1976), such as increased cortisol, catecholamine, and antidiuretic hormone release. Increased protein catabolism, lipolysis, and hyperglycemia can ensue. Therefore, advantages of pain control in critical care patients may be an attenuation of the stress response (Bryan-Brown, 1986; El-Baz & Goldin, 1987) and prevention of other deleterious physiological and psychological consequences of pain. The reader is directed to Chapter 3, which presents a foundation for understanding the psychological consequences of pain.

CONCLUSION

The total pain experience of critically ill patients results from transmission, integration, and modulation of physiological responses to real or potential tissue injury. This chapter described the physiology of pain in a stepwise manner, from peripheral to spinal cord to brain sites. The benefit of this approach is that it delineates the multiple causes for variations in perceived pain sensations and identifies the many potential sites for therapeutic interventions. It must be remembered, however, that an individual's pain experience does not always occur in the sequence outlined. Nevertheless, whatever the exact sequence of physiology, health care professionals have the challenging responsibility to limit pain and its consequences in critically ill patients.

REFERENCES

Andersson, S.A., & Rydenhag, B. (1985). Cortical nociceptive systems. In A. Iggo, L.L. Iverson, & F. Cervero (Eds.), *Nociception and pain* (pp. 347–355). London: The Royal Society.

Basbaum, A.I., & Fields, H.L. (1984). Endogenous pain control systems: Brainstem spinal pathways and endorphin circuitry. *Annual Review of Neurosciences, 7*, 309–338.

Bonica, J.J. (1953). *The management of pain*. Philadelphia: Lea & Febiger.

Bonica, J.J. (1981). The relation of pain and stress. In *Research in Stress in Health and Disease* (Report of the Institute of Medicine, National Academy of Sciences, to the Executive Office of the President).

Bonica, J.J., & Benedetti, C. (1980). Postoperative pain. In R.E. Condon & J.J. DeCosse (Eds.), *Surgical care: A physiologic approach to clinical management* (pp. 394–414). Philadelphia: Lea & Febiger.

Bouckoms, A.J. (1988). Pain relief in the intensive care unit. *Journal of Intensive Care Medicine, 3*, 32–51.

Bryan-Brown, C.W. (1986). Development of pain management in critical care. In M.J. Cousins & G.D. Phillips (Eds.), *Acute pain management* (pp. 1–19). New York: Churchill Livingstone.

Bunney, W.E., Pert, C.B., Klee, W., Costa, E., Pert, A., & Davis, G.C. (1979). Basic and clinical studies of endorphins. *Annals of Internal Medicine, 91*, 239–250.

Butler, S. (1984). Present status of tricyclic antidepressants in chronic pain therapy. *Advances in Pain Research and Therapy, 7*, 173–197.

Cervero, F. (1985). Visceral nociception: Peripheral and central aspects of visceral nociceptive systems. In A. Iggo, L.L. Iverson, & F. Cervero (Eds.), *Nociception and pain* (pp. 325–337). London: The Royal Society.

Cervero, F. (1988). Visceral pain. In R. Dubner, G.F. Gebhart, & M.R. Bond (Eds.), *Proceedings of the fifth world congress on pain* (pp. 216–226). Amsterdam: Elsevier Science.

Chapman, C.R., & Bonica, J.J. (1983). *Acute Pain.* Kalamazoo, Mich.: Upjohn.

Craig, D.B. (1981). Postoperative recovery of pulmonary function. *Anesthesia and Analgesia, 60*, 46–52.

El-Baz, N., & Goldin, M. (1987). Continuous epidural infusion of morphine for pain relief after cardiac operations. *Journal of Thoracic and Cardiovascular Surgery, 93*, 878–883.

Fields, H.W. (1987). *Pain: Mechanisms and management.* New York: McGraw-Hill.

Fields, H.L., Meyer, G.A., & Partridge, L.D. (1970). Convergence of visceral and somatic input onto spinal neurons. *Experimental Neurology, 26*, 36–52.

Ganong, W.F. (1985). *Review of medical physiology* (12th ed.). Los Altos, CA: Lange Medical Publications.

Goldstein, A. (1976). Opioid peptides (endorphins) in pituitary and brain. *Science, 193*, 1081–1086.

Hoffert, M. (1986). The gate control theory revisited. *Journal of Pain and Symptom Management, 1*, 39–41.

Iggo, A., Steedman, W.M., & Fleetwood-Walker, S. (1985). Spinal processing: Anatomy and physiology of spinal nociceptive mechanisms. In A. Iggo, L.L. Iverson, & F. Cervero (Eds.), *Nociception and pain* (pp. 235–252). London: The Royal Society.

Inman, V.T., & Saunders, J.B. (1944). Referred pain from skeletal structures. *Journal of Nervous and Mental Disease, 99*, 660–667.

Jaffe, J.H., & Martin, W.R. (1988). Opioid analgesics and antagonists. In A.G. Gilman, L.S. Goodman, T.W. Rall, & F. Murad (Eds.), *Goodman and Gilman's pharmacological basis of therapeutics* 7th ed., (pp. 491–531). New York: Macmillan.

James, E.C., Kolberg, H.L., Iwen, G.W., & Gellatly, T.A. (1981). Epidural analgesia for post-thoracotomy patients. *Journal of Thoracic and Cardiovascular Surgery, 82*, 898–903.

Kandel, E.R., & Schwartz, J.H. (1984). *Principles of neural science.* New York: Elsevier–North Holland.

Kehlet, H. (1986). Pain relief and modification of the stress response. In M.J. Cousins & G.D. Phillips (Eds.), *Acute pain management* (pp. 49–75). New York: Churchill Livingstone.

Kellgren, J.H. (1937–38). Observations on referred pain arising from muscle. *Clinical Science, 3*, 175–190.

Kenshalo, D.R., & Isensee, O. (1983). Responses of primate SI cortical neurons to noxious stimuli. *Journal of Neurophysiology, 59*, 1479–1496.

Lassen, N.A., Ingvar, D.H., & Skinhoj, E. (1978). Brain function and blood flow. *Scientific American, 239*, 62–71.

Leek, B.F. (1977). Abdominal and pelvic visceral receptors. *British Medical Bulletin, 33*, 163–168.

Levine, J. (1984). Pain and analgesia: The outlook for more rational treatment. *Basic Review, 100*, 269–276.

Lewis, J.W., Cannon, J.T., & Liebeskind, J.C. (1980). Opioid and nonopioid mechanisms of stress analgesia. *Science, 208*, 623–625.

Livingston, R.B. (1978). *Sensory processing, perception, and behavior.* New York: Raven.

Lloyd, J.W., Smith, A.C., & O'Connor, B.T. (1965). Classification of chest injuries as an aid to treatment. *British Medical Journal, 1*, 1518–1523.

Lynn, B. (1977). Cutaneous hyperalgesia. *British Medical Bulletin, 33*, 103–108.

Mather, L.E., & Cousins, M.J. (1986). Local anesthetics: Principles of use. In M.J. Cousins & G.D. Phillips (Eds.), *Acute pain management* (pp. 105–131). New York: Churchill Livingstone.

Mayer, D.J., Wolfle, T.L., Akil, H., Carder, B., & Liebeskind, J.C. (1971). Analgesia from electrical stimulation in the brainstem of the rat. *Science, 174*, 1351–1354.

Melzack, R., & Casey, K.L. (1968). Sensory, motivational, and central control determinants of pain. In D.R. Kenshalo (Ed.), *The skin senses* (pp. 423–443). Springfield, IL: Thomas.

Melzack, R., & Wall, P. (1965). Pain mechanisms: A new theory. *Science, 150*, 971–978.

Melzack, R., & Wall, P. (1983). *The challenge of pain.* New York: Basic Books.

Mense, S., & Schmidt, R.F. (1974). Activation of group IV afferent units from muscle by analgesic agents. *Brain Research, 72*, 305–310.

Mense, S., & Stahnke, M. (1983). Responses in muscle afferent fibres of slow conduction velocity to contractions and ischaemia in the cat. *Journal of Physiology, 342*, 383–397.

Meyer, R.A., Campbell, J.N., & Raja, S.N. (1985). Peripheral neural mechanisms of cutaneous hyperalgesia. *Advances in Pain Research and Therapy, xx*, 53–71.

Mountcastle, V.B. (1980). Pain and temperature sensibilities. In V.B. Mountcastle (Ed.), *Medical physiology* (pp. 391–427). St. Louis, MO: Mosby.

Noback, C.R., & Demarest, R.J. (1981). *The human nervous system: basic principles of neurobiology* (3rd ed.). New York: McGraw-Hill.

O'Gara, P.T. (1988). The hemodynamic consequences of pain and its management. *Journal of Intensive Care Medicine, 3*, 3–5.

Pasternak, G.W. (1988). Multiple morphine and enkephalin receptors and the relief of pain. *Journal of the American Medical Association, 259*, 1362–1367.

Price, D.D., Hayashi, H., Dubner, R., & Ruda, M.A. (1979). Functional relationships between neurons of marginal and substantia gelatinosa layers of primate dorsal horn. *Journal of Neurophysiology, 42*, 1590–1608.

Reynolds, D.V. (1969). Surgery in the rat during electrical analgesia induced by focal brain stimulation. *Science, 164*, 444–445.

Sabbe, M.B., & Yaksh, T.L. (1990). Pharmacology of spinal opioids. *Journal of Pain and Symptom Management, 5*, 191–203.

Terenius, L. (1984). The endogenous opioids and other central peptides. In P.D. Wall & R. Melzack (Eds.), *Textbook of pain* (pp. 133–141). Edinburgh: Churchill Livingstone.

Torebjork, E. (1985). Nociceptor activation and pain. In A. Iggo, L.L. Iverson, & F. Cervero (Eds.), *Nociception and pain* (pp. 227–234). London: The Royal Society.

Vander, A.J., Sherman, J.H., & Luciano, D.S. (1990). *Human physiology: The mechanisms of body function* (5th ed., p. 705). New York: McGraw-Hill.

Veselis, R.A. (1988). Sedation and pain management for the critically ill. *Critical Care Clinics, 4*, 167–181.

Wall, P.D. (1978). The gate control theory of pain mechanisms: A re-examination and re-statement. *Brain, 101*, 1–18.

Watkins, L.R., & Mayer, D.J. (1982). Organization of endogenous opiate and nonopiate pain control systems. *Science, 216*, 1185–1191.

Willis, W.D. (1985). Nociceptive pathways: Anatomy and physiology of nociceptive ascending pathways. In A. Iggo, L.L. Iverson, & F. Cervero (Eds.), *Nociception and pain* (pp. 253–268). London: the Royal Society.

Wilmore, D.W., Long, J.M., Mason, A.D., & Pruitt, B.A. (1976). Stress in surgical patients as a neurophysiologic reflex response. *Surgery, Gynecology & Obstetrics, 142*, 257–269.

Zaloga, G.P., Hostinsky, C., & Chernow, B. (1984). Endogenous opioid peptides: Critical care implications. *Heart & Lung, 13*, 421–430.

Zamir, N., & Shuber, E. (1980). Altered pain perception in hypertensive humans. *Brain, 201*, 471–474.

RECOMMENDED READING

Benedetti, C. (1990). Acute pain: A review of its effects and therapy with systemic opioids. In, C. Benedetti, C.R. Chapman, & G. Giron (Eds.), *Advances in pain research and therapy*, vol. 14 (pp. 367–424). New York: Raven Press.

Bonica, J.J. (1990). Postoperative pain. In, J.J. Bonica (Ed.), *The management of pain*, 2nd ed. (pp. 461–480). Philadelphia: Lea & Febiger.

Cousins, M.J., & Phillips, G.D. (Eds.). (1986). *Acute pain management*. New York: Churchill Livingstone.

Puntillo, K. (1988). The phenomenon of pain and critical care nursing. *Heart & Lung 17*, 262–271.

Chapter 3

Psychological Aspects of Pain and Coping in Critical Care

Julia Faucett

Pain is a multifaceted experience that has psychological as well as physiological features. What patients learn about pain from their own or others' experiences affects how they respond to noxious stimuli. Thus past experiences and previously acquired coping skills in addition to events associated with the critical care admission influence patients' cognitive, emotional, and behavioral responses to pain. Patient's abilities to cope effectively with pain in the critical care unit may also depend on how they cope with the dependence or helplessness that inevitably accompanies severe illness. This chapter considers the responses of the patient in the critical care unit to pain in the context of theories of helplessness, coping, and control.

As noted in the preceding chapter, Melzack and Wall (1965, 1982) initially delineated multiple components of the pain experience. They contrasted the sensory-discriminative component of pain associated with tissue damage with the emotional-motivational component or the "unique, distinctly unpleasant, affective quality" (Melzack, 1985, p. 3) of pain, which produces the drive to avoid the noxious stimulus. The gate control theory proposed that different nervous system processes mediate these components (Melzack, 1985). Neural impulses associated with tissue damage due to underlying disease processes or injuries, for example, are transmitted centrally along sensory pathways. The eventual perception of pain is influenced not only by transmission from the periphery, however, but also by descending central control mechanisms (Melzack, 1985). Central reticular, limbic, and cortical systems, for example, influence pain perception (Casey, 1982). It may be through these central systems that cognition and emotion modulate pain.

Research on both clinical and experimental pain has demonstrated the utility of studying the psychological aspects of pain. Research on the influence of cognition and emotion on pain perception has led to various interventions for both acute and chronic pain. Virtually all the psychological in addition to the physiological interventions for pain currently in use have implications for the critical care nursing management of patients and many may be applied independently by nurses (see Part II). Interventions related to the psychological concepts presented in this chapter are discussed in Chapter 8.

RESPONSES TO PAIN IN CRITICAL CARE

In the critical care unit, inability to control pain, mental alertness, bodily functions, or surrounding events may be emotionally overwhelming and, additionally, may lead to maladaptive thoughts and behaviors. Furthermore, the usual coping skills of critically ill patients may be ineffective as a result of the severity of their pain or illness condition. The following section discusses responses to loss of control and the inability to cope with pain in the critical care unit.

Learned Helplessness

Extreme dependence, unfamiliarity, and lack of capability or opportunities to exercise personal control are likely to make patients in critical care feel confused and powerless. Their lack of control may put them at risk for learned helplessness, an acquired response to situations in which there appears to be little connection between what one does in response to noxious stimuli and the outcome of the situation. Helplessness is mediated by personal attributions of failure or inability to control events and is characterized by passivity, slowed thought processes, and negative emotions (Abramson, Seligman, & Teasdale, 1978; Seligman, 1974). If persistent pain is perceived by the critically ill patient as uncontrollable, for example, this may contribute to the experience of learned helplessness. The significance of the clinical outcomes in critical care further contributes to feelings of being overpowered and helpless.

Depression

Learned helplessness theory predicts that, when severe pain and illness are perceived as persistent and inevitable or fatal and when patients believe that there is nothing they personally can do to modify or prevent undesirable outcomes, depression develops (Garber, Miller, & Abramson, 1980). Weiner, Russell, and Lerman (1978) suggested that the belief that one's own inability contributes to the inevitability of undesirable outcomes further increases depression, apathy, and resignation. Because patients in critical care are so severely impaired and may easily perceive themselves to be in a hopeless and helpless situation, they may be especially vulnerable to depression.

Depression has been associated with specific patterns of thought (Beck, 1976). Called cognitive errors, examples of these patterns include overgeneralization, catastrophizing, personalization, and selective abstraction. These errors reflect beliefs about the impact of life events. Overgeneralization is assuming that the outcome of one experience will happen over and over again in related experiences; catastrophizing is assuming that the outcome will be devastating in impact; personalization is taking personal responsibility for negative events; and selective abstraction is focusing on the negative aspects of experiences (Beck, 1976). Cognitive therapies specific for depression propose that depressive symptomology arises from these faulty and unrealistically negative inferences about oneself and the world and seek to correct maladaptive patterns of thinking. In fact, observing patients for maladaptive thinking may be a more useful technique for identifying the onset of depression in the critical care unit than relying on other common indicators of depression, such as sleep disruption or appetite suppression. Helping patients talk about their responses to being in the critical care unit may uncover unrealistic thinking. Patients who consistently focus on the negatives of their day-to-day course in critical care, who feel personally responsible for their illness condition, or who assume that the worst is inevitable may be at risk for depression.

Fields (1987) speculated that depression lowers tolerance for aches and pains by lowering serotonin, norepinephrine, or endogenous opiate levels associated with the inhibition of pain. Feedback cycles between pain and depression could result in worsening of the symptoms of each. Tricyclic medication, which is commonly given for depression, augments the body's production and cycling of these neurotransmitters. Thus pharmacological therapy for depression may reduce pain in the critical care unit. At low doses, tricyclics given in the absence of signs of depression also have been shown to be useful for specific pain syndromes as a result of their effects on neurotransmitters (Fields, 1987).

Both pharmacological and brief psychological therapies for depression may facilitate pain management in the critical care unit. Supporting patients in the unit by identifying concrete, positive outcomes, crediting patients for their role in effecting outcomes, and providing adequate pain relief when possible and pharmacological treatment for depression when appropriate helps break the cycle of pain and depression.

Anxiety

Helplessness in connection with uncertainty about what outcomes will occur produces feelings of anxiety (Garber, Miller, & Abramson, 1980). In the critical care unit, dependency on others for one's well-being and survival coupled with the unpredictability of health outcomes fuels anxiety. When pain relief is in the hands of strangers, when unfamiliar procedures threaten increased pain, or when pain is affected by day-to-day or hour-to-hour fluctuations in physical condition, patients may have difficulty coping with uncertainty and may become increasingly anxious.

Acute pain typically represents impending danger and signals the need for escape or avoidance. The intensity of the impending danger is relative to the degree of harm that it represents in terms of further injury, tissue damage, or survival itself. Feelings of anxiety and helplessness arise in response to an unfavorable imbalance between the perceived potential for harm and the ability to cope with it (Lazarus & Folkman, 1984). Patients in critical care are highly dependent on the protective responses of others to compensate for their incapacitation. Any uncertainty they have about the vigilance or competence of others increases the threat of danger. For example, awakening to the pain of ischemia due to having one's arm trapped under one's torso poses relatively low threat for the healthy intact individual at home in bed. The threat increases anxiety dramatically for the paralyzed individual who is mute on a respirator and dependent on nursing surveillance.

Anxiety is characterized by inhibition of ongoing behavior, heightened arousal, and increased attention to stimuli (Gray, 1979). Physiological changes associated with arousal, increased vigilance over activities and people in the critical care unit, heightened responsiveness to environmental as well as internal stimuli, and abrupt changes in voluntary movement may be signals that a patient's anxiety is increasing. Heightened arousal and attention to one's bodily state may lower the threshold of pain sensation or one's ability to endure pain.

Building on Melzack and Wall's (1965) gate control system, Schalling (1986) suggested four ways in which anxiety might contribute to pain perception: (1) by potentiating activity in the sensory-discrimination system, (2) by altering the cognitive evaluation of the pain, (3) by increasing the aversiveness of the pain through the emotional-motivational component, and (4) by increasing that portion of the pain complaint related to the needs for support, sympathy, and other anxiety-relieving interventions. For example, anxiety may increase pain by increasing sympathetic nervous system activity, by altering the meaning of pain, by increasing the unpleasantness of pain, or by changing relationships with others.

Weisenberg, Aviram, Wolf, and Raphaeli (1984) have, however, emphasized the importance of the source of anxiety to pain perception. Anxiety related to pain or a painful procedure may amplify pain, whereas anxiety related to task performance may lower pain intensity. The performance of nonpainful procedures or treatments in the critical care unit, thus, may serve to distract patients from their pain. If, however, patients fear that unfamiliar or difficult procedures will hurt, then pain may be intensified.

Nursing can facilitate pain management in the critical care patient by assessing the contribution that anxiety is making to pain, the source of anxiety, and needs for interpersonal support. Interventions to reduce unnecessary uncertainty and arousal, to provide emotional support, and to enhance the patient's own sense of competence in the critical care environment will help reduce anxiety.

Pain Behavior

Critical care nurses assess patient pain by observing and evaluating verbal and nonverbal behavior (See Chapter 4). Pain behaviors consist of verbal complaints, moaning and groaning, grimacing, guarding, limping, bracing or splinting, and voluntary restriction of activities. Pain behaviors have multiple effects, serving to communicate the presence of pain to others, to reduce the sensation of pain, and to increase pain endurance. In addition to increasing with pain severity, they may also increase as a result of helplessness and anxiety, particularly if they elicit attention and sympathy from others.

Pain behaviors are distinguished from reflex responses to noxious stimuli in that they are learned, acquired responses that are socioculturally influenced. Because they are learned, pain behaviors may increase in frequency in response to positive reinforcement (Fordyce, 1974, 1982). For example, successful reduction of pain during coughing due to the use of a pillow as a splint acts as a reinforcer for splinting and increases the likelihood that splinting will be used again for that activity.

As a result of reinforcement, however, patterns of self-protective or other pain-related behavior may be perpetuated after the pain itself has resolved and may complicate pain assessment (Fordyce, Shelton, & Dundore, 1982). For example, the association of an activity such as wound dressing changes with previous increases in pain may lead to anxious anticipation of pain, to guarding and protective behavior, and to heightened awareness of pain when the procedure is repeated, even though improvements in physical condition indicate that the patient will be increasingly able to tolerate the dressing change. Providing concrete information to the dependent, fearful, or demonstrative patient about progress in healing and strength may help change patient attitudes and behaviors related to anxiety-provoking and painful procedures.

Under certain circumstances, attention and sympathy from nurses and family members may reinforce and thus increase pain behavior and dependent behavior among patients, especially when they are in the hospital for a long period of time (Minarik & Sparacino, 1989). Attention, esteem, affection, and relief from unpleasant activities elicited in response to pain behavior are referred to as secondary gains, a term borrowed from psychiatry (Freedman, Kaplan, & Sadock,

1977; in psychiatry, primary gain is the reduction of internal conflict and tension). Although such gains are desirable outcomes of many of our social interactions, they are undesirable as reinforcers of pain behavior and may interfere with both pain management and the patient's ability to cope with pain and pain-inducing nursing care activities.

Staff members may feel manipulated and angry if they believe that increases in or maintenance of pain behaviors is related to seeking secondary gains. Patients should not be held responsible for this type of reinforcement, however, because they are generally unaware of the relationship between pain behavior and reinforcement. Discussing concerns about pain behavior with patients, relieving anxiety, and praising positive patient contributions to care will help promote pain behavior that accurately communicates pain severity. Changing the behavior of an overly dependent, fearful, or demonstrative patient in pain, however, requires a well-considered and coordinated plan, and consultation with a psychiatric clinician skilled in behavior modification may be helpful.

COPING WITH PAIN

In contrast to helplessness, successful coping represents mastery over the events that affect one's well-being. People learn how to cope with pain and their cognitive and emotional responses to it from their previous experiences and the experiences of others.

Experiential Learning about Coping with Pain

People learn about pain and their ability to cope with pain from four major sources: their immediate physical sensations, their personal past experiences, watching and listening to others in pain, and the critical and persuasive comments of others about their coping efforts. Such information affects the focus of coping, the kinds of coping behaviors that people use, the effort that will be expended in attempting to cope (Bandura, 1986).

Through previous experiences, people acquire cognitive and behavioral techniques for coping with pain that they bring to the critical care unit. Patients draw upon their repertoire of techniques in their initial efforts to cope with pain whether it is by applying personal skills and strategies or by enlisting support from others (Lazarus & Folkman, 1984). The patient who has endured numerous surgeries to combat chronic problems will have a quite different repertoire of coping skills than the critically ill patient who has never experienced severe pain of any kind. Adequate nursing assessment of past experiences with pain may facilitate coping, for example by leading to the resolution of unfounded fears about narcotics or by the incorporation of previously acquired relaxation and imagery skills.

The unique meanings patients have for pain, based on their previous experiences and on their current experience in the critical care unit, will also influence their attempts to cope with pain. The meanings patients have for pain influence their appraisal of events, coping needs, and abilities (Lazarus & Folkman, 1984). For the patient in critical care, pain taken as a sign of decline and mortality, for example, may be accompanied by depression and withdrawal. Pain associated with culpability in a traumatic accident may be perceived as just punishment, which perhaps is a more desirable outcome than unalleviated guilt. If loss of self-esteem or heightened family distress from unsuccessful management of pain is more threatening than the intensity of the pain, pain may be stoically tolerated. Chest pain may be denied by the myocardial infarction patient who sees it as the only limit on the ability to return to home, and recovery may be delayed by lack of treatment. Pain as proof of survival, competence, or recovery, on the other hand, can boost the exercise of coping skills and expenditure of effort. The patient who is unable to create meaning for pain, however, may be the least able to cope with pain in the critical care environment (Lowery, Jacobsen, & Murphy, 1983). Responses to pain of patients in the critical care unit become more understandable and amenable, if necessary, to intervention when patients' meanings for pain, previous experiences with pain, and coping skills have been assessed.

Spouses and families, other patients, and health care providers may influence the success of pain management through vicarious learning and social modelling (Block, Kremer, & Gaylor, 1980; Fagerhaugh & Strauss, 1977; Funch & Gale, 1986). Previous modeling in the family about pain and ways to cope with it and patient models in the critical care unit are likely to influence the expression of pain, the behaviors utilized for control of pain, and the endurance of pain (Craig, 1983; Edwards, Zeichner, Kuczmierczyk, & Boczkowski, 1985; Fagerhaugh & Strauss, 1977; Mohamed, Weisz, & Waring, 1978; Violon & Giurgea, 1984). Patients on a burn unit, for example, learn vicariously about debridement pain, the efficacy of analgesic premedication, and expected and acceptable pain behavior from watching and listening to other burn patients during daily procedures (Fagerhaugh & Strauss, 1977).

Thus the willingness of an elderly patient to engage in painful coughing after coronary vessel bypass surgery is influenced by what current sensations may mean to the patient, by previous experience with pain and with the procedure or similar procedures, by the information and feedback provided by the nurse and family members, and by observation of other patients in the unit. The initial agreement to use premedication or pillows for splinting and decisions about persisting in the face of pain will be influenced by what is learned from these sources.

By using knowledge about sources of learning, critical care nurses can gauge activities to expand but not overwhelm patients' coping capabilities. Therefore, patients may be willing to learn new techniques for pain management if they build on previous coping skills or familiar experiences. Timely information may help patients interpret physical sensations and persuasion and positive comparisons with other patients in critical care may help to sustain hope and appropriate levels of activity.

Problem-Focused and Emotion-Focused Coping

Coping with pain and mastering the feelings of threat associated with it involve both problem-focused and emotion-focused coping strategies (Lazarus & Folkman, 1984). The first requires effective problem-solving skills, including problem identification, the generation of alternative solutions, and decision making. Requesting analgesics, rest periods from procedures, or privacy during painful treatments are examples of problem-focused coping strategies to minimize pain and preserve self-esteem despite pain.

When pain is inevitable, managing the feelings associated with it requires emotion-focused coping. Controlling the experience and display of fear, anxiety, anger, and sadness associated with pain requires such strategies as distancing, minimizing, reappraisal, and selective attention. Occasionally, the patient's coping focus is inappropriate for the situation. For example, ineffective coping occurs when the patient denies or minimizes a potentially solvable problem or persists in using problem-solving approaches for an irremediable situation. Ineffective coping contributes to feelings of anxiety and helplessness and reduces the efficacy of pain management.

Support from family, friends, and health care providers can supplement both problem-focused coping and emotion-focused coping (Thoits, 1986) in the critical care unit. Others facilitate problem-focused coping by providing information, suggesting solutions, making decisions, and acting to resolve difficulties faced in the critical care environment or related to roles and responsibilities outside the unit. They facilitate emotion-focused coping by calming and sustaining the critical care patient, diverting attention from pain and distress, and helping the patient to reappraise the situation. Belief in the availability of physical aid, information, and emotional support from others is often a substantial boost to individual coping ability. Conversely, the ability of the individual to cope with pain and distress may be overwhelmed if unit policies bar access to family and friend support. Because of the severe incapacitation of the patient in the critical care unit, it is important that the nursing staff work with both the patient and the family to identify the most adaptive coping focus for particular situations and to facilitate appropriate coping strategies.

PERCEIVED CONTROL AND ITS INFLUENCE ON PAIN

Control over pain varies with the type of pain and with the person who experiences it. Controllability is a feature of the noxious stimulus and varies with the type of pain. For example, incisional pain generally responds to analgesic medication, whereas central pain from a thalamic infarct is extremely difficult to relieve. Perceived control, on the other hand, varies with personal beliefs about mastery of a situation. Thompson (1981) has defined perceived control as "the belief that one has at one's disposal a response that can influence the aversiveness of an event" (p. 89). The perception that a controlling response is available affects the awareness and endurance of pain (Glass, Singer & Friedman, 1969; Miller, 1980). Individuals, however, vary widely in their ability to summon coping skills and resources to control their pain and, thus, in their perception of personal control over pain. Nurses in critical care are in an excellent position to enhance individual coping and promote a sense of mastery or control.

Types of Control

Thompson (1981) identified four types of personal control over pain: behavioral, cognitive, information, and retrospective. In the clinical setting, these types of control may reduce patient anxiety, arousal, and pain severity, and increase endurance of pain.

Behavioral Control

Behavioral control is the sense of control derived from the belief that one has a behavioral response that can affect the painfulness of an event (Thompson, 1981). Experimentally, it relates to a method, generally a button, supplied by investigators that allows a research subject to initiate or stop a painful event. Experimental behavioral controls have been shown to reduce anxiety and to increase pain endurance even though they appear to have little effect on the intensity of experimental pain (for review see Thompson, 1981).

Clinically, behavioral control for pain refers to externally applied techniques used to modify pain or to control the onset of painful procedures. Patient-controlled analgesia, transcutaneous nerve stimulation, massage, rest breaks, and applications of heat and cold are all examples of behavioral techniques which may increase the patient's perception of control over pain. If the patient cannot independently apply behavioral pain controls, the nurse's availability and responsiveness to requests also may facilitate perceived control.

Cognitive Control

Cognitive control refers to the belief that one has a mental strategy that will alter the painfulness of an event (Thompson, 1981). Mental strategies to ignore, reappraise, or dissociate from pain fall into this category. Examples include music and relaxation tapes, distraction, and guided imagery exercises. Cognitive methods have been found to decrease anxiety, arousal, and pain severity and increase pain endurance. Not all methods are equally effective, and aspects of both patient personality and context affect their applicability (for reviews see Thompson, 1981; Weisenberg, 1977). Limitations due to the nature of the critical care environment and the cognitive status of the critically ill individual may necessitate modifications of these techniques (see Chapter 8).

Information

In the laboratory, information is generally provided as a warning signal that allows preparation before an aversive event. In the clinical setting, facts about sensations or procedures also provide information that allows patients to predict events and prepare for them. Preparatory information about sensations that may occur during medical procedures, however, has been found to reduce distress better than information about the procedure itself (Johnson, 1973, 1984; Thompson, 1981). Information about the causes of pain, on the other hand, may actually increase anxiety and arousal prior to an event (Thompson, 1981).

Retrospective Control

Thompson (1981) defined retrospective control as beliefs about the causes of previous events that preserve one's sense of personal control. Reconstructing meaning for past events may help to maintain a sense of order and meaningfulness about the world. Taylor (1983), for example, theorized that the search for meaning after major crisis events, such as those in critical care, accompanies efforts to regain mastery. Furthermore, the ability to make sense of past events may serve to modify their long range emotional impact (Wortman & Dintzer, 1978). Considering the event precipitating the critical care episode as a teaching from God, for example, or as an opportunity to reconsider life goals may serve to lessen intolerable feelings of loss or anxiety. Patients who are unable to find coherent explanations of the experiences that led to their critical care admission may be prone to helplessness and distress, which compounds their pain and suffering.

Self-Efficacy

Self-efficacy expectations about control over pain refer not only to the belief that one has available a response or technique that can affect the outcome of a painful event but also to the confidence that one is capable of competently and dependably performing such a technique (Bandura, 1986). For example, one may have a patient-controlled analgesia pump at hand, but the fear that one cannot operate it safely will discourage attempts to use it. One may have learned a breathing or distraction technique to use during dressing changes, but lack of faith in one's ability to perform it consistently will reduce the effort invested in it during the procedure. Judgments about increasing patient's coping skills and perceived control require assessment not only of the pain and its characteristics but also of the patient's often fragile confidence.

Because they lack confidence in their abilities, not all critical care patients will prefer or desire control. Control that is perceived as inadequate, furthermore, may be worse than no control in its effects on pain and arousal (Weisenberg, Wolf, Mittwoch, Mikulincer, & Aviram, 1985). Ill and injured individuals in the critical care setting will be likely to relinquish much of their role in pain management to nurses because they doubt their own ability to manage pain consistently. Critical care patients who perceive nurses to be more stable or dependable in their ability to control pain than themselves will turn the control of pain management over to them (Miller, 1980). Some Type A personalities may prefer to retain control, however, even when they believe that they are not better at controlling pain, implying that control may be more important than pain relief to the occasional patient (Miller, 1980). As patients begin to feel competent and secure in their control of pain, they will be more likely to prefer at least a collaborative role in pain management.

Increases in feelings of self-efficacy reduce the fear, anxiety, and pain associated with specific interventions and alter their neurophysiological correlates as well (Bandura, 1986; Bandura, Taylor, Williams, Mefford, & Barchas, 1985; Bandura, O'Leary, Taylor, Gauthier, & Gossard, 1987; Miller, 1980; O'Leary, 1985). Beliefs about competence in performing pain-reduction techniques, regardless of the technique used, have been shown to be significantly related to pain endurance and pain sensation threshold (Litt, 1986; Reese, 1982). For example, belief in personal competence for performing muscle relaxation exercises, regardless of actual ability to decrease muscle tension, has been shown to reduce clinical pain severity (Holroyd et al., 1984) and to increase endurance of experimental pain (Neufeld & Thomas, 1977). Similarly, women in labor who have higher confidence for using childbirth training techniques have been shown to request fewer pain medications and to endure pain longer before asking for medication (Manning & Wright, 1983). Although there is no research on self-efficacy for cognitive-behavioral techniques in critical care, these results indicate that patients' confidence for performing even simple control measures is at least as important as their belief that the measures will help.

Patients gain confidence in their abilities as they become increasingly able to tolerate activity or treatments. Nursing encouragement is often required to persuade patients who lack confidence in their ability to manage or endure pain to participate in painful procedures. If completed with minimal pain, those procedures enhance confidence and perceived control, and, thus reinforced, patients become less reluctant the next time. When successful management of activities and related pain allows sensations to be reinterpreted as temporary and tolerable, patients' beliefs in their capabilities are also enhanced (Bandura, 1986). Nursing rehabilitation plans that ensure progressive patient mastery will promote gains in personal self-efficacy for pain management and activity tolerance. Explicit feedback on successes related, for example, to tolerating coughing exercises, dressing changes, repositioning, or advancing from the bedpan to the commode will support self-efficacy for pain endurance. Likewise, feedback on the skilled use of breathing or distraction exercises or on the use of patient-controlled analgesia pumps or transcutaneous nerve stimulation units promotes self-efficacy for using those pain management measures.

IMPLICATIONS FOR PAIN MANAGEMENT IN CRITICAL CARE

To assess and manage pain adequately in critically ill patients, it is important to understand what pain and dependency may mean to them. Information about patients' previous experiences with pain and typical patterns of coping will help to establish a baseline for understanding their responses to pain while in critical care. The unique experience of being a patient in critical care may further influence perceptions of pain and of competence for coping with it if patients are threatened or overwhelmed by their lack of control. Cognitive, emotional, and behavioral responses to pain, thus, will vary with patients' appraisals of pain, their perceived self-efficacy for controlling it, and their evaluation of the nurse's competence and pain-relief methods. By building on information about the previous experiences and coping patterns of patients, nurses may assist patients to understand their pain in a way that allows them to feel confident that pain can be controlled or endured and that they can develop or access resources to manage it.

REFERENCES

Abramson, L.Y., Seligman, M.E.P., & Teasdale, J.D. (1978). Learned helplessness in humans: Critique and reformulation. *Journal of Abnormal Psychology, 87*, 49–74.

Averill, J. (1973). Personal control over aversive stimuli and its relationship to stress. *Psychological Bulletin, 80*, 286–303.

Bandura, A. (1986). *Social foundations of thought and action*. Englewood Cliffs, NJ: Prentice-Hall.

Bandura, A., O'Leary, A., Taylor, C.B., Gauthier, J., & Gossard, D. (1987). Perceived self-efficacy and pain control: Opioid and nonopioid mechanisms. *Journal of Personality and Social Psychology, 53*, 563–571.

Bandura, A., Taylor, C., Williams, S., Mefford, I., & Barchas, J. (1985). Catecholamine secretion as a function of perceived efficacy. *Journal of Consulting and Clinical Psychology, 53*, 406–414.

Beck, A.T. (1976). *Cognitive therapy and the emotional disorders*. New York: International Universities Press.

Block, A., Kremer, E., & Gaylor, M. (1980). Behavioral treatment of chronic pain: The spouse as a discriminative cue for pain behavior. *Pain, 9*, 243–252.

Casey, K.D. (1982). Neural mechanisms of pain: An overview. *Acta Anaesthesia Scandinavia, 74*(suppl), 13–20.

Craig, K.D. (1983). Modelling and social learning factors in chronic pain. In J.J. Bonica (Ed.), *Advances in pain research and therapy* (pp. 813–825). New York: Raven.

Edwards, P.W., Zeichner, A., Kuczmierczyk, A.R., & Boczkowski, J. (1985). Familial pain models: The relationship between family history of pain and current pain experience. *Pain, 21*, 379–384.

Fagerhaugh, S., & Strauss, A. (1977). *Politics of pain management: Staff-patient interaction*. Menlo Park, CA: Addison-Wesley.

Fields, H. (1987). *Pain*. San Francisco: McGraw-Hill.

Fordyce, W. (1974). Pain viewed as learned behavior. *Advances in Neurology, 4*, 415–422.

Fordyce, W. (1982). A behavioural perspective on chronic pain. *British Journal of Clinical Psychology, 21*, 313–320.

Fordyce, W.E., Shelton, J.L., & Dundore, D.E. (1982). The modification of avoidance learning pain behaviors. *Journal of Behavioral Medicine, 5*, 405–415.

Freedman, A., Kaplan, H., & Sadock, B. (1977). *Modern synopsis of comprehensive textbook of psychiatry/II* (2nd ed.). Baltimore: Williams & Wilkins.

Funch, D.P., & Gale, E.N. (1986). Predicting treatment completion in a behavioral therapy program for chronic temporomandibular pain. *Journal of Psychosomatic Research, 30*, 57–62.

Garber, J., Miller, S.M., & Abramson, L.Y. (1980). On the distinction between anxiety and depression: Perceived control, certainty, and probability of goal attainment. In J. Garber & M. Seligman (Eds.), *Human Helplessness* (pp. 131–169). New York: Academic Press.

Glass, D., Singer, J., & Friedman, L. (1969). Psychic cost of adaptation to an environmental stressor. *Journal of Personality and Social Psychology, 12*, 200–210.

Gray, J.A. (1979). A neuropsychological theory of anxiety. In C.E. Izard (Ed.), *Emotions in personality and psychopathology* (pp. 303–335). New York: Plenum.

Holroyd, K., Penzien, D., Hursey, K., Tobin, D., Rogers, L., Holm, J., Marcille, P., Hall, J., & Chila, A. (1984). Change mechanisms in EMG biofeedback training: Cognitive changes underlying improvements in tension headache. *Journal of Consulting and Clinical Psychology, 52*, 1039–1053.

Johnson, J. (1973). Effects of accurate expectations about sensations on the sensory and distress components of pain. *Journal of Personality and Social Psychology, 27*, 261–275.

Johnson, J. (1984). Psychological interventions and coping with surgery. In A. Baum, S. Taylor, & J. Singer (Eds.), *Handbook of psychology and health* (Vol. 4). Hillsdale, NJ: Erlbaum.

Lazarus, R.S., & Folkman, S. (1984). *Stress, appraisal, and coping*. New York: Springer.

Litt, M. (1986). *Self-efficacy and perceived control: Cognitive mediators of pain tolerance*. Unpublished doctoral dissertation, Yale University, New Haven, CT.

Lowery, B., Jacobsen, B., & Murphy, B. (1983). An exploratory investigation of causal thinking of arthritics. *Nursing Research, 25*, 29–35.

Manning, M.M., & Wright, T.L. (1983). Self-efficacy expectancies, outcome expectancies, and the persistence of pain control in childbirth. *Journal of Personality and Social Psychology, 45*, 421–431.

Melzack, R. (1985). *Pain measurement and assessment*. New York: Raven.

Melzack, R., & Wall, P. (1965). Pain mechanisms: A new theory. *Science, 150*, 971–979.

Melzack, R., & Wall, P. (1982). *The challenge of pain*. New York: Basic Books.

Miller, S. (1980). Why having control reduces stress: Why if I can stop the roller coaster, I don't want to get off. In J. Garber & M. Seligman (Eds.), *Human helplessness: Theory and research* (pp. 71–95). New York: Academic Press.

Minarik, P., & Sparacino, P. (1989). Clinical nurse specialist collaboration in a university medical center. In P. Sparacino, D. Cooper, & P. Minarik (Eds.), *The clinical nurse specialist: Implementation and impact* (pp. 231–260). Norwalk, CT: Appleton & Lange.

Mohamed, S.N., Weisz, G.M., & Waring, E.M. (1978). The relationship of chronic pain to depression, marital adjustment, and family dynamics. *Pain, 5*, 285–292.

Neufeld, R., & Thomas, P. (1977). Effects of perceived efficacy of a prophylactic controlling mechanism on self-control under painful stimulation. *Canadian Journal of Behavioural Science, 9*, 224–232.

O'Leary, A. (1985). Self-efficacy and health. *Behavior Research Therapy, 23*, 437–451.

Reese, L. (1982). *Pain reduction through cognitive, self relative, and placebo means: A self-efficacy analysis*. Unpublished doctoral dissertation, Stanford University, Stanford, CA.

Schalling, D. (1986). Anxiety, pain, and coping. In C. Spielberger & I. Sarason (Eds.), *Stress and anxiety* (pp. 437–460). Washington, DC: Hemisphere.

Seligman, M. (1974). *Helplessness*. San Francisco: Freeman.

Taylor, S.E. (1983). Adjustment to threatening events: A theory of cognitive adaptation. *American Psychologist, 38*, 1161–1173.

Thoits, P.A. (1986). Social support as coping assistance. *Journal of Community Psychology, 54*, 416–423.

Thompson, S. (1981). Will it hurt less if I can control it? A complex answer to a simple question. *Psychological Bulletin, 90*, 89–101.

Violon, A., & Giurgea, D. (1984). Familial models for chronic pain. *Pain, 18*, 199–203.

Weiner, B., Russell, D., & Lerman, D. (1978). Affective consequences of causal ascriptions. In J.H. Harvey, W.J. Ickes, & R.F. Kidd (Eds.), *New directions in attribution research* (Vol. 3). Hillsdale, NJ: Erlbaum.

Weisenberg, M. (1977). Pain and pain control. *Psychological Bulletin, 84*, 1008–1044.

Weisenberg, M., Aviram, O., Wolf, Y., & Raphaeli, N. (1984). Relevant and irrelevant anxiety in the reaction to pain. *Pain, 20*, 371–383.

Weisenberg, M., Wolf, Y., Mittwoch, T., Mikulincer, M., & Aviram, O. (1985). Subject versus experimenter control in the reaction to pain. *Pain, 23*, 187–200.

Wortman, C.B., & Dintzer, L. (1978). Is an attributional analysis of the learned helplessness phenomenon viable? A critique of the Abramson-Seligman-Teasdale reformulation. *Journal of Abnormal Psychology, 87*, 75–90.

Chapter 4

Assessment of Pain in the Critically Ill

Kathleen A. Puntillo and Diana J. Wilkie

Assessment is integral to the nursing process and is a major critical care nursing activity and responsibility. As a result of assessment, diagnoses are made and treatments initiated. Assessment involves the collection of subjective and objective information about a patient's status, including the patient's pain. Pain assessment is the evaluation of the individual's particular pain experience, including both the felt sensation and the emotional, physiological, cognitive, and behavioral responses to pain. Pain measurement is the quantification of this experience; it is the transformation of subjective information into objective information.

This chapter stresses the importance of pain assessment, discusses some of the barriers to adequate pain assessment in critically ill adult patients, and presents a review of pain assessment methods. Because little has been written about pain assessment in the critically ill, suggestions are made about the application of current pain assessment methods to the critical care population.

IMPORTANCE OF PAIN ASSESSMENT

Pain assessment is an extremely important nursing activity for a number of reasons. First, without appropriate assessment, many erroneous assumptions can be made about the cause, location, or extent of a patient's pain and can result in improper or inadequate treatment. For example, if a surgical patient is bothered by exacerbation of chronic back pain due to lying on the operating table, the pain treatment plan could be very different from a plan for incisional pain.

Second, improper or ineffective pain assessment can lead to adverse physiological and psychological consequences. For example, pain has been reported to be associated with impaired respiratory performance, development of myocardial ischemia in compromised patients (Phillips & Cousins, 1986), and activation of the stress response (Bryan-Brown, 1986). In addition, anxiety, sleeplessness

45

(Phillips & Cousins, 1986), confusion, and delirium (Baker, 1984; Noble, 1979) have been associated with pain.

Third, nurses' assessments of their patients' pain can have a significant impact on physician decision making and prescriptions. Collaborative decision making and practice are highly valued in critical care and can significantly influence pain relief for the critically ill.

Pain experts distinguish between nociception and pain. Nociception is the stimulation of neural pathways by noxious stimuli, whereas pain, by definition, requires perceptual activity for noxious stimuli to be interpreted as pain (see Chapter 2). Critical care clinicians sometimes may believe that their patient's status precludes the ability to perceive pain (e.g., the comatose patient). Current evidence, however, has not determined a definitive anatomical location where nociception becomes pain. Thus, even when perception is deemed improbable, if nociceptive stimuli are present the conclusion cannot be made that pain does not occur. Given this ambiguity, a conservative and humanitarian approach is to consider all nociceptive stimuli painful. It is crucial, therefore, that any potentially painful procedure be treated properly.

BARRIERS TO ASSESSMENT

Pain assessment in a critical care environment presents a significant challenge. There are certain characteristics of the person in pain, the critical care environment, and critical care health professionals that can create barriers to successful assessment. Each of these three components—person, environment, and health professional—are discussed below so that a better appreciation of the complexity of pain assessment can be gained.

Characteristics of the Person

Individuals are products of their psychological, familial, and cultural environments. Each of these environments contributes to the manner in which an individual's pain is tolerated and conveyed to others. At times these intrinsic characteristics make the assessment of pain formidable. For example, a person who is depressed may withdraw from others and may not be willing to give adequate verbal descriptions of the pain. On the other hand, a person from a Mediterranean country may be expressive when in pain and viewed by health professionals as overreacting. Either the depressed or the expressive person may not be given appropriate attention by health professionals (see Chapters 3 and 5).

In addition to these intrinsic barriers, other factors may compromise pain assessment in critical care. Because of the presence of endotracheal tubes, patients may be physically unable to verbalize their pain, which usually is the most effective method of reporting pain. In some patients, an altered level of consciousness may affect pain perception, pain communication, or both. Other patients may have an alteration in mobility due to their pathological processes, such as paralysis due to spinal cord injury, which interferes with behaviors that typically suggest pain. Some patients may be subject to iatrogenic interferences with these normal behaviors, such as when protective restraints or paralyzing agents are used. To provide quality nursing care, it is important for staff to identify these and other problems that patients may have in verbally or behaviorally communicating their pain.

Characteristics of the Environment

Pain assessment requires time, knowledge, and a method of communicating findings. Because the complexity and acuity levels of critical care environments are increasing at a rapid pace, critical care clinicians need to prioritize their actions. Thus interventions for life-threatening patient problems may, understandably, be given a higher priority than pain assessment. Consequently, clinicians may be left with insufficient time to do a complete pain assessment. Additionally, lack of pain assessment knowledge is a barrier. For example, although critical care nurses have become knowledgeable and adept at respiratory assessment, they may not be so knowledgeable about pain assessment. The intent here is not to minimize the importance of respiratory assessment but to stress the importance of deliberative pain assessment and to encourage its performance.

Finally, documentation practices (or the lack thereof) are barriers to assessment. One method of accountability for practice is through written documentation. What has not been charted may or may not have been done. It is probable that, if there was a section on a critical care flowsheet for pain documentation, pain assessment would be given a higher priority, would be more uniform and systematic, and would be communicated more effectively among health team members. Research is needed to substantiate this hypothesis.

Characteristics of the Health Professional

Pain assessment also may be affected by a number of factors related to the individual providing care to the critically ill person. Clinicians, like patients, come to a particular clinical situation with their own beliefs, attitudes, and knowledge base about pain. These factors may influence clinicians' judgments about the nature of their patients' pain, the effectiveness of specific analgesics, and the amount of analgesics administered.

Beliefs and attitudes about pain arise from health professionals' cultural and educational experiences. Clinicians are most familiar with verbal and nonverbal expressions of pain that are similar to their own. Yet there is tremendous variability in pain expression among persons from different cultures (See Chapter 5). If clinicians are not educated about the significance of cultural differences in pain expression, they tend to rely on their own cultural heritages when making inferences about the pain experienced by the critically ill patient. Hence there may be a great discrepancy among clinicians, with each being convinced of the validity of his or her assessment of the patient's pain experience.

A health professional's knowledge about pain and pain management also may interfere with adequate pain assessment in the critically ill patient. Although there has been an explosion of pain research in the past two decades, a deficiency of basic pain content in medical and nursing education persists. Therefore, clinicians may not understand the influence of physiological variables on the amount of pain that the patient perceives. For example, low extracellular sodium concentrations decrease the amplitude of an action potential, resulting in a smaller amount of neurotransmitter release at the synapse (Koester, 1985). Therefore, a noxious stimulus could be perceived as less intense by a patient with hyponatremia. Additionally, morphine binding to opiate receptors is improved in the presence of low concentrations of sodium (Pasternak, Snownan, & Snyder, 1975; Pert & Snyder, 1973). Hence physiological differences such as variable serum sodium levels may account for some of the individual differences seen in response to pain and pain therapy in critical care settings.

Education about pain and pain management appears to alter barrier-producing attitudes, beliefs, and knowledge deficits (Hauck, 1986; Meyers, 1985). Nevertheless, additional research is needed to determine whether changes occur in clinical practice as a result of pain education.

Finally, health professionals' goals for therapy may be another barrier to accurate pain assessment. In fact, investigators have found that only 9% to 25% of clinicians cite complete pain relief as their goal when providing analgesic therapy (Grier, Howard, & Cohen, 1979; Weis, Sriwatanakul, Alloza, Weintraub, & Lasagna, 1983). Most clinicians indicate that they expect less than complete pain relief from their therapy, and pain assessment may reflect this bias.

UNIDIMENSIONAL METHODS OF ASSESSING PAIN

Pain is a sensation that elicits physiological, emotional, behavioral, and cognitive responses. It is through these responses that nurses learn about the subjective pain experience and assist in pain alleviation. Because no objective measure is available to accurately evaluate sensations and feelings, a crucial variable is the patient's subjective report (Wallenstein & Houde, 1975). The individual's description and quantification of the experienced pain is by far the most direct method of measuring pain. Although this pain report can be influenced by many factors, such as culture (Zborowski, 1952), psychological factors (Murray, 1975), and environment (Beecher, 1956), it nevertheless is based on the individual's assessment rather than the assessment of others.

Until recently, however, most pain assessment instruments measured a single dimension, most frequently the sensory dimension. The best-known unidimensional measures depend on the patient's report of pain perception or emotional state, but methods are now available to measure sensory, physiological, affective, cognitive, and behavioral dimensions of pain.

Assessing the Sensory Dimension

Assessment of the sensory dimension of pain includes gathering information about pain quality, location, and intensity. The qualitative nature of pain is described through the use of adjectives such as sharp, burning, tearing, and aching. Some of the qualitative words correspond to what is known about the specificity of pain fibers. For example, Aδ fibers carry sharp, well-localized pain, whereas the sensation carried by C fibers is frequently described as burning (see Chapter 2 for a discussion of pain pathways). Usually quality of pain is assessed when multidimensional tools are used; these tools are described later.

Assessing the location of pain is certainly an important prerequisite to appropriate intervention. This information may be elicited by asking the patient to name or point to the body area where pain is felt (McGuire, 1981). The use of a body outline is advantageous, especially when a person's mobility is impaired and for record-keeping purposes (Margoles, 1983). As a map of the pain location, the body outline is useful to follow pain extension or resolution over time. Drawings on a body outline frequently reflect dermatomal distribution and help localize the spinal segment involved in the pain. When interpreting pain location on a body outline, however, it is important to keep in mind that visceral pain is a more diffuse sensation and is difficult to localize to a discrete area. The diffuseness of visceral pain can be explained by the observation that there are fewer afferent nociceptive visceral fibers. Generally these are C fibers, which carry less discriminate sensations (Cervero, 1988). In addition, pain may be referred from one site to another, probably because both visceral and somatic fibers converge on the same cells in lamina V of the spinal cord dorsal horn (Cervero, 1988; Wall, 1984).

Pain intensity is the magnitude of the pain sensation and is the most frequently assessed dimension of pain. Various tools have been devised to document patient's self-report of pain intensity. Because of their widespread use, these tools are now described in some detail.

Category Scales

Category scales have verbal pain severity descriptors such as mild, moderate, and severe (verbal descriptor scale) or a gradation of numbers such as 0 to 10 (numerical rating scale; Fig. 4-1). An advantage of category scales is their ease in administration and scoring (McGuire, 1984). Patients simply state or circle the word or number that best fits their level of pain. A disadvantage is that the patient must choose categories that may not seem to be equally spaced (Chapman, Casey, Dubner, Foley, Gracely, & Reading, 1985). Also, words may not mean the same thing to different people (Ohnhaus & Adler, 1975). Visual disturbances and poor motor strength and coordination in critically ill patients may be additional disadvantages to the use of these scales. To circumvent these problems, nurses can ask the patient to nod his or her head in reply or to hold up the number of fingers that describes the level of pain.

Visual Analogue Scales

A visual analogue scale (VAS) is a horizontal, vertical, or curved line with word anchors at each end denoting the extremes of what is being measured. Figure 4-1 depicts a VAS with commonly used word anchors. The length of the line is usually 10 cm. The patient marks or points to the place on the line that he or she judges to

---

Verbal Descriptor Scale

No Pain	Mild Pain	Moderate Pain	Severe Pain	Worst Pain Possible

Numerical Rating Scale

---

0   1   2   3   4   5   6   7   8   9   10

Visual Analogue Scale

No Pain				Worst Pain Ever

Figure 4-1 Pain intensity scales.

represent the intensity of pain or pain relief. VASs are more sensitive than verbal descriptor or numerical rating scales because the patient rates his or her pain anywhere along a continuum (Huskisson, 1983; McGuire, 1984). Additionally, VASs are useful for the patient who judges the pain intensity to be between two verbal descriptors.

The linear VASs are easy to use in most patient populations, but they may pose problems for the critically ill, in whom impaired visual perception and muscle coordination are frequent problems. Modified visual analogue scales that may be more applicable to a critical care setting have been developed. An analog chromatic continuous scale (ACCS) is a 160-mm long and 33-mm wide color-coded tool (Grossi, Borghi, & Montanari, 1985). The patient moves a slider to a point along a 100-mm by 20-mm, pink to red colored line that depicts his or her pain intensity. The corresponding value in millimeters can be read by the clinician on the opposite side of the instrument. The ACCS was found to correlate well with the VAS, having comparable sensitivity, accuracy, and reliability when used preoperatively for assessment of pain from intravenous cannulation in a gynecological population (Grossi et al., 1985). In this same group postoperatively, when motor coordination and sight were impaired, traditional VAS ratings were found to be unreliable whereas ACCS ratings were well defined. Use of the ACCS warrants exploration in a critically ill population.

Other Scales

Two other pain intensity scales that may be relevant to critical care are the light analogue recorder (Nayman, 1979) and a computerized VAS (Bhachu, Kay, Healey, & Beatty, 1983). In the former, the patient pushes a button to turn on different colored lights that depict various intensities of pain. In the latter, the patient presses a button that extends a horizontal bar on a computer screen, the length of the bar representing his or her pain intensity. This is accompanied by an audible tone, which increases in pitch as the bar length increases. Although these types of tools are costly and not feasible for all settings, they may be appropriate in critical care units, where verbal communication often is a problem.

Assessing the Physiological Dimension

A physiological correlate of pain is a physiological event that occurs along with a patient's report of pain (Chapman et al., 1985), suggesting an interrelationship between the two. However, this relationship does not imply causality. Pain automatically activates both voluntary and involuntary defense systems (Sicuteri, Del Bene, & Poggioni, 1984). Although the voluntary system (i.e., withdrawal of a body part from a painful stimulus) can be controlled by the individual, frequently in acute pain the involuntary system cannot. When pain is sudden and severe, a whole series of autonomic nervous system (ANS) physiological responses is evidenced. As yet unanswered is the question of how much these changes are the result of emotions evoked by the pain rather than the result of the nociceptive stimulus or the sensation of pain itself (Sicuteri et al., 1984). Nonetheless, clinicians note changes in vital signs when patients report pain, particularly when the pain is moderate to severe and acute.

When using ANS changes as indicators of pain, one must remember that many medications used in critical care (e.g., β-blocking agents) may blunt these ANS responses to pain. Therefore, lack of expected increased heart rate and blood pressure, for example, does not mean absence of pain. Many postoperative pain studies have used ANS changes as measures of pain (e.g., Flaherty & Fitzpatrick, 1978; McBride, 1967; Miller & Perry, 1990; Mogan, Wells, & Robertson, 1985).

In one study of intensive care unit patients, investigators observed physiological variables (tachycardia, pupil dilation, and hypertension) as signs of pain in those treated with morphine sulfate (Rawal & Tandon, 1985). They concluded that a decrease in pulse to nearly normal levels is one indicator that the patient is pain free. This was certainly a reasonable conclusion to make, but in this and the other studies in which ANS changes were measured there were some methodological and design problems. Therefore, it is difficult to know how confident clinicians can be about the relationship between ANS changes and pain in their patients.

Further research is needed to determine how these ANS parameters correlate and change with pain to improve assessment and treatment practices. In the interim, these measures should continue to be part of a pain assessment. This is especially true in a critical care setting, where the ability to verbalize pain is often impaired and where these physiological variables are easily measured and documented.

Assessing the Affective Dimension

A number of emotional responses to pain are believed to influence and be influenced by pain perception, even though the precise mechanisms of their action have not been described. Anxiety, fear, depression, anger, helplessness, hopelessness, and joy have been associated with pain modulation (Bonica, 1985; Cousins, 1983). One or more of these affective states may be present in critically ill patients.

Beecher's (1956) classic research suggested that perceived pain intensity was influenced in part by reactions to the pain. He proposed that anxiety level influences the amount of pain. On the basis of this hypothesis, Johnson and Rice (1974) demonstrated that in laboratory conditions the distress of pain could be measured separately from the sensory component. Since that time, however, these affective and sensory components of pain have not always been easily separated.

Taenzer (1983), for example, asked 40 patients with postoperative cholecystectomy pain to report pain distress on a 10-cm VAS anchored on one end with "no distress" and on the other with "severe distress." Distress decreased daily from postoperative day 1 to 6. This distress was strongly associated with the amount of pain that the patient reported, but it was only moderately associated with other measures of emotional state, such as anxiety or depression. These findings suggest that the measure of affective state was not clearly separate from the pain intensity.

Conversely, Ahles, Blanchard, and Ruckdeschel (1983) found that 77 patients with cancer were able to use VASs to measure anxiety and depression. These scales were anchored on the left with "I am not anxious (depressed)" and on the right with "I am as anxious (depressed) as I can possibly imagine myself being." The 40 patients with cancer pain reported significantly higher anxiety and depression scores than the 37 patients without pain. Yet pain intensity was not strongly associated with anxiety or depression scores, suggesting that the tools were measuring dimensions different from but somewhat related to the sensory dimension.

Because of the relative simplicity of a VAS, perhaps the affective dimension could be assessed in critical care through use of this type of scale. Patients require careful explanation of how to use a VAS, however, and practice using it. Similar recommendations are important for VAS anxiety and depression scales.

A number of other scales have been used to measure the affective dimension of pain; because of their complexity, however, these scales are not appropriate for use with most patients requiring critical care. Examples include the Profile of Mood States (McNair, Lorr, & Droppleman, 1971), the State-Trait Anxiety Inventory (Speilberger, 1983), and the Beck Depression Inventory (Beck, Ward, Mendelsohn, Mock, & Erbaugh, 1961). Each has been used to measure acute and chronic pain, but because more than 20 questions are included in each tool their clinical use in the critical care environment is probably not feasible.

Assessing the Cognitive Dimension

Beliefs and attitudes about pain, pain therapy, illness, and one's resources and abilities to manage or cope with pain are cognitive dimension variables that may influence perception of pain (Ahles et al., 1983; Daut & Cleeland, 1982). The cognitive dimension has been the focus of limited systematic research in acutely ill populations, however.

Beecher (1956) found that wounded soldiers reported less pain and requested less analgesic medication than civilian surgical patients with similar wounds. He suggested that the injury was interpreted by the soldiers as an indication that they would be sent home. Hence the soldiers did not perceive the amount of pain that would be expected, given the extent of their injuries. These data suggest that the meaning that the individual gives to pain may influence the amount of pain perceived and reported.

Unidimensional measures of the cognitive dimension of pain are sparse and not developed for use in critical care environments. Locus of control (Rotter, 1966) and self-efficacy (O'Leary, 1985) tools are the most commonly used measures of the cognitive dimension of pain (see Chapter 3).

Assessing the Behavioral Dimension

Behavioral indicators of pain are vital to accurate assessment of pain in critically ill patients. Even for those patients with intact ability to verbalize their pain, observation of behavior may provide important clues about the pain that could be useful as a pain management plan is devised.

Behaviors may be defined rather broadly to include physiological manifestations of pain, verbalizations about pain, vocalizations, facial expressions, and gross body activities. Variations in pain may be reflected by the behaviors summarized in Table 4-1. Although many of these behaviors may be expressions

---

Table 4-1 Behaviors Associated with Pain

Type of Behavior	Examples
Facial Expression	Grimacing (1)*, clenching teeth (2), tightly shutting lips (2), gazing/staring (3,4), wrinkling forehead (2), tearing (2)
Vocalization (2)	Moaning (4), groaning (3), grunting (2), sighing (2), gasping, crying (3), screaming (3)
Verbalization	Praying (3), counting (3), swearing or cursing (3), repeating nonsensical phrases (3)
Body action	Thrashing (2), pounding (3), biting (3), rocking (3), rubbing (4)
Behaviors	Massaging (3,4), immobilizing (4), guarding (1,4), bracing (1), eating/drinking (4), applying pressure (3,4)/heat (3,4)/cold (3), assuming special position/posture (3,4), reading (3,4), watching television (4), listening to music (4)

*Numbers in parentheses refer to references: (1) Keefe & Dolan (1986); (2) Roberts (1986); (3) Copp (1974); (4) Wilkie et al. (1988).

of pain, some have been identified by patients as their attempts to control their pain (Copp, 1974; Wilkie, Lovejoy, Dodd, & Tesler, 1988). For example, patients may be reducing pain through use of visualization or distraction methods when they gaze, stare, count, repeat nonsensical phrases, watch television, listen to music, or read. Patients also recognize that massaging or rubbing a painful area helps control pain. Critical care clinicians must exert caution when drawing a conclusion about the amount of pain a critically ill patient has if the patient engages in pain-controlling behaviors without exhibiting pain-expression behaviors (e.g., moaning, crying, or thrashing).

In adult populations, most behavioral scales have been developed to assess chronic pain and are not relevant to the critical care setting. Tools developed for pediatric populations commonly include behavioral indices of pain, but many of these behaviors are inappropriate for the adult critical care patient. Hence measurement of the behavioral dimension of acute pain is hampered by lack of valid and reliable tools that are easily used with the critically ill.

MULTIDIMENSIONAL TOOLS FOR ASSESSING PAIN

A multidimensional pain assessment tool is one that assesses more than one aspect of a person's pain and therefore captures more of the pain experience. Use of such a tool is more consistent with nurses' attention to the wholeness of a patient's pain experience. Table 4-2 describes a number of multidimensional tools that might be feasible for use in selected critical care populations.

Multidimensional pain assessment tools differ in the attention devoted to the various dimensions of the pain experience. Usually some measure of the sensory dimension is included. Of course, pain intensity is the most frequently measured sensory component (Fishman, Pasternak, Wallenstein, Houde, Holland, & Foley, 1987; Gaston-Johansson, Fridh, & Turner-Norvell, 1988; McGuire, 1981; Melzack, 1987; Mount, Melzack, & Mackinnon, 1978; Tursky, 1976). Pain quality is most comprehensively measured with the McGill-Melzack Pain Questionnaire (Mount et al., 1978), but other tools also address this aspect of the sensory dimension (McGuire, 1981; Melzack, 1987; Tursky, 1976). Pain location is assessed less frequently with multidimensional tools (e.g., McGuire, 1981; Mount et al., 1978).

The physiological dimension of pain seldom is a component of multidimensional pain-assessment tools. If the dimension is considered broadly, the McGill-Melzack Pain Questionnaire addresses physiological symptoms such as sleep, nausea, and vomiting (Mount et al., 1978). Otherwise, this dimension is inadequately measured with current tools.

Numerous tools measure the affective dimension of pain (Fishman et al., 1987; Gaston-Johansson et al., 1988; Melzack, 1987; Mount et al., 1978; Tursky,

Table 4-2 Selected Multidimensional Pain Instruments

Instrument	Studies	Description	Dimensions Measured
Memorial Pain Assessment Card (Fig. 4-2)	Fishman, Pasternak, Wallenstein, Houde, Holland, & Foley (1987)	Single 8.5″ × 11″ card folded in half, four sided; three sides have VASs to measure pain intensity, pain relief, and mood; fourth side has randomly placed set of pain intensity words	Sensory, affective (measures general psychological distress; may not be pain related)
Pain-O-Meter	Gaston-Johansson & Asklund-Gustaffsson (1985); Gaston-Johansson, Fridh, & Turner-Norvell (1988); Gaston-Johansson, personal communication (1988)	Plastic 8″ × 2″ × 1″ card; side one has 11 affective words; side two has 10-cm VAS	Sensory, affective
Pain Assessment Tool	McGuire (1981)	One page; includes demographic information; questions about intensity, location, quality, onset, patient's view of pain; area to document intervention plan	Sensory, behavioral, physiological
Short-form McGill Pain Questionnaire	Melzack (1987)	One page; includes 11 sensory and 4 affective word descriptors, verbal intensity scale, VAS	Sensory, affective
McGill-Melzack Pain Questionnaire	Mount, Melzack, & Mackinnon (1978); Melzack & Torgerson (1971); Melzack (1975); Dubuisson & Melzack (1976); Turk, Rudy, & Salorvey (1985); Graham, Bond, Gerkovich, & Cook (1980); Chen & Treede (1985)	One page; includes 78 word descriptors in 20 categories; 3 pattern words, body outline, associated symptoms (e.g., sleep, food, activity), intensity scale	Sensory, affective, physiological, cognitive, behavioral
Pain Perception Profile	Tursky (1976); Tursky, Jamner, & Friedman (1982)	Four-part protocol; part III may be useful in critical care; includes three-column word list with 12 intensity, 12 unpleasantness, 13 feeling descriptors that have been quantified by means of scaling techniques	Sensory, affective

Validity	Reliability	Completion Time	Scoring Methods	Populations
Construct, correlation with McGill Pain Questionnaire and among subscales	Not reported	Less than 20 seconds for experienced patient	Patient marks on VASs; response measured by clinician; pain intensity words circled	Hospitalized adult cancer patients without severe physical disability or cognitive impairments
Construct	Test-retest	Less than 2 minutes	Sensory and affective words assigned numbers 1–5	Labor, post-operative, cancer, chronic pain
Not reported	Not reported	10–15 minutes	Patient points to or traces area of pain; uses own words to describe pain; rates intensity of pain on 0–10 number scale; answers series of questions about onset, alleviation, aggravation of pain	Chronic
Concurrent	Not reported	2–5 minutes	Words are read to patient, who selects as many words as describe pain; intensity of each quality of pain (word) is rated by patient (none, mild, moderate, severe); patient selects word to describe intensity of pain and marks VAS	Postoperative, obstetric, dental, musculoskeletal
Content, concurrent, predictive, construct	Test-retest	Less than 15 minutes	Words are read to patient, who selects no more than one word/group; predetermined rank values of sensory, affective, evaluative, miscellaneous words summed for subscale scores; patient marks body outline and picks intensity word (scored as 0–5)	Acute, chronic, cancer, experimental
Content, concurrent	Stable	Not reported	Patient selects one word per group; score based on a priori value assigned to word	Chronic headache, experimental

1976). Usually these measures are verbal or VAS-like. A major limitation of the affective measures, however, is that not all emotions related to pain are assessed by the tools. Additional research is needed to expand the affective component of pain-assessment tools to include joy, anger, hopelessness, helplessness, and other pain-related emotions.

The McGill-Melzack Pain Questionnaire is one of the few multidimensional tools to include measures of the cognitive dimension by including evaluative pain descriptors. Only five evaluative words are included, however. The behavioral dimension of pain is measured briefly with some multidimensional tools (McGuire, 1981; Mount et al., 1978). Pain-aggravating and pain-alleviating behaviors are types of behaviors measured by these tools. Again, additional research is needed to develop other measures of the cognitive and behavioral dimensions of pain.

Despite the limitations of the available multidimensional pain-assessment tools, many have been used in multiple patient populations and have some degree of validity and reliability. Administration and scoring times vary from a few seconds to 15 minutes. Although 15 minutes may be too long for pain assessment in critical care, administration of some multidimensional pain-assessment tools can be accomplished in a reasonable time period.

INSTRUMENTS FOR ASSESSING PAIN IN CRITICAL CARE PATIENTS

In spite of the large number of pain assessment instruments that have been developed and used in various clinical situations, research on the appropriateness of these instruments in critical care settings is lacking. Until such research is available, it is suggested that pain in critical care patients be assessed by instruments that meet two criteria: (1) The instruments have been shown to be valid and reliable in other patient populations, and (2) use of the instrument is feasible in a critical care setting. Feasibility means that the instrument is completed by the patient in a brief time period and that its use is not physically or mentally taxing.

Figures 4-2 and 4-3 are examples of two pain-assessment measures that are possible options for critical care. Figure 4-2 presents the four sections of the Memorial Pain Assessment Card (Fishman et al., 1987; see Table 4-2). Three of the sections are VASs used to assess intensity, mood, and pain relief. The fourth section is a categorical scale of pain intensity; patients circle or point to the word that best describes their pain severity.

Figure 4-3 presents a body outline to which a patient can point to indicate the area or areas of present pain. After patients localize their pain on the body outline, they can be asked whether the pain is near the skin or deeper. This question

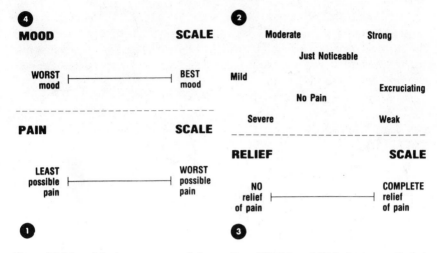

Figure 4-2 Memorial pain assessment card. *Source:* From ''The Memorial Pain Assessment Card: A Valid Instrument for the Evaluation of Cancer Pain'' by B. Fishman et al., 1987, *Cancer, 60.* Copyright 1987 by The American Cancer Society, Inc. Reprinted by permission.

attempts to determine whether the patient's pain is superficial, deep somatic, or visceral in origin. Clinical experiences indicate that patients prefer to first report the location of their pain, then the intensity and quality of their pain. Nurses usually ask about pain intensity first, but pain assessment is facilitated by using the order preferred by the patient.

Use of these recommended pain instruments usually requires little time (less than 3 minutes) and effort for both the critical care patient and the health professional assessing the pain. Furthermore, these instruments elicit information that is valuable for planning pain relief interventions and evaluating their effectiveness. Once again, however, research on the appropriateness of these and other instruments in a critical care setting is needed.

CONTINUITY OF PAIN ASSESSMENT

As with most nursing care activities, pain assessment is a process. This chapter provided content essential to adequate pain assessment of critically ill patients, but the process of assessing pain involves more than application of this content by using the multidimensional pain assessment tools. To draw logical and accurate conclusions about the data obtained from use of the tools, the critical care nurse

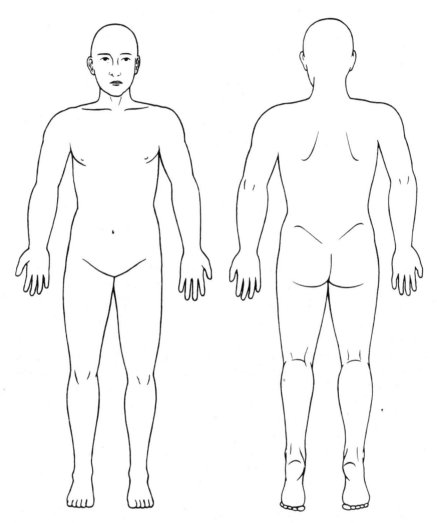

Figure 4-3 Body outline for pain location report. *Source:* Copyright © 1989 by D. Wilkie and K. Puntillo. Reprinted with permission.

must recognize his or her beliefs and attitudes about pain that could influence the pain assessment process, understand basic pain mechanisms, and understand the expected effect of the various pain-management strategies. Then, when using an instrument feasible for the critical care setting, the nurse has greater ability objectively to evaluate the patient's pain.

The pain-assessment process is ongoing. Although the process begins with an initial assessment, follow-up assessment is essential. For the initial assessment, it is important to use multidimensional assessment tools such as those described above. Follow-up assessments may emphasize fewer dimensions, such as pain intensity or amount of pain relief.

Timing of follow-up assessments is important. Optimally, follow-up assessment times should correspond to the onset or peak effect of administered analgesic therapy. Certainly, follow-up assessment time should correspond to the expected dissipation of the analgesic effect. Therefore, timing of the follow-up assessment is contingent on the expected pattern of the pain and pain relief. Use of the multidimensional tools in this manner, by a critical care nurse aware of his or her personal beliefs, has the potential to provide an accurate assessment of the subjective pain experience.

CONCLUSION

Under even the best of circumstances, pain assessment is a complex process. In a critical care setting, it is a significant challenge. To date, little research exists on pain assessment in critical care, but a number of valid and reliable pain-assessment methods can be adapted for use in critical care settings.

Despite the barriers to pain assessment in critical care settings, adequate assessment is an essential prerequisite to initiating and evaluating the effectiveness of pain-relieving interventions. Critical care nurses can best serve their patients in pain by using interventions that are based on systematic and sensitive assessment practices.

REFERENCES

Ahles, T.A., Blanchard, E.B., & Ruckdeschel, J.C. (1983). The multidimensional nature of cancer-related pain. *Pain, 17*, 277–288.

Baker, C.F. (1984). Sensory overload and noise in the ICU: Sources of environmental stress. *Critical Care Quarterly, 6*, 66–80.

Beck, A.T., Ward, C.H., Mendelsohn, M., Mock, J., & Erbaugh, J. (1961). An inventory for measuring depression. *Archives of General Psychiatry, 4*, 561–571.

Beecher, H.K. (1956). Relationship of significance of wound to the pain experienced. *Journal of the American Medical Association, 161*, 1609–1613.

Bhachu, H.S., Kay, B., Healey, E.J., & Beatty, P. (1983). Grading of pain and anxiety. *Anaesthesia, 38*, 875–878.

Bonica, J.J. (1985). Treatment of cancer pain: Current status and future needs. *Advances in Pain Research and Therapy, 9*, 589–616.

Bryan-Brown, C.W. (1986). Development of pain management in critical care. In M.J. Cousins & G.C. Phillips (Eds.), *Acute pain management* (pp. 1-19). New York: Churchill Livingstone.

Cervero, F. (1988). Visceral pain. In R. Dubner, G.F. Cervero, & M.R. Bond (Eds.), *Pain research and clinical management* (Vol. 3, pp. 216–226). Amsterdam: Elsevier.

Chapman, C.R., Casey, K.L., Dubner, R., Foley, K.M., Gracely, R.H., & Reading, A.E. (1985). Pain measurement: An overview. *Pain, 22,* 1–31.

Chen, A.C.N., & Treede, R.D. (1985). The McGill Pain Questionnaire in the assessment of basic and tonic experimental pain: Behavioral evaluation of the "pain inhibiting pain" effect. *Pain, 22,* 67–79.

Copp, L.A. (1974). The spectrum of suffering. *American Journal of Nursing, 74,* 491–495.

Cousins, N. (1983). *The healing heart.* New York: Norton.

Daut, R.L., & Cleeland, C.S. (1982). The prevalence and severity of pain in cancer. *Cancer, 50,* 1913–1918.

Dubuisson, D., & Melzack, R. (1976). Classification of clinical pain descriptions by multiple group discriminant analysis. *Experimental Neurology, 51,* 480–487.

Fishman, B., Pasternak, S., Wallenstein, S.L., Houde, R.W., Holland, J.C., & Foley, K.M. (1987). The Memorial Pain Assessment Card: A valid instrument for the evaluation of cancer pain. *Cancer, 60,* 1151–1158.

Flaherty, G.C., & Fitzpatrick, J.J. (1978). Relaxation technique to increase comfort level of postoperative patients: A preliminary study. *Nursing Research, 27,* 325–355.

Gaston-Johansson, F., & Asklund-Gustafsson, M. (1985). A baseline study for the development of an instrument for the assessment of pain. *Journal of Advanced Nursing, 10,* 539–546.

Gaston-Johansson, F., Fridh, G., Turner-Norvell, K. (1988). Progression of labor pain in primiparas and multiparas. *Nursing Research, 37,* 86–90.

Graham, C., Bond, S.S., Gerkovich, M.M., & Cook, M.R. (1980). Use of the McGill Pain Questionnaire in the assessment of cancer pain: Replicability and consistency. *Pain, 8,* 377–387.

Grier, M.R., Howard, M., & Cohen, F. (1979). Beliefs and values associated with administering narcotic analgesics to terminally ill patients. In American Nurses' Association Division on Practice (Ed.), *Clinical and scientific sessions* (pp. 211–222). Kansas City, MO: American Nurses Association.

Grossi, E., Borghi, C., & Montanari, M. (1985). Measurement of pain: Comparison between visual analog scale and analog chromatic continuous scale. *Advances in Pain Research and Therapy, 9,* 371–376.

Hauck, S.L. (1986). Pain: Problem for the person with cancer. *Cancer Nursing, 9,* 66–76.

Huskisson, E.C. (1983). Visual analogue scales. In R. Melzack (Ed.), *Pain measurement and assessment* (pp. 33–37). New York: Raven.

Johnson, J.E., & Rice, Y.N. (1974). Sensory and distress components of pain: Implications for the study of clinical pain. *Nursing Research, 23,* 203–209.

Keefe, F.J., & Dolan E. (1986). Pain behavior and pain coping strategies in low back pain and myofascial pain syndrome patients. *Pain, 24,* 49–56.

Koester, J. (1985). Voltage-gated channels and the action potential. In E.R. Kandel & J.H. Schwartz (Eds.), *Principles of neural science* (2nd ed., pp. 75–88). New York: Elsevier.

Margoles, M.S. (1983). The pain chart: Spatial properties of pain. In R. Melzack (Ed.), *Pain measurement and assessment* (pp. 215–225). New York: Raven.

McBride, M.A. (1967). Nursing approach, pain, and relief: An exploratory experiment. *Nursing Research, 16,* 337–341.

McGuire, D.B. (1984). The measurement of clinical pain. *Nursing Research, 33,* 152–156.

McGuire, L. (1981). A short simple tool for assessing your patient's pain. *Nursing '81, 11,* 48–49.

McNair, D.M., Lorr, M., & Droppleman, L.F. (1971). *Profile of mood states.* San Diego, CA: Educational and Industrial Testing Service.

Melzack, R. (1975). The McGill Pain Questionnaire: Major properties and scoring methods. *Pain, 1,* 277–299.

Melzack, R. (1987). The short-form McGill Pain Questionnaire. *Pain, 30,* 191–197.

Melzack, R., & Torgerson, W.S. (1971). On the language of pain. *Anesthesiology, 34,* 50–59.

Meyers, J.S. (1985). Cancer pain: Assessment of nurses' knowledge and attitudes. *Oncology Nursing Forum, 12,* 62–66.

Miller, K.M., & Perry, P.A. (1990). Relaxation techniques and postoperative pain in patients undergoing cardiac surgery. *Heart & Lung, 19,* 136–146.

Mogan, J., Wells, N., & Robertson, E. (1985). Effects of preoperative teaching on postoperative pain: A replication and expansion. *International Journal of Nursing Studies, 22,* 267–280.

Mount, B.M., Melzack, R., & Mackinnon, K.J. (1978). The management of intractable pain in patients with advanced malignant disease. *Journal of Urology, 120,* 720–725.

Murray, J.B. (1975). Psychology of the pain experience. In M. Weisenberg (Ed.), *Pain: Clinical and experimental perspectives* (pp. 36–44). St. Louis, MO: Mosby.

Nayman, J. (1979). Measurement and control of postoperative pain. *Annals of the Royal College of Surgeons of England, 61,* 419–426.

Nobel, M.A. (1979). Modifying the ICU environment. In M.A. Noble (Ed.), *The ICU environment: Directions for nursing* (pp. 303–323). Reston, VA: Reston Publishing.

Ohnhaus, E.E., & Adler, R. (1975). Methodological problems in the measurement of pain: A comparison between the verbal rating scale and the visual analogue scale. *Pain, 1,* 379–384.

O'Leary, A. (1985). Self-efficacy and health. *Brain Research Therapy, 23,* 437–451.

Pasternak, G.W., Snownan, S.M., & Snyder, S.H. (1975). Selective enhancement of [^{1}H]-opiate agonist binding by divalent cations. *Molecular Pharmacology, 11,* 735–744.

Pert, C.B., & Snyder, S.H. (1973). Opiate receptor: Its demonstration in nervous tissue. *Science, 179,* 1011–1014.

Phillips, G.D., & Cousins, M.J. (1986). Neurological mechanisms of pain and the relationship of pain anxiety and sleep. In M.J. Cousins & G.D. Phillips (Eds.), *Acute pain management* (pp. 21–48). New York: Churchill Livingstone.

Rawal, N., & Tandon, B. (1985). Epidural and intrathecal morphine in intensive care units. *Intensive Care Medicine, 11,* 129–133.

Roberts, S.L. (1986). *Behavioral concepts and the critically ill patient* (2nd ed.). Norwalk, CT: Appleton-Century-Crofts.

Rotter, J.B. (1966). Generalized expectancies for internal versus external control of reinforcement. *Psychological Monographs: General and Applied, 80,* 1–28.

Sicuteri, F., Del Bene, E., & Poggioni, M. (1984). Changes of vegetative parameters under pain. In B. Bromm (Ed.), *Pain measurement in man: Neurophysiological correlates of pain* (pp. 111–126). Amsterdam: Elsevier Science.

Speilberger, C.D. (1983). *State-trait anxiety inventory manual.* Palo Alto, CA: Consulting Psychologists Press.

Taenzer, P. (1983). Postoperative pain: Relationships among measures of pain, mood, and narcotic requirements. In R. Melzack (Ed.), *Pain measurement and assessment* (pp. 111–118). New York: Raven.

Turk, D.C., Rudy, T.E., & Salovey, P. (1985). The McGill Pain Questionnaire reconsidered: Confirming the factor structure and examining appropriate uses. *Pain, 21*, 385–397.

Tursky, B. (1976). Development of pain perception profile. In M. Weisenberg & B. Tursky (Eds.), *Pain: New perspectives in therapy and research* (pp. 171–174). New York: Plenum.

Tursky, B., Jamner, L.D., & Friedman, R. (1982). The Pain Perception Profile: A psychophysical approach to the assessment of pain report. *Behavior Therapy, 13*, 376–394.

Wall, P.D. (1984). The dorsal horn. In P.D. Wall & R. Melzack (Eds.), *Textbook of pain* (pp. 80–87). Edinburgh: Churchill Livingstone.

Wallenstein, S.L., & Houde, R.W. (1975). The clinical evaluation of analgesic effectiveness. In S. Ehrenpreis & A. Neidle (Eds.), *Methods in narcotics research* (pp. 127–145). New York: Dekker.

Weis, O.F., Sriwatanakul, K., Alloza, J.L., Weintraub, M., & Lasagna, L. (1983). Attitudes of patients, housestaff, and nurses toward postoperative analgesic care. *Anesthesia and Analgesia, 62*, 70–74.

Wilkie, D.J., Lovejoy, N., Dodd, M., & Tesler, M. (1988). Cancer pain control behaviors: Description and correlation with pain intensity. *Oncology Nursing Forum, 15*, 723–731.

Zborowski, M. (1952). Cultural components in response to pain. *Journal of Social Issues, 8*, 16–30.

RECOMMENDED READING

Donovan, M.I. (1987). Clinical assessment of cancer pain. In D.B. McGuire & C.H. Yarbro (Eds.), *Cancer pain management* (pp. 105–132). Orlando, FL: Grune & Stratton.

Donovan, M.I., & Dillon, P. (1987). Incidence and characteristics of pain in a sample of hospitalized cancer patients. *Cancer Nursing, 10*, 85–92.

Donovan, M.I., Dillon, P., & McGuire, L. (1987). Incidence and characteristics of pain in a sample of medical-surgical inpatients. *Pain, 30*, 69–78.

Houde, R.W. (1982). Methods for measuring clinical pain in humans. *Acta Anaesthesia Scandinavia* (Suppl. 74), 25–29.

Huskisson, E.C. (1974). Measurement of pain. *Lancet, 2*, 1127–1131.

Jensen, M.P., Karoly, P., & Braver, S. (1986). The measurement of clinical pain intensity: A comparison of six methods. *Pain, 27*, 117–126.

McCaffery, M., & Beebe, A. (1989). *Pain: Clinical manual for nursing practice*. St. Louis, MO: Mosby.

McGuire, D.B. (1988). Measuring pain. In, M.F. Stromborg (Ed.). *Instruments for clinical nursing research* (pp. 333–356). Norwalk, CT: Appleton & Lange.

Chapter 5

Cultural Diversity in the Response to Pain

Marilyn Kuhel Douglas

Being ill [in Spain] calls for loud complaint—an exercise of Latin spontaneity rather than Anglo-Saxon self-control. (Kenny, 1962, p. 284)

Not everyone defines and expresses pain in the same way. Individual differences in the response to pain have long been recognized by bedside clinicians and investigators alike.

Any experienced nurse can recall at least one instance in which two patients, side by side, underwent the same painful procedure or had the same pathology and yet responded to the pain in totally different ways. Many factors account for these differences, such as gender, personality characteristics, or socioeconomic class. Also among those variables found to influence pain behaviors is the culture of the patient. This chapter focuses on the cultural component and its relationship to pain, particularly in critical care.

STUDIES OF CULTURAL DIFFERENCES

A few cross-cultural pain studies have been performed both in the laboratory and in the clinical setting. Most, however, have not been well controlled for the many other variables that affect pain behaviors. Therefore, the true relationship between culture and the response to pain has yet to be determined.

Laboratory Studies

Experiments of induced pain performed in the laboratory on subjects of various cultures found no significant differences among the groups in pain threshold, the

65

point at which pain begins. On the other hand, pain tolerance, the point at which the subject winces and withdraws, did differ significantly according to cultural group. In one such study, the groups tested were "Yankees" (Protestants of British descent), first-generation Irish, Italians, and Jews. The "Yankees" recorded the highest pain-tolerance levels and the Italian subjects the lowest (Sternbach & Tursky, 1965).

The generalization of these findings to the clinical setting is questionable, however. Because pain in the laboratory setting is experimentally controlled, the meaning and significance of the pain experience is not the same as in the clinical situation.

Clinical Studies

Cross-cultural studies performed in the clinical setting have been limited, especially in the critical care area.

Hospitalized Patients

The work of Zborowski (1952, 1969) remains the classic study of cross-cultural pain responses in hospitalized patients. Zborowski studied 103 medical-surgical unit patients of four cultural groups: "Old-American," Italian, Irish, and Jewish. These subjects were controlled for age but not for socioeconomic status, gender, or pain-causing pathology.

Various qualitative methods were used in this study, including questionnaires, unstructured interviews, and direct observation of patients' behaviors and manner of describing their perceptions of and feelings about pain. The specific elements of the pain experience, such as its intensity, duration, and quality, as well as its interpretation and significance were compared across the four cultural groups.

From these observations, Zborowski made the following conclusions. The "Old-American" tends to be precise in the description of pain and its significance, displays little emotion, and prefers to withdraw from other people when in pain. The Irish patients were similar to the "Old-Americans" in that they showed little emotion with pain and tended to deemphasize the pain. They differed from that group, however, in that they had difficulty in describing and talking about their pain.

Both the Jewish and the Italian patients shared a lack of inhibitions in expressing pain, admitting freely that they show their pain and do so by crying, moaning, complaining, and being more demanding. Both groups also preferred the company of others, especially relatives, while they were experiencing pain. The difference between these two groups, however, was manifested in their response to treatment. Once the pain was alleviated the Italian patients reported no further symptoms, whereas the Jewish patients continued to complain after their pain had diminished.

Zborowski interpreted these differences to reflect the time orientation of their respective cultures. The Italians' present orientation is reflected in their demand for immediate relief. A future orientation is attributed to both the Jewish and the "Old-American" groups and thus indicates a concern over the significance and implications of the pain. Unlike their "Old-American" counterparts, however, the Jewish patients tended to be more pessimistic.

The major deficiencies of this study arise from the lack of control of the pain-causing pathology as well as such intervening variables as gender, level of education, and socioeconomic status. In addition, the analysis focused more on the traits in each culture that contribute to the observed behaviors rather than on the discrete differences in overt behavior. Nevertheless, this work remains the cornerstone of cross-cultural comparisons of pain responses.

Zola (1983) also studied the differences in pain response between 63 Italian and 81 Irish hospitalized subjects. Both men and women were included, and the pain-causing pathologies consisted of 18 distinct diagnoses. Substantiating Zborowski's findings, this study concluded that the Irish more often tended to deny pain whereas the Italians would more readily admit the presence of pain. Compared to the Irish, the Italians presented significantly more symptoms in more bodily locations and noted more types of bodily dysfunctions. Cluster analysis revealed that the variable that most consistently correlated strongly with the illness behavior was the ethnic group membership of the subject.

Obstetrical Patients

Conflicting results have been reported. Flannery, Sos, and McGovern (1981) found no significant differences in the pain response to an episiotomy among 75 women in five cultural groups: African-American, Italian, Jewish, Irish, and Anglo-Saxon Protestant. This is one of only a few studies controlling for the type of pain as well as for sex and age.

Dental Pain and Anxiety

In another study in which the type of pain was held constant, pain anxiety and pain attitudes were studied in African-American, white, and Puerto Rican dental patients (Weisenberg, Kreindler, Schachat, & Werboff, 1975). No significant between-group differences were observed in the amount of pain or the number and type of symptoms that the patient experienced.

Significant cross-cultural differences were recorded on the State-Trait Anxiety Inventory and the Dental Anxiety Scale, however. The Puerto Rican patients were more anxious by most measures and most interested in denying, getting rid of, and not dealing with the pain. The white patients reported significantly less anxiety and were most willing to face and deal with the pain. The African-American subjects fell between these two groups.

One limitation of this study was the lack of control for socioeconomic status and level of education, variables that are suggested to affect the pain response.

Pain in Children

Children of various cultural groups also have been studied. Abu-Saad (1984) explored how Arab-American, Asian-American, and Latin-American school-age children perceive, describe, and respond to painful experiences. The range of physical and psychological causes of pain did not differ widely among the groups, but the descriptions about the feelings when in pain varied by cultural group. The Arab-American and Latin-American children were more likely to use sensory words to describe pain, whereas the Asian-American children tended to use relatively more words in the affective and evaluative domains.

Summary

In summary, trends in the studies conducted thus far plus empirical evidence from clinicians at the bedside indicate that there may be cultural differences in the way in which patients respond to pain. Because of incompletely controlled studies and conflicting results, however, the relationship between culture and pain behaviors remains essentially unestablished, especially in critical care (Wolff & Langley, 1977).

CULTURE AND ILLNESS BEHAVIOR

There is no human activity which we could regard as purely physiological, that is "natural" or "untutored." . . . Not even the simplest need, nor yet the physiological function most independent of environmental influences, can be regarded as completely unaffected by culture. (Malinowski, 1944, p. 34)

Anthropologists define culture as "the set of learned beliefs, values and behaviors generally shared by a society" (Ember & Ember, 1973, p. 24). Culture also can be defined as "patterned behavior [both mental and physical] that individuals learn and are taught as members of groups, and that is transmitted from generation to generation" (Hunter & Whitten, 1976, p. 582).

Health Belief Systems

Within each culture are belief systems that provide uncritically accepted truths about the universe. These beliefs, which are organized around central components of survival such as eating, shelter, and health and illness, give meaning to life experiences. They exist in all cultures and tend to encompass broad concepts, such as the nature of illness and the reason for its existence, as well as specific details of curing practices.

Within a health belief system are attitudes about health and illness, how the community maintains health, who helps them when they are ill, and what folk remedies and curing techniques they use (Foster & Anderson, 1978). These belief systems contain models explaining disease causation, the experience of symptoms, the severity of the illness, the sick role, treatment alternatives, and outcome criteria (Kleinman, 1978).

Figure 5-1 depicts pain behaviors in an explanatory model of illness. An example of such an explanatory model is the hot-cold principle of health maintenance found in many Oriental and Latin communities. Derived from the Greek humoral theory, the hot and cold classifications refer to the intrinsic quality (not the temperature) of food, medicine, or particular body conditions. The organs of the body are also believed to have these qualities. The heart and blood, for example, are considered hot (Maduro, 1983; Rose, 1978).

Illness is often attributed to an imbalance between heat and cold; consequently, curing is directed toward the restoration of the proper balance. For example, cold illnesses, such as convulsions, would be treated with hot foods and medicines.

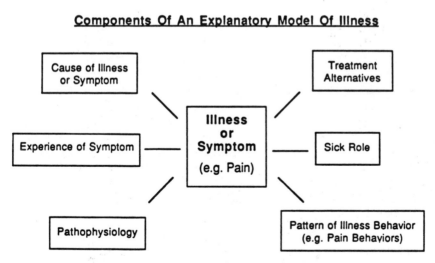

Figure 5-1 Elements of Kleinman's (1978) explanatory model of illness. The symptom of pain is depicted in this framework. *Source:* From "Concepts and a Model for the Comparison of Medical Systems as Cultural Systems" by A. Kleinman, 1978, *Social Science and Medicine, 12B*, pp. 85–93.

Every individual, as well as the members of the health care team, have explanatory models about health and illness. When the client and the health care professional are from different cultures, these explanatory models may conflict, resulting in miscommunication and ultimately poor care.

Meaning and Significance of Pain

The explanatory model approach was used to study the meaning of "heart distress" (*narahatiye galb*) in an Iranian city. The term *semantic illness networks* is used to label the "network of words, situations, symptoms and feelings that are associated with the illness and give it meaning for the sufferer" (Good, 1977, p. 40).

In one case study, heart distress signified old age, sorrow, sadness, ritual mourning, and worries over poverty. In another case, in which a young woman on birth control pills was experiencing tachycardia, the core symbol of heart distress linked childbirth, miscarriage, pregnancy, oral contraceptives, infertility, sorrow, and old age. The complete meaning of the illness or symptom to the individual is derived from this network of symbols of the illness experience.

Sick Role Behaviors

The sick role and illness behaviors in health belief systems have particular relevance to analyzing the phenomenon of pain. In Spain, as previously noted, "Being ill calls for loud complaint—an exercise of Latin spontaneity rather than Anglo-Saxon self-control" (Kenny, 1962, p. 284).

This "Latin spontaneity" contrasts even more with the behavior observed in a native American hospital in the southwestern United States. A nurse in such a hospital, commenting on pain responses, states "We have learned from experience that when a Papago complains of pain or requests medication, such requests should receive prompt attention, for he is usually in serious trouble" (Christopherson, 1971, p. 36).

For example, a person may experience pain, self-treat it with aspirin, and continue working. The sick role, however, is not assumed until a person is unable to fulfill some of his or her normal roles, thereby adding extra demands to the roles of others. In this role the person decides to stay home from work and to be cared for by family members.

A further extension of the sick role is the patient role. Once the person consults a formal therapeutic organization for advice and treatment, the patient role is assumed. At this point, when the individual decides to become a patient, a "hierarchy of resort'' provides alternative choices and a potential order for choosing treatments of illness or symptoms such as pain (Romanucci-Schwartz, 1969).

For example, the first preference may be to seek a medical physician; this may be followed by prayers and other religious rituals if the pain is seen as a punishment for sins. A subsequent alternative may be to visit a folk healer to determine whether a curse is the cause of the illness or pain. In this case, the individual has utilized various treatment options in a specific order of preference to deal with all the aspects of the illness: physical, spiritual, and social.

Pain Behaviors

Human interaction is based on the communication of symbols or gestures that have social meanings. Zborowski (1952, 1969) suggests that pain behaviors are culturally learned and culturally specific. Each culture has patterned attitudes toward pain behaviors that are passed down from one generation to another. The gestures and symbols of stoicism, for example, may be sanctioned in one culture, whereas more expressive symbols are encouraged in another culture.

The following case study provides an example in which the patient and health care professionals have different expectations regarding the expression of pain and other symptoms:

> A 53-year-old Navajo woman came to the emergency room stating she was having difficulty in breathing. She did not appear distressed and reported no other symptoms, so she was sent to the main waiting room. The patient did not protest the wait and did not indicate any sense of urgency. The woman spoke no English but brought with her a Navajo interpreter who stated simply that the patient was generally healthy and "drank a lot."
>
> The work-up process started approximately 1 hour later when the triage nurse ordered an X-ray study of the chest, which showed no abnormalities. During the physical examination, chest auscultation revealed high-pitched wheezes in the mainstem bronchus. An examination of the throat showed an extensive, inflamed pseudomembrane extending over the tonsils and down the trachea. Her airway was severely compromised. Despite an emergency tracheotomy and administration of diphtheria antitoxin, a cardiac arrest occurred and the patient ultimately expired within 24 hours.
>
> The examining physician's reaction was "Why didn't she SAY something? Why didn't she TELL us that she also had a sore throat and painful swallowing" (Excerpted from Weaver & Sklar, 1980).

In the above case, the pain was not considered a symptom that needed to be reported nor one to be physically expressed. The admitting clerk or nurse would need specifically to ask the patient whether she had pain anywhere to elicit this information.

In another culture, the ladino—who is said to be of direct Spanish descent—describes pain in a constellation of elements. Pain was not viewed as a distinct sensation, but rather as a part of a complex whole (Fabrega, 1980). Instead of simply stating ''I have pain in my chest,'' the response of the ladino would more likely include a cluster of meanings and interpretations about that pain. For example, ''I am having the pain of 'X' (e.g., chest pain), brought on by doing 'Y' (breathing in of cold air) after having experienced 'Z' (*susto* or fright).'' The word pain itself (*dolor*) has limited use. ''What we observe frequently are 'heaviness,' 'burningness,' 'squeezingness' etc., which (although viewed as instances of pain by the observer) are often seen as phenomena different from ''pain'' by the ladino'' (Fabrega, 1980, p. 240).

Thus the description of pain may have many elements: an emotional or an interpersonally incited cause; the mechanism and components of the process that resulted; a description of the pain as a bodily, psychic, and social entity; the duration of all these; and various ways of controlling the pain.

The population of the United States is becoming increasingly more culturally diverse. In the care of this population, the nurse needs to determine the network of meanings about pain and illness for the specific client in his or her cultural context to provide effective and therapeutic pain management.

CULTURE OF THE NURSE

The nurse brings to the interaction his or her own set of attitudes about pain and its expression. These attitudes, often culturally learned, ultimately may influence how the nurse assesses the pain behaviors of the patient and subsequently treats the pain.

A large-scale, continuing study of the cross-cultural differences in pain inferences among nurses has been conducted in up to 13 countries (Davitz & Davitz, 1980, 1981; Davitz, Davitz, & Higuchi, 1977a, 1977b). The original sample consisted of 544 female registered nurses currently employed in the United States, Japan, Puerto Rico, Korea, Thailand, and Taiwan. The sample was later extended to include nurses in Uganda, India, Nigeria, England, Israel, Belgium, and Nepal.

The instrument, the Standard Measure of Inferences of Suffering, was translated into the native languages of all subjects. It consisted of 60 brief case studies describing the following: a particular illness or injury (five categories), gender of the patients, and age of the patients (three age groups). The nurses were asked to rate, on a 7-point magnitude estimation scale, the degree of both psychological and physical pain for each of these case studies.

Korean and Japanese nurses inferred the highest amount of pain: They ranked first and second, respectively, among all the nurses in the amount of physical pain inferred and first and third, respectively, in the amount of psychological distress inferred for patients in their countries.

The nurses from the United States and England ranked the lowest among all the nurses, 12th and 13th, respectively, in the amount of inferred physical pain. These findings are consistent with those of Bond (1980) and Fagerhaugh (1974), who found that British and American nurses tended to value stoicism and minimal expression of pain. In the category of psychological distress, however, the American and British nurses ranked 7th and 9th, respectively, among the 13 countries.

The Puerto Rican nurses were the only representatives from Latin America. This group of nurses inferred a relatively low (tenth rank) amount of physical pain but high (second rank) amounts of psychological distress for the case studies presented.

Interestingly, there was also considerable difference in seemingly similar groups. Nurses from Taiwan and Thailand differed significantly from the top-ranking Korean and Japanese nurses. The Taiwanese and Thai nurses ranked 6th and 9th, respectively, in the amount of physical pain inferred and 12th and 8th, respectively, in psychological distress inferred. Hence the Western assumption that all Oriental groups view pain similarly was not substantiated by these findings.

In a smaller segment of this study (Davitz & Davitz, 1981), American nurses were given the ethnic background of the patients in the case studies. For both physical pain and psychological distress, cultural differences were evident. The Jewish patients were seen as experiencing the greatest amount of pain, the Spanish patients were seen as experiencing the second greatest amount, and the Oriental and Anglo-Saxon and Germanic patients were seen as experiencing the least amount.

In summary, significant cross-cultural differences were found in nurses' perceptions of the amount of physical pain and psychological distress experienced by their patients. This perception is a crucial component of pain assessment and forms the basis of subsequent decision making regarding the type and efficacy of pain control.

NURSING INTERVENTIONS

Every day critical care nurses must assess patients in pain. The task is not an easy one. There is a wide variety of ways in which people respond to pain; these are due in part to culture. The nurse's difficult task is to assess and interpret these pain behaviors accurately and then to plan and monitor pain-relieving interventions.

Communication is the basis of accurate assessment. At a particular disadvantage is the patient who is unable to speak the language of the nurse. A word board at the bedside with a list of translated common words and phrases can be used by all nurses or health professionals who have contact with the patient. The list may contain both English and translated questions such as "Do you have pain? (or discomfort)?" "Where do you have pain?" "How strong is your pain? Light, moderate, severe?" The list should be left open-ended so that additional words and phrases can be continuously added by staff and family alike.

Besides language differences, there also is a wide range of gestures used to express pain. In a critical care unit with a multicultural patient population, nurses need a broad theory base of possible accepted pain behaviors, especially of those cultures seen most frequently in their units. In addition, the nurses' own culturally learned attitudes and values regarding pain may be different from their patients' value systems. This discrepancy could affect the nurses' ability to assess accurately and then to manage their patients' pain.

A potential area for miscommunication arises when the cause and meaning of pain or the expectations of care are different from the classic biomedical approach. For example, in some religions and cultures pain is seen as having a "cleansing" quality and hence is to be endured. The patient may be experiencing pain but does not want relief. Therefore, the nurse needs to assess not only whether the patient is experiencing pain and how much pain is present but also whether the patient is requesting pain relief.

More frequent communication and continuous validation with the patient is necessary if the patient is from a culture other than the dominant culture. "Are you still having pain, Sra. Garcia?" the nurse might ask of a Mexican woman who moans continuously during her second day after surgery. She may not necessarily be asking for more analgesic but rather may be "releasing" the pain through physical expression.

If at all possible, the patient's beliefs and practices should be incorporated into the plan of care. A special crucifix or charm to help healing and to ward off pain could be pinned to the sheet at the head of the bed instead of worn around the neck of an intubated patient. On the other hand, not all requests are feasible, such as a lighted candle at the bedside of a patient on a mechanical ventilator with oxygen.

CONCLUSION

The nurse provides the therapeutic environment for the patient in pain. That therapeutic environment includes trust that the pain will be relieved when necessary and acceptance and respect for the patient's beliefs and practices.

Nurses caring for patients of cultural groups other than their own need a broad knowledge of health beliefs and practices to interpret accurately their patients' pain and to control it effectively. American nurses in particular, because of the cultural diversity of the population, are confronted with a broad range of pain beliefs and behaviors. Miscommunication is possible because of differences in language, expressive patterns, and meanings of pain. Continuous validation with the patient is necessary for accurate communication and assessment and, ultimately, adequate pain control.

REFERENCES

Abu-Saad, H. (1984). Cultural group indicators of pain in children. *Maternal-Child Nursing Journal, 13*, 187–196.

Bond, M.R. (1980). Characteristics of families of chronic pain patients attending a psychiatric pain clinic. In T. Yokata & R. Dubner (Eds.), *Current topics on pain research and therapy* (pp. 79–87). New York: Elsevier.

Christopherson, V.A. (1971). Sociocultural correlates of pain response. *Social Science, 46*, 33–37.

Davitz, L.L., & Davitz, J.R. (1980). *Nurses' responses to patients' suffering.* New York: Springer.

Davitz, J.R., & Davitz, L.L. (1981). *Inferences of patients' pain and psychological distress.* New York: Springer.

Davitz, L.L., Davitz, J.R., & Higuchi, Y. (1977a). Cross-cultural inferences of physical pain and psychological distress: 1. *Nursing Times, 73*, 521–523.

Davitz, L.L., Davitz, J.R., & Higuchi, Y. (1977b). Cross-cultural inferences of physical pain and psychological distress: 2. *Nursing Times, 77*, 556–558.

Ember, C.R., & Ember, M. (1973). *Cultural anthropology.* New York: Appleton-Century-Crofts.

Fabrega, H. (1980). *Disease and social behavior: An interdisciplinary perspective.* Cambridge: Massachusetts Institute of Technology Press.

Fagerhaugh, S.Y. (1974). Pain expression and control on a burn care unit. *Nursing Outlook, 22*, 645–650.

Flannery, R.B., Sos, J., & McGovern, P. (1981). Ethnicity as a factor in the expression of pain. *Psychosomatics, 22*, 39–50.

Foster, G.M., & Anderson, B.G. (1978). *Medical anthropology.* New York: Wiley.

Good, B.J. (1977). The heart of what's the matter: The semantics of illness in Iran. *Culture, Medicine and Psychiatry, 1*, 25–58.

Hunter, D.E., & Whitten, P. (1976). *The study of anthropology.* New York: Harper & Row.

Kenny, M. (1962). Social values and health in Spain: Some preliminary considerations. *Human Organization, 21*, 280–285.

Kleinman, A. (1978). Concepts and a model for the comparison of medical systems as cultural systems. *Social Science and Medicine, 12B*, 85–93.

Maduro, R. (1983). Curanderismo and Latino views of disease and curing. *Western Journal of Medicine, 139*, 868–884.

Malinowski, B. (1944). *A scientific theory of culture.* Chapel Hill: University of North Carolina Press.

Romanucci-Schwartz, L. (1969). The hierarchy of resort in curative practices: The Admiralty Islands, Melanesia. *Journal of Health and Social Behavior, 10*, 201–209.

Rose, L.C. (1978). *Disease beliefs in Mexican-American communities.* San Francisco: R & E Research.

Sternbach, R.A., & Tursky, B. (1965). Ethnic differences among housewives in psychophysical and skin potential responses to electrical shock. *Psychophysiology, 1*, 241–246.

Weaver, C., & Sklar, D. (1980). Diagnostic dilemmas and cultural diversity in emergency rooms. *Western Journal of Medicine, 133*, 356–366.

Weisenberg, M., Kreindler, M.L., Schachat, R., & Werboff, J. (1975). Pain: Anxiety and attitudes in Black, White and Puerto Rican patients. *Psychosomatic Medicine, 37*, 123–135.

Wolff, B.B., & Langley, S. (1977). Cultural factors and the response to pain. In D. Landy (Ed.), *Culture, disease and healing* (pp. 313–319). New York: Macmillan.

Zborowski, M. (1952). Cultural components of the response to pain. *Journal of Social Issues, 8*, 16–30.

Zborowski, M. (1969). *People in pain*. San Francisco: Jossey-Bass.

Zola, I.K. (1983). *Socio-medical inquiries: Recollections, reflections and reconsiderations*. Philadelphia: Temple University Press.

Part II

Nursing and Pain Management

Chapter 6

Intravenous Methods of Analgesia for Pain in the Critically Ill

Lorie Wild

For many years, intravenous (IV) opioids have been the mainstay of analgesic therapy for the critically ill patient. Introduction of IV opioids in the critical care setting was, in part, based on the need for rapid relief of moderate to severe pain in the critically ill or injured and the availability of close monitoring by highly skilled nurses.

The IV route has several distinct advantages over the traditional intramuscular (IM) route for the critically ill patient. The absorption of IM medications is highly variable, especially in critically ill patients, who may have marked alterations in perfusion and cardiac output. The rapid onset and short duration of action of IV opioids allows them to be titrated easily for patient comfort. In addition, the rapid onset of action of IV narcotics helps modify the emotional response to prolonged pain. The physiological consequences of stress, which can be elicited by emotion, may be harmful to the critically ill patient, who is already compromised.

INDICATIONS FOR THE USE OF INTRAVENOUS ANALGESICS

Acute Postoperative Pain

Since the advent of modern surgery, the importance of preventing serious postoperative complications, particularly pulmonary complications, has been well known. A key element in the strategies to prevent postoperative complications is the control of postoperative pain. A major cause of pulmonary complications after surgery is a marked reduction in functional residual capacity (FRC) with subsequent hypoxemia. Pain in the postoperative period contributes to the reduction in FRC. If effective analgesia is provided FRC can be improved, and patients will be more likely to have improved respiratory function (Alexander, Spence, Parikh, &

79

Stuart, 1973). IV narcotics can provide adequate analgesia, permitting earlier mobility for postoperative patients.

Trauma

Because the critically ill trauma patient often undergoes extensive surgical procedures, the goals of pain management with IV analgesics are similar to those for normal postoperative recovery. Again, the primary goal is to prevent pulmonary complications by providing adequate analgesia. For example, the patient who has multiple rib fractures or flail chest as a result of trauma may require large doses of IV narcotics to provide adequate analgesia to allow coughing and deep breathing and thereby to enhance respiratory function. The use of IV analgesics enables the nurse to titrate carefully the amount of narcotic necessary for the respiratory care yet to avoid oversedation during rest periods.

Burns

The patient with burns undergoes intermittent, extensive wound care that typically is associated with intense pain. These intermittent wound scrubs and debridements require intense analgesia. IV narcotics can be used effectively during these procedures because of their rapid onset of action and short duration.

Myocardial Infarction and Congestive Heart Failure

The need for relief of chest pain during myocardial infarction (MI) has been well described. The body's sympathetic response to pain further taxes the compromised myocardium. The emotional response to the pain intensifies the problem as well. The rapid relief of pain with IV narcotics such as morphine can interrupt the sympathetic response to pain. In addition, the hemodynamic effects of IV morphine, such as arterial and venous dilation, may be beneficial in both MI and congestive heart failure (CHF). Morphine also may reduce myocardial oxygen consumption and cardiac workload in the heart (Jaffe & Martin, 1985). Finally, morphine may help alleviate some of the anxiety associated with pain of MI and the respiratory difficulties seen in CHF.

Mechanically Ventilated Patients

Critically ill patients who are intubated or mechanically ventilated may have difficulty communicating pain. Because anxiety often accompanies pain, adequate analgesia may help alleviate the anxiety and agitation frequently seen with mechanical ventilation and consequently reduce the need for paralytic drugs or excessive sedation.

PHARMACOLOGIC ACTIONS OF INTRAVENOUS OPIATE ANALGESIA

IV opiates provide pain relief through systemic circulation. Morphine continues to be the standard opiate against which all other opiates are compared. All opiates bind with specific receptors in the brain and spinal cord and alter the perception of pain. The relief of pain resulting from IV opiates is not at the expense of other sensory modalities such as touch or vibration (Jaffe & Martin, 1985). Chapter 2 details the physiology of pain and analgesia.

Central Nervous System

Drowsiness is a frequent effect of opiates. The drowsiness and sedation caused by opiates is probably modulated by various neurotransmitters in the brain and spinal cord (Jaffe & Martin, 1985). In part, the opiate helps alleviate not only the pain but also the emotional response to the pain. In this sense, the narcotics are effective for producing sedation; narcotics are not as effective when used solely for sedation, however. Narcotics also can produce euphoria, although the mechanisms that produce the euphoria and other mood changes are not clear.

Hemodynamic System

Critically ill patients receiving IV opiates may experience orthostatic hypotension as a result of peripheral arteriolar and venous dilation as well as an inhibition of the baroreceptor reflexes. Nonpostural changes in blood pressure also can occur as a result of both the vasodilation and a release of histamine induced by opiates. Thus IV opiates should be administered cautiously in patients who are hypovolemic (Jaffe & Martin, 1985).

In addition, IV morphine can blunt the peripheral reflex vasoconstrictive response to elevated carbon dioxide tension. Although cerebral circulation is relatively unaffected by morphine, cerebral vasodilation can still occur in response to hypercarbia (Jaffe & Martin, 1985).

Meperidine has some vagolytic actions and should be used cautiously in patients with supraventricular tachycardias (McEvay, 1988). Tachycardia and increases in ventricular response to cardiac rhythms such as atrial flutter or atrial fibrillation could be detrimental to critically ill patients, particularly in those with reduced cardiac reserve.

Respiratory System

Opiates can cause respiratory depression, even in small doses. Opiates can depress pontine and medullary centers, which normally regulate respiratory rhythmicity (Jaffe & Martin, 1985). Hence changes in respiratory rate and volume and, consequently, minute ventilation can occur after administration of opiates. As minute ventilation decreases, carbon dioxide tension (Pco_2) begins to rise. Opiates also directly affect the respiratory center in the brainstem by reducing its responsiveness to carbon dioxide. The combination of decreased minute ventilation and decreased responsiveness to hypercarbia leads to clinically evident respiratory depression.

Evidence of respiratory depression may surface within 7 minutes of IV opiate administration. The respiratory depressant effects of IV opiates may persist for as long as 5 hours.

Although the concern for respiratory depression in the critically ill patient is genuine, it is imperative to balance the need for adequate analgesia with that for respiratory protection. For example, in the patient who is being weaned from mechanical ventilation or is newly extubated, goals are to avoid excessive sedation and to preserve respiratory drive. Yet, an often overlooked goal is the avoidance of pain, which may lead to splinting, shallow breathing, and a marked reduction in respiratory effort and tidal volume. Careful titration of IV analgesics can help balance the need for pain control and respiratory protection.

Pruritus

Narcotics, especially IV narcotics, can cause pruritus. The precise cause of the pruritus is not known. Histamine release may play a part, but central neural mechanisms are a more likely cause because the pruritus can respond to naloxone.

Nausea and Vomiting

Nausea and vomiting seen with IV narcotics are caused by stimulation of the chemoreceptor trigger zone in the medulla. Opiates also may increase vestibular sensitivity. The nausea observed with IV narcotics also tends to be postural in nature, with most patients experiencing nausea when upright rather than when supine (Jaffe & Martin, 1985).

Urinary Retention

Opiates can alter the tone of the detrusor muscle and vesical sphincter of the bladder. The augmented tone may lead to urinary retention. Urinary catheterization may be needed for some patients who do not already have Foley catheters in place.

Gastrointestinal Motility

Opiates can slow gastric emptying and gastrointestinal motility throughout the small and large intestine. The constipating effects of narcotics are seldom seen in the critically ill patient, but it is important to keep in mind the slowed emptying and motility when enteral feedings or oral medications are given.

NARCOTICS USED INTRAVENOUSLY

Table 6-1 summarizes the characteristics of commonly used intravenous opioids and includes both opiate agonists and mixed agonist-antagonist agents. The characteristics of IV narcotic agents can be distinguished by their respective actions at four types of opioid receptors: μ, κ, δ, and σ. For example, morphine is an opioid agonist primarily active at the μ and κ receptors. Naloxone is a potent opioid antagonist that has a high affinity for the μ receptors. The class of agents known as mixed agonists-antagonists are agonists at some receptors and antagonists at other receptors. The therapeutic goal in using mixed agonist-antagonist agents is to provide analgesia by their agonist actions yet to avoid side effects such as respiratory depression through their antagonist actions.

Metabolism of opioids occurs primarily in the liver, and most undergo significant first-pass metabolism. The narcotic agents are largely protein bound and are distributed widely throughout body tissues. Although opioids can be absorbed by the gastrointestinal tract, the agents work quickly and efficiently when given IV. Generally, agents that are more lipid soluble (e.g., fentanyl and sufentanyl) are rapidly absorbed and distributed in body tissues, producing a rapid onset of effects (Jaffe & Martin, 1985). Lipophilic agents also are rapidly metabolized and thus have a short duration of action.

The predominant route of excretion for opioids after metabolism in the liver is via the renal system into the urine. Some agents are partially excreted through the biliary system as well (Table 6-1). Critically ill patients experiencing hepatic or renal insufficiency or failure not only require lower doses of narcotics but also are at a higher risk for side effects resulting from reduced clearance of the drug (Jaffe & Martin, 1985; McEvay, 1988).

Table 6-1 Intravenous Opioids

Drug	Dose (mg)	Infusion (mg/hour)	Onset (minutes)	Peak (Minutes)	Duration (hours)	Excretion (First Pass/ Second Pass)
Agonists						
Morphine	2–10	2–8	2–3	20	4–5	Urine/bile
Meperidine (Demerol)	10–30	15–35	1	5–7	2–4	Urine
Hydromorphone (Dilaudid)	0.5–1.0	0.2–1.0	10–15	15–30	2–3	Urine
Methadone (Dolophine)	2.5–10.0	NR*	2–3	15–30	3–4†	Urine/bile
Oxymorphone (Numorphan)	1.0–1.5	NR	5–10	15–30	3–4	Urine
Fentanyl (Sublimaze)	50–100 mcg	50–100 mcg	1–2	3–5	0.5–1.0	Urine
Sufentanyl (Sufenta)	25–50 mcg	NR	Immediate	1.3–3.0	5 min	Urine/bile
Mixed agonists-antagonists						
Buprenorphine (Buprenex)	0.3–0.6	NR	2–5	15–30	6–8	Bile
Butorphanol (Stadol)	0.5–2.0	NR	1	4–5	3–4	Urine/bile
Nalbuphine (Nubain)	10	NR	2–3	30	3–4	Urine
Pentazocine (Talwin)	30–60	NR	2–3	15–30	2–3	Urine/bile

*Not reported for analgesic doses.
†Duration lengthens with subsequent doses.

Sources: From *Goodman and Gilman's Pharmacologic Basis of Therapeutics*, 7th ed., by A. Gilman, A.G. Gilman, and L.S. Goodman (Eds.). 1985, New York, NY: Macmillan, and from *Drug Information* by G.K. McEvoy (Ed.), 1988, Bethesda, MD: American Society of Hospital Pharmacists.

Of special note for patients receiving meperidine is that normeperidine, the drug's active and toxic metabolite, can accumulate after long-term usage, especially when high doses are used. Normeperidine can cause excessive central nervous system stimulation, leading to seizures (Jaffe & Martin, 1985). The risk of seizures from normeperidine accumulation is an important consideration in critically ill patients, especially those whose seizure threshold may already be lowered from other causes such as neurologic injury or electrolyte imbalance.

INTRAVENOUS MODALITIES

Intermittent Bolus

The use of intermittent bolus doses of narcotics has been the mainstay of analgesic therapy for the critically ill patient for many years. The strategy for using intermittent, or p.r.n. doses involves slowly administering small doses every 15 to 20 minutes, two to three times, and titrating to patient comfort (Benedetti, Bonica, & Bellucci, 1984). After the initial loading doses, the critical care nurse can extend dosing intervals on the basis of patient's demonstrated need for additional analgesia.

Intermittent bolus doses of narcotics are effective for the relief of moderate to severe pain, which most critically ill patients are likely to experience. Regular dosing, preferably on a "non-p.r.n." schedule, can provide adequate, ongoing analgesia for many critically ill patients. Clinical situations in which intermittent dosing may be advantageous include those in which short-term analgesia of high intensity is needed, for example during wound debridement or painful dressing changes. The intermittent regime is particularly helpful when the patient is comfortable between painful procedures.

One of the major advantages of using intermittent bolus dosing is its familiarity to both nurses and physicians. In this case the analgesic treatment and pain medications are both administered and monitored by experienced professionals. Another distinct advantage of the use of intermittent bolus dosing is its low cost. No additional equipment or technology is necessary.

The intermittent bolus regime also carries with it several disadvantages. First, there is wide individual variation among patients regarding the dosage and timing necessary to obtain and maintain adequate analgesia. Some critically ill patients may have optimal comfort with small doses of IV opiates whereas others may require much higher doses, even if both types of patients have undergone the same surgical procedure. Protocols for pain medications often fall short of what would be optimal for patient comfort. Studies indicate that many prescriptions for and administrations of pain medications are inadequate to provide appropriate analgesia (Bonica, 1983; Cohen, 1980; Marks & Sachar, 1973; Mather & Mackie, 1983).

Coupled with the wide individual variation among patients regarding the need for pain medications is the variability among nurses in their assessment of patients' pain levels. This is particularly true in situations in which the patient is unable to communicate effectively (e.g., the intubated patient). In these cases, the nurse or physician makes a judgment about a patient's need for pain medication, which may or may not be accurate.

Frequently, the pain cycle is in operation for the critically ill patient (Fig. 6-1). This cycle not only involves the nurse's assessment of the patient's level of discomfort but also depicts the time needed to obtain and administer the pain medication. From a practical standpoint, when intermittent bolus doses of narcotics are employed increased nursing time may be needed to secure narcotics between

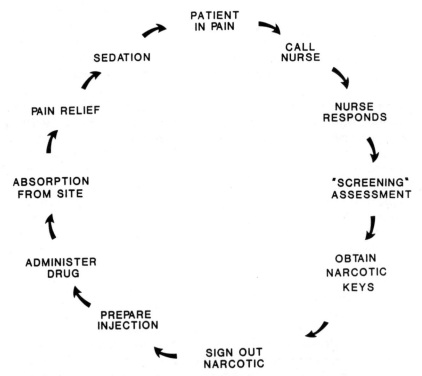

Figure 6-1 The pain cycle. *Source:* From ''Patient-controlled Analgesia'' by D.A. Graves, T.S. Foster, R.L. Batenhorst, R.L. Bennett, and T.J. Baumann, 1983, *Annals of Internal Medicine, 99,* pp. 360–366. Copyright 1983 by American College of Physicians. Adapted by permission.

doses, or there may be high wastage of narcotics when small amounts are used and the remainder is subsequently discarded.

Finally, there can be additional infection control risks for critically ill patients associated with intermittent bolus doses of IV narcotics. Multiple IV push injections require repeated access of the IV line. Studies indicate that the risk of IV catheter–related infection increases with multiple entries into the closed system (Maki, Botticelli, LeRoy, & Thielke, 1987).

Continuous Infusion

Continuous infusion of opiates such as morphine, meperidine, hydromorphone, and fentanyl can provide constant blood levels of a prescribed analgesic. An adequate, consistent serum level of narcotic will help provide an even comfort level for the critically ill patient, avoiding distressing episodes of pain and related physiologic stress. In addition to avoiding peaks and valleys of comfort and pain, a continuous narcotic infusion helps maintain adequate analgesic levels during sleep, eliminating the increase in pain often seen when patients awaken.

For optimal use of continuous narcotic infusions, the patient should be given an adequate loading dose to raise circulating blood levels of the drug. Once an analgesic level is attained, the continuous infusion can be set at a basal rate to maintain those levels. For example, with morphine a loading dose can be given in 1- to 2-mg increments every 10 to 20 minutes, titrating to patient comfort. At this time the continuous infusion may be started at 2 to 3 mg/hour (Benedetti et al., 1984). It is important to remember, however, that as with intermittent bolus dosing there is wide, individual variation in the amount of narcotic needed to provide adequate analgesia for critically ill patients. Similar types of regimes for loading doses and basal infusions are used for other narcotics, such as meperidine, hydromorphone, and fentanyl.

Although continuous narcotic infusions can provide steady-state analgesia for most patients, the basal level may be inadequate to cover procedures or events that cause extra pain (e.g., ambulation, suctioning, coughing, and dressing changes), especially for patients who are unable to communicate their pain. Additional bolus doses of narcotic should be used to provide analgesic coverage for these periods of time or procedures.

Another disadvantage of continuous narcotic infusions is the need for special equipment, such as infusion control devices, to control and monitor the IV infusion. Typically, IV narcotic solutions are mixed in the pharmacy, which can increase costs to the patient and sometimes creates unavoidable delays in supplying the narcotic IV solution.

Patient-Controlled Analgesia

Recently, computerized pumps that allow the patient to self-administer small boluses of pain medication have been introduced clinically (Fig. 6-2). These devices, referred to as patient-controlled analgesia (PCA) pumps, have been shown to be valuable in a variety of clinical settings, including the critical care unit (Atwell, Flanigan, Bennett, Allen, Lucas, & McRoberts, 1984; Baumann, Gutschi, & Bivins, 1986; Bennett, Batenhorst, Bivins, et al., 1982; Dunwoody, 1987; Kleiman, Lipman, Hare, & MacDonald, 1987; Panfill, Brunckhorst, & Dundon, 1988; Tamsen, Hartvig, Fagerlund, Dahlstrom, & Bondesson, 1982). When using PCA, patients are able to balance pain relief and sedation levels. The use of PCA avoids the large peaks and valleys of analgesia and sedation often seen with intermittent IV or IM doses (Fig. 6-3). Other side effects of IV narcotics also can be balanced, to a large degree, because blood levels can be kept within a narrow range by the patient. Adequate loading doses should still be administered before PCA is initiated.

The infusion parameters on the PCA pump are set by the clinician, including the incremental or bolus dose amount and the minimum time between doses (lockout interval). Incremental doses usually range between 1 and 3 mg for morphine and between 10 and 30 mg for meperidine. The lockout interval is typically set

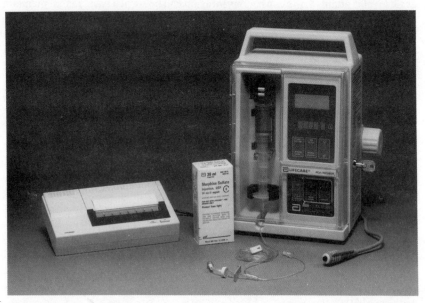

Figure 6-2 Patient-controlled analgesia (PCA) pump. *Source:* Courtesy of Abbott Labs, Hospital Products Division, Abbott Park, Illinois.

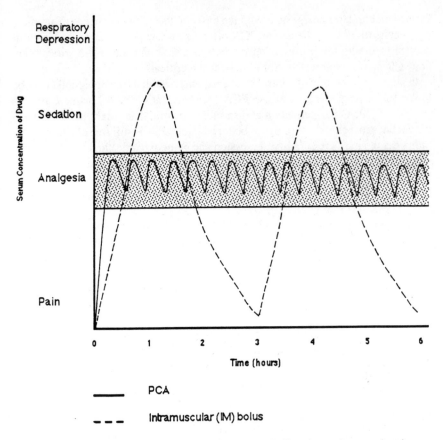

Figure 6-3 Relationships of dosing and effects with narcotics administered by IM compared to PCA routes.

between 5 and 15 minutes. Some PCA pumps also limit the amount of narcotic that can be self-administered over a 1- or 4-hour period. The newer, second-generation PCA devices can provide a background continuous narcotic infusion in addition to the patient-demand modality (Vickers, Derbyshire, Burt, Bagshaw, Pearson, & Smith, 1987). This can be particularly beneficial for patients because the continuous infusion can maintain adequate circulating levels of narcotic for analgesia, even when the patient is asleep, yet allow the patient access to a bolus dose for painful procedures or activities.

One of the major advantages of PCA over conventional parenteral narcotic therapy is that it can confer improved pain relief for the critically ill patient because the patient regulates analgesic use on the basis of his or her own needs (Tammisto & Tigerstedt, 1982). The use of PCA offers the critically ill patient one area of control in the highly professionally controlled environment of the critical care unit. Chapter 3 explores control issues for the critically ill patient.

In addition to improved control by the patient, overall usage of narcotic may be lower for some patients who use PCA (Keeri-Szanto, 1979; Lange, Dahn, & Jacobs, 1988). Other patients may use more narcotic than might have been expected but subsequently experience better analgesia that is still free of side effects. Side effects such as respiratory depression and hemodynamic changes also can be minimized with PCA (Graves, Foster, Batenhorst, Bennett, & Baumann, 1983). Pulmonary function may improve for patients who use PCA (Bennett, Batenhorst, Bivins, et al., 1982; Bennett, Batenhorst, Foster, Griffen, & Wright, 1982; Lange et al., 1988; Tamsen et al., 1982).

Although there are numerous benefits to critically ill patients who use PCA, there are also limitations to its use. The ability to discern a need for pain relief and to respond by pushing a button is an underlying prerequisite for critically ill patients to use PCA effectively (Dunwoody, 1987; Scheidler, 1987; Ward, Pauli, & Serafin, 1987). Some patients may be fearful of self-administering pain medications. Effective use of PCA also requires trust and thorough patient teaching by nurses and physicians.

Other drawbacks to PCA include the need for specialized equipment and the education needed for nurses to initiate and monitor the pumps. Any time specialized equipment is used, costs may be increased.

OTHER INTRAVENOUS METHODS OF ANALGESIA

Narcotic Adjuvants

Occasionally, narcotic adjuvants such as hydroxyzine or dextroamphetamine may be used in combination with IV narcotics. Agents such as hydroxyzine can potentiate the analgesic effect of the narcotic as well as relieve the anxiety associated with pain (Benedetti et al., 1984). Hydroxyzine also may help reduce nausea and vomiting associated with the use of narcotics. The parenteral form of hydroxyzine is for IM use only and should never be given by the IV route.

Dextroamphetamine is used less commonly but also has been shown to reduce the amount of narcotic needed to provide analgesia. The mechanism of action for dextroamphetamine appears to be an increase in secretion of serotonin, thus counteracting the nervous system depression seen with opiate use, and a concurrent decrease in anxiety and improvement in the feeling of well-being (Benedetti et al., 1984). Because dextroamphetamine is only available as an oral preparation, its use in the critically ill patient is limited.

Benzodiazepines

Critically ill patients frequently receive benzodiazepines, such as lorazepam, diazepam, or midazolam, on an intermittent basis to treat the anxiety that often accompanies pain. These anxiolytic agents are highly effective in managing patients who are anxious and are powerful adjuncts to opioid analgesics. The benzodiazepines have the added benefit of producing mild amnesia for many patients.

A new concept in the use of benzodiazepines is the use of patient-controlled anxiolysis. By using a short-acting benzodiazepine such as midazolam in a PCA pump, critically ill patients can control their level of sedation (Loper, Ready, & Brody, 1988). Patient-controlled anxiolysis with midazolam may be used alone or in conjunction with a PCA narcotic. Although this technique is still experimental, improved patient control over the need for sedation while in the critical care unit is a promising advance.

Anesthetics

Short-acting agents such as ketamine or other barbiturates may be helpful in providing analgesia during short periods of severe pain, such as wound debridement, in the critically ill patient (Stanley, Allen, & Bryan-Brown, 1985). These agents are highly effective in producing brief yet intense analgesia, but usually they require administration by an anesthesiologist or a nurse anesthetist. Patients receiving these agents require careful monitoring.

CONCLUSION

IV opioids continue to be a standard therapy for treating pain in the critically ill patient. The availability of venous access combined with problems associated with IM or oral routes of administration makes the IV route preferable for these patients. By reviewing the indications for using IV analgesics and their pharmacologic actions, the critical care nurse can make knowledgeable judgments regarding interventions for pain management. The variety of IV modalities currently available provides the nurse with a wide armamentarium of therapeutic strategies. New technologies such as PCA infusion devices are a positive addition for both patients and nurses. As new technology and medication delivery systems emerge, managing pain in the critically ill patient will continue to progress and ultimately result in improved patient outcomes.

REFERENCES

Alexander, J.I., Spence, A.A., Parikh, R.K., & Stuart, B. (1973). The role of airway closure in postoperative hypoxemia. *British Journal of Anaesthesia, 5*, 34–40.

Atwell, J.R., Flanigan, R.C., Bennett, R.L., Allen, D.C., Lucas, B.A., & McRoberts, J.W. (1984). The efficacy of patient-controlled analgesia in patients recovering from flank incisions. *Journal of Urology, 132*, 701–703.

Baumann, T.J., Gutschi, L.M., & Bivins, B.A. (1986). The safety and efficacy of a new patient-controlled analgesia device in hospitalized trauma and surgery patients. *Henry Ford Hospital Medical Journal, 34*, 105–108.

Benedetti, C., Bonica, J.J., & Bellucci, G. (1984). Pathophysiology and therapy of postoperative pain: A review. *Advances in Pain Research and Therapy, 7*, 373–407.

Bennett, R.L., Batenhorst, R.L., Bivins, B.A., Bell, R.M., Graves, D.A., Foster, T.S., Wright, B.D., & Griffen, W.O. (1982). Patient-controlled analgesia: A new concept of postoperative pain relief. *Annals of Surgery, 195*, 700–705.

Bennett, R.L., Batenhorst, R.L., Foster, T.S., Griffen, W.O., & Wright, B.D. (1982). Postoperative pulmonary function with patient controlled analgesia. *Anesthesia and Analgesia, 61*, 171.

Bonica, J.J. (1983). Current status of postoperative pain therapy. In T. Yokota & R. Dubner (Eds.), *Current topics in pain research and therapy*. Amsterdam: Exerpta Medica.

Cohen, F.L. (1980). Postsurgical pain relief: Patient's status and nurse's medication choice. *Pain, 9*, 265–274.

Dunwoody, C.J. (1987). Patient-controlled analgesia: Rationale, attributes, and essential factors. *Orthopaedic Nursing, 6*, 31–36.

Graves, D.A., Foster, T.S., Batenhorst, R.L., Bennett, R.L., & Baumann, T.J. (1983). Patient-controlled analgesia. *Annals of Internal Medicine, 99*, 360–366.

Jaffe, J.H., & Martin, W.R. (1985). Opioid analgesics and antagonists. In A. Gilman, A.G. Gilman, & L.S. Goodman (Eds.), *Goodman and Gilman's pharmacologic basis of therapeutics* (7th ed., pp. 491–531). New York: MacMillan.

Keeri-Szanto, M. (1979). Drugs or drums: What relieves postoperative pain? *Pain, 6*, 217–230.

Kleiman, R.L., Lipman, A.G., Hare, B.D., & MacDonald, S.D. (1987). PCA vs. regular IM injections for severe postop pain. *American Journal of Nursing, 87*, 1491–1492.

Lange, M.P., Dahn, M.S., & Jacobs, L.A. (1988). Patient-controlled analgesia versus intermittent analgesia dosing. *Heart & Lung, 17*, 495–498.

Loper, K.A., Ready, L.B., & Brody, M. (1988). Patient-controlled anxiolysis with midazolam. *Anesthesia and Analgesia, 67*, 1118–1119.

Maki, D.G., Botticelli, J.T., LeRoy, M.L., & Thielke, T.S. (1987). Prospective study of replacing administration sets for intravenous therapy at 48- and 72-hour intervals. *Journal of the American Medical Association, 258*, 1777–1781.

Marks, R.M., & Sachar, E.J. (1973). Undertreatment of medical inpatients with narcotic analgesics. *Annals of Internal Medicine, 78*, 173–181.

Mather, L., & Mackie, J. (1983). The incidence of postoperative pain in children. *Pain, 15*, 271–281.

McEvay, G.K. (Ed.). (1988). *Drug information*. Bethesda, MD: American Society of Hospital Pharmacists.

Panfill, R., Brunckhorst, L., & Dundon, R. (1988). Nursing implications of patient-controlled analgesia. *Journal of Intravenous Nursing, 11*, 75–77.

Scheidler, V.R. (1987). Patient-controlled analgesia. *Current Concepts in Nursing, 1*, 13–16.

Stanley, T.H., Allen, S.A., & Bryan-Brown, C.W. (1985). Management of pain and pain-related problems in the critically ill patient. *Critical Care: State of the Art, 6*, 33–80.

Tammisto, T., & Tigerstedt, I. (1982). Narcotic analgesics in postoperative pain relief. *Acta Anaesthesiologica Scandinavia, F4* (Suppl.), 161–164.

Tamsen, A., Hartvig, P., Fagerlund, C., Dahlstrom, B., & Bondesson, U. (1982). Patient controlled analgesic therapy: Clinical experience. *Acta Anaesthesiologica Scandinavia, F4*(Suppl.), 157–160.

Vickers, A.P., Derbyshire, D.R., Burt, D.R., Bagshaw, P.F., Pearson, H., & Smith, G. (1987). Comparison of the Leicester micropalliator and the Cardiff palliator in the relief of postoperative pain. *British Journal of Anaesthesia, 59*, 503–509.

Ward, L.K., Pauli, M., & Serafin, M.B. (1987). Patient-controlled analgesia: A case study. *Journal of the National Intravenous Therapy Association, 10*, 34–39.

RECOMMENDED READING

Abu-Saad, H., & Tesler, M. (1986). Pain. In V.K. Carrieri, A.M. Lindsey, & C.M. West (Eds.), *Pathophysiological phenomena in nursing* (pp. 235–269). Philadelphia: Saunders.

Chapman, C.R., & Bonica, J.J. (1983). *Acute pain: Current concepts.* Kalamazoo, MI: Upjohn.

Ellis, J.A. (1988). Using pain scales to prevent undermedication. *Maternal Child Nursing, 13*, 180–182.

Fitzgerald, K.A. (1984). Pain management demands creativity and flexibility. *Critical Care Monitor, 4*, 4–5.

Kane, N.E., Lehmman, M.E., Dugger, R., Hansen, L., & Jackson, D. (1988). Use of patient-controlled analgesia in surgical oncology patients. *Oncology Nursing Forum, 15*, 29–32.

King, K.B., Norsen, L.H., Robertson, R.K., & Hicks, G.L. (1987). Patient management of pain medication after cardiac surgery. *Nursing Research, 36*, 145–150.

O'Brien, S.W., & Konsler, G.K. (1988). Alleviating children's postoperative pain. *Maternal Child Nursing, 13*, 183–186.

White, P.F. (1987). Mishaps with patient-controlled analgesia. *Anesthesiology, 66*, 81–83.

White, P.F. (1988). Use of patient-controlled analgesia for management of acute pain. *Journal of the American Medical Association, 259*, 243–247.

Chapter 7

Epidural and Intrathecal Methods of Analgesia in the Critically Ill

Katherine M. Vivenzo Dyble

Acute pain is generally associated with subjective and objective physical signs and hyperactivity of the autonomic nervous system. The International Association for the Study of Pain (1979) defines pain as "an unpleasant sensory and emotional experience associated with actual or potential tissue damage or described in terms of such damage" (p. 249). In the critical care environment pain represents one of the most common patient problems, yet the alleviation of that pain can be one of the most challenging of nursing goals. Balancing optimal pain relief against the many pathophysiological events that may be occurring is a frequent role of the health professional because maintaining adequate pulmonary and hemodynamic function has always taken priority over traditional methods of complete analgesia.

In recent years various new techniques and drugs that provide an improved quality of pain control have become available. One such technique is the administration of spinal opioids. These may be administered into either the epidural space or the intrathecal space.

Spinal opioids, whether intrathecal or epidural, are remarkable for the high quality of pain relief that can be achieved from small quantities of medication. They can be used to treat pain in the lower extremities, abdomen, and thorax. Perhaps most important, they are associated with little to no sedation and no hemodynamic changes (Cousins & Bridenbaugh, 1988), and, when correctly administered with appropriate nursing care, they rarely result in respiratory depression. The patient treated with spinal opioids has an increased ability to cooperate with postoperative self-care, earlier ambulation, and pulmonary toilet. Such a patient also may have a shorter hospital stay.

Today this technique of pain control promises to be an important advancement toward realizing optimal pain relief. This chapter reviews the present role of epidural and intrathecal analgesia in alleviating pain, discusses various methods for administration of spinal opioids, and describes implications for nursing care.

PHYSIOLOGICAL MECHANISMS OF PAIN TRANSMISSION
AND SITE OF ACTION OF SPINAL OPIOIDS

Physiological pain can result from chemical, thermal, or mechanical modalities. In critical care the types of pain that nurses see most often are postoperative, posttraumatic, and related to acute medical diseases (e.g., myocardial infarction). Receptors for nociceptive pain are most abundant in superficial skin layers, periosteum of bone, arterial walls, joint surfaces, and the cranial vault.

Signals are transmitted from a peripheral nerve to the spinal cord and ascend via intraspinal tracts to the brain. Both visceral and somatic nociceptive afferents converge in the substantia gelatinosa in the dorsal horn (gray matter) of the spinal cord. The spinal cord, then, is the first link in the central neuronal network involved in pain perception. It is here that information is processed for delivery to the brainstem and cortical structures for response generation. A significant proportion of the substantia gelatinosa neurons receive A-δ and C fiber input (Fine & Hare, 1985; see Chapter 2).

In the dorsal horn, several discrete opioid receptors have been identified. The mu (40%), delta (10%), and kappa (50%) receptors are thought to be the major sites where opioids produce their analgesic effects. Different receptor affinities for various spinal opioids also are present (e.g., one mu agonist is morphine). Spinal opioids also have both presynaptic and postsynaptic sites of action.

Activation of mu and delta receptors could result in hyperpolarization of membranes and decrease neuronal responses to excitatory transmitters. Activation of kappa receptors could result in blockade of calcium ion influx in axonal terminals to inhibit transmitter release (Cousins & Bridenbaugh, 1988).

MECHANISMS OF ACTION: SPINAL ANALGESIA COMPARED
TO SPINAL ANESTHESIA

Spinal anesthesia with local anesthetics has been used since 1921. Currently the same administration technique is used but with different drugs (i.e., opioids).

In 1979, Behar, Olshwang, Magorai, and Davidson reported cases of epidural opioids being used to treat pain, and Wang, Nauss, and Thomas reported on intrathecal opioids being used to treat pain. At this same time, Cousins, Mather, and Glynn (1979) suggested the term *selected spinal analgesia* to emphasize the difference between analgesia obtained from local anesthetics and that obtained from spinal opioids.

At the outset it is important to recognize the differences between local anesthetics and opioids because at some institutions therapies involving both methods are being used outside the operating room for analgesia (Table 7-1). In general, local

Table 7-1 Comparison of Actions of Spinal Opioids and Local Anesthetics

	Spinal Opioids	*Local Anesthetics*
Site of Action	Pre- and postsynaptic receptors in dorsal horn of spinal cord	Axonal membrane block, predominantly in spinal nerve roots
Type of Block	Inhibition of neuron cell excitation	Block of nerve impulse conduction
Modalities Blocked	Nociception only	Sympathetic, pain, sensory, and motor

anesthetics produce blockade first in small-diameter nerves and then in large-diameter nerves. Pain, sympathetic, sensory, and then motor blockade might be the expected order for a thoracic epidural placement, whereas a lumbar catheter might produce pain, sensory, and then motor blockade. Some sympathetic activity may be blocked from a lumbar placement as well, but the impact probably will not be the same as with a higher thoracic placement (see Chapter 2).

The major factors contributing to the extent of the block seen are the insertion site of the catheter, the volume and strength of the solution administered, and the specific kind of local anesthetic used (e.g., lidocaine or bupivacaine). Small volumes of weak solutions (e.g., 0.125%), slowly infused, appear to provide good pain relief without untoward effects to the patient.

Spinal opioids produce dose-dependent, stereospecific, and naloxone-reversible analgesia. To date, there remains a great deal of interpatient variability in response to the administration of all opioids, whether parenteral or spinal. When spinal opioids are administered, the pharmacodynamic aspects of these drugs should be considered. Studies have demonstrated that an intramuscular dose of Demerol produces peak blood concentrations similar to those of a spinal dose (Gustafsson, Johannisson, & Garle, 1986; Max, Inturrisi, Kaiko, Grabinski, Li, & Foley, 1985). The analgesia from spinal opioids, however, appears to last much longer than that from plasma concentrations of opioids. In addition, less total opioid is needed when administered epidurally over time to produce the same or better analgesia.

The absorption and spread of these opioids is dependent on the rate of diffusion from the site of administration to the active receptor sites in the spinal cord (Fig. 7-1). Intrathecal opioids are placed directly into the cerebrospinal fluid (CSF) and attach readily to spinal cord receptor sites (Fig. 7-2). The quality of epidural actions is related to dural penetration, fat deposition, and systemic absorption of the opioids.

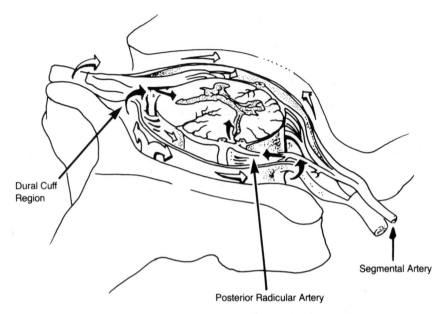

Figure 7-1 Cross-section of spinal cord and epidural space. Opioid spread in epidural space is depicted by white arrows, and spread into CSF and spinal cord is depicted by black arrows. In dural cuff region, posterior radicular spinal artery is readily accessible to opioid, and this artery directly supplies the dorsal horn region of the spinal cord. Its role is currently speculative. *Source*: From *Neural Blockade in Clinical Anesthesia and Management of Pain*, 2nd ed., (p. 983) by M.J. Cousins and P.O. Bridenbaugh (Eds.), 1988, Philadelphia, PA: J.B. Lippincott Company. Copyright 1988 by J.B. Lippincott Company. Reprinted by permission.

The rate of diffusion, spread, and clearance from the neuroaxial structures is dependent on the lipid solubility, molecular weight, mode of delivery (bolus or continuous infusion), volume, and specific receptor affinities of the drug. Volume refers to the amount of preservative-free normal saline (PFNS) used to dilute the drug. An average volume is 10 mL for bolus administration. However, to meet the analgesia needs of a patient with shoulder pain from a diaphragmatic incision (e.g., from thoracic surgery), when that patient has a lumbar catheter in place and a more lipophilic drug is being administered, a larger volume (e.g., 10 to 20 mL) of PFNS may need to be given (Brodsky, 1985). In clinical experience, 15 to 20 mL of PFNS mixed with 100 μg of fentanyl has provided excellent analgesia as a "rescue bolus" for this referred pain.

A lipid-soluble opioid such as fentanyl penetrates the dura rapidly and thus has a rapid onset of action. It undergoes rapid receptor binding as well as dissociation, which results in a short duration of action. Rapid CSF clearance results in a low residual CSF concentration (Fig. 7-3). In contrast, a water-soluble opioid, such as

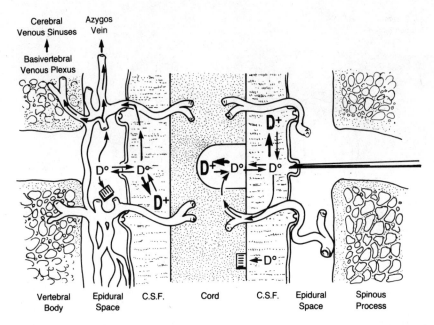

Figure 7-2 Pharmacokinetic model: Subarachnoid injection of a hydrophilic opioid such as morphine. D^0 = unionized drug; D^+ = ionized hydrophilic drug. A spinal needle is shown delivering opioid directly to the CSF. Nearby spinal arteries are in proximity to arachnoid granulations. In the spinal cord, equilibria of D^0 and D^+ on spinal receptors are shown as well as nonspecific lipid binding sites (*shaded squares*). Epidural veins, in proximity to arachnoid granulations, are depicted as the major spinal route of clearance of intrathecal opioid. The two alternative routes of venous drainage are shown. *Source*: From *Neural Blockade in Clinical Anesthesia and Management of Pain*, 2nd ed., (p. 963) by M.J. Cousins and P.O. Bridenbaugh (Eds.), 1988, Philadelphia, PA: J.B. Lippincott Company. Copyright 1988 by J.B. Lippincott Company. Reprinted by permission.

---

morphine penetrates the dura slowly and thus has a longer onset of action. Slower, stronger receptor binding results in a long duration of action. These opioids have slow CSF clearance and low lipid solubility, which may yield a high residual CSF concentration (Fig. 7-4).

Hydromorphone (Dilaudid) might be thought of as an intermediate-acting opioid. With the administration of this opioid, the patient's pain may be relieved in a shorter length of time than with morphine. The duration of action is shorter, however (Table 7-2), but there is also less residual CSF concentration of hydromorphone because it is more lipid soluble. Therefore, the occurrence of long-delayed side effects is not as likely.

Spinal opioids may be removed via the choroid plexus and the cerebral venous drainage system or via epidural veins to the azygos system and then to the superior vena cava.

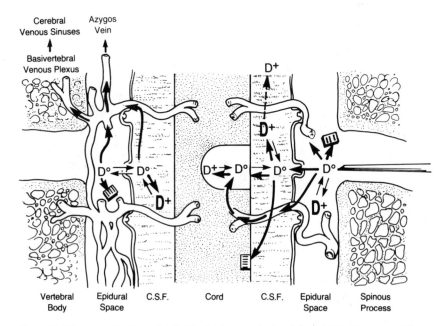

Cerebral Venous Sinuses   Azygos Vein

Basivertebral Venous Plexus

D+

D+

D+ → D° ⇌ D° ⇌ D° ⇌ D°

D°←D°

D+

D+

| Vertebral | Epidural | C.S.F. | Cord | C.S.F. | Epidural | Spinous |
| Body | Space | | | | Space | Process |

Figure 7-3 Pharmacokinetic model: Epidural injection of a lipophilic opioid such as meperidine or fentanyl. Symbols as in Fig. 7-2. Note the rapid passage of unionized species (D^0) into CSF and thence to spinal opioid receptors. Thus the amount of ionized species (D^+), which remains to migrate to the brain, is less than that for morphine (see Fig. 7-4). *Source*: From *Neural Blockade in Clinical Anesthesia and Management of Pain*, 2nd ed., (p. 989) by M.J. Cousins and P.O. Bridenbaugh (Eds.), 1988, Philadelphia, PA: J.B. Lippincott Company. Copyright 1988 by J.B. Lippincott Company. Reprinted by permission.

INDICATIONS, ADVANTAGES, AND DISADVANTAGES OF SPINAL OPIOIDS

Intrathecal Opioids

Intrathecal applications for spinal opioids may have a limited scope of indications in the acute hospital environment. A single bolus dose given intraoperatively may be more discretionary than a catheter remaining in situ. It is imperative that medical staff be able to recognize the site of placement, especially in view of the difference in the dose given intrathecally compared to that given epidurally. The intrathecal dose is currently thought to be 3% to 5% of the epidural dose, whether it is given by bolus or by continuous infusion. There are no current controlled studies to support this, however.

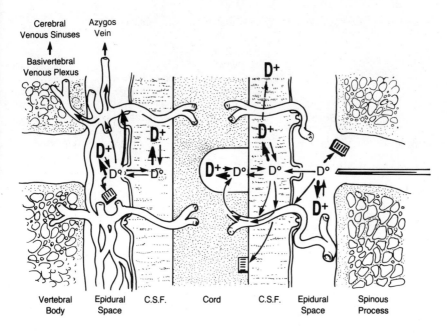

Figure 7-4 Pharmacokinetic model: Epidural injection of a hydrophilic opioid such as morphine. D^0 = unionized lipophilic drug; D^+ = ionized hydrophilic drug. An epidural needle is shown delivering drug to epidural space. Model otherwise similar to Fig. 7-2. The role of absorption by way of radicular arteries remains speculative. The shaded squares are nonspecific lipid-binding sites. *Source*: From *Neural Blockade in Clinical Anesthesia and Management of Pain*, 2nd ed., (p. 987) by M.J. Cousins and P.O. Bridenbaugh (Eds.), 1988, Philadelphia, PA: J.B. Lippincott Company. Copyright 1988 by J.B. Lippincott Company. Reprinted by permission.

Intrathecal opioids have been used for pain associated with open heart surgery, orthopedic surgery, selected general surgeries, labor pain, complicated obstetrics, acute myocardial infarction, and cancer (Cousins & Mather, 1984). Single-dose treatment provides good pain relief, especially when long-acting opioids are used in procedures associated with relatively little pain after the immediate postoperative period (e.g., some orthopedic and some neurosurgical back procedures). Also, blood concentrations after administration are low because of direct placement. A catheter remaining in the subarachnoid space may only be advantageous practically for treatment of severe cancer pain.

The incidence of side effects also may be higher with intrathecal dosing (Cousins & Mather, 1984), including a greater potential for postdural puncture (spinal) headache and infection in deep cerebral structures. The onset of postdural headache is from several hours to days after the procedure. It usually appears in the first or second day after puncture. Severity varies from mild to severe, and an

Table 7-2 Epidural Opioids: Latency and Duration of Postoperative Analgesia

Drug	Dose (mg)	Detectable Onset (min; mean ± standard deviation [SD] or range)	Complete Pain Relief (min; mean ± SD or range)	Duration (hours; mean ± SD or range)
Meperidine	30–100	5–10	12–30	6 (median) 4–20 6.6 ± 3.3
Morphine*	5–10 5 2–6	23.5 ± 6.0	60 37 ± 6 60–90	20 18.1 ± 6.8 12.3 ± 7.7 8–15
Methadone	5	12.5 ± 2.0	17 ± 3	7.2 ± 4.6 8.7 ± 5.9
Hydromorphone	1	13 ± 4	23 ± 8	11.4 ± 5.5
Fentanyl	0.1 0.1	4–10	20	5.7 ± 3.7 2.6–4.0
Diamorphine	5 6	15 5	30 15	8.4 ± 1 12.4 ± 6.5 2–21
Phenoperidine	2	15	30	6.0 ± 0.4

*Increasing the dose from 2 mg to 6 mg of morphine increases the duration of pain relief from approximately 514 minutes to 938 minutes.

Source: From *Neural Blockade in Clinical Anesthesia and Management of Pain*, 2nd ed., (p. 997) by M.J. Cousins and P.O. Bridenbaugh (Eds.), 1988, Philadelphia, PA: J.B. Lippincott Company. Copyright 1988 by J.B. Lippincott Company. Reprinted by permission.

upright position and vagal maneuvers seem to accentuate it. The supine position alleviates the headache. Treatment modalities have varied considerably. Hydration and the epidural injection of autologous blood (blood patch procedure) are the most frequently utilized (Albright, Ferguson, Joyce, & Stevenson, 1986; Cousins & Bridenbaugh, 1988; Orkin & Cooperman, 1983).

A blood patch procedure is usually reserved for those debilitating headaches refractory to less invasive treatments and/or which have not abated in a reasonable length of time. It requires placement of a needle into the patient's lumbar epidural space, followed by epidural injection of 5ccs to 10ccs of blood drawn aseptically from the patient's anticubital vein. The clot formed at the site, is thought to stem escape of CSF (Orkin & Cooperman, 1983). The needle is removed and the patient is requested to remain supine for a period of time. A single treatment is usually all that is necessary.

Epidural Opioids

Epidural applications for spinal opioids are gaining an increasingly broader scope. When a regional technique is used for part or all of the anesthesia in surgical patients, it is especially advantageous to leave the catheter in place for the provision of postoperative analgesia. Postsurgical indications for use are reported for thoracotomy, orthopedic surgery (e.g., total hip or total knee replacement), prostatectomy, abdominal and general surgery, gynecologic surgery, vascular surgery (intraabdominal or peripheral), and nephrectomy. Other indications include cancer pain, as for patients who are unresponsive to oral opioids and other measures (see Chapter 14); chronic pain (e.g., back pain) to assist in mobilization; ischemic rest pain (for acute or chronic episodes); acute medical conditions (e.g., thrombophlebitis, herpes zoster or nephrolithiasis); and posttraumatic injury (e.g., crushed chest) (Cousins & Bridenbaugh, 1988; Cousins & Mather, 1984; Cousins & Phillips, 1986; Foley, 1985).

The advantages associated with the use of epidural analgesia appear to be compared most often in the literature with those of local anesthesia. The selective blockade of pain by spinal opioids is a major advantage compared to the potential multimodal blockade (sympathetic, sensory, and motor) of local anesthetics. Other advantages of epidural analgesia are that the patient is comfortable and that patients ambulate in about half the time compared to patients receiving parenteral narcotics (Rawal, Sjostrand, Christoffersson, Dahlstrom, Arvill, and Rydman, 1984). They cough and deep-breathe sooner and with less discomfort and are much more alert and aware. It is extrapolated from this that these patients may have fewer respiratory complications (e.g., pulmonary emboli) because they have better compliance with their prescribed regimes. At one large West Coast university teaching hospital nearly all thoracotomy patients have spinal opioid analgesia, and it is routine for them to begin incentive spirometry a few hours after their surgery. The vast majority are transferred to general care areas the next day.

The total narcotic requirement is much less with spinal opioids (see Table 7-2). This is especially important in the elderly and the narcotic-naive or narcotic-sensitive patient. The ease of repeated administration through the catheter by either bolus or continual infusion is a clear advantage over the intramuscular administration of narcotics. Depending on the opioid used, the patient may not need to be dosed as often as with parenteral narcotics. This advantage also can save nursing time, and when continuous infusions are used to help ensure a steady state of pain relief both the patient and the nurse benefit.

Contraindications to the utilization of spinal opioids include site infections, dermatological conditions, septicemia or bacteremia, shock or severe hypovolemia, preexisting disease of the spinal cord, increased intracranial pressure, gross abnormality of blood clotting mechanisms (whether iatrogenic or pathophysiological in origin), and patient refusal or physician inexperience with spinal techniques.

SIDE EFFECTS ASSOCIATED WITH THE ADMINISTRATION OF SPINAL OPIOIDS

Early and Late Respiratory Depression

The first cases of respiratory depression from spinal opioids were reported in 1980, shortly after the introduction of opioid use to clinical practice (Boas, 1980). Respiratory depression, although rare, occurs more frequently in patients who are naive to narcotics. Other factors that may pose an increased risk to patients are concomitant severe respiratory disease, age greater than 65 years, American Society of Anesthesiologists status greater than 2, moderate or large amounts of narcotics or long-acting sedatives used before or during surgery, raised intrathoracic or intraabdominal pressure, obstruction of inferior vena cava, severe illness due to any cause, and use of unusually high doses of opioid for analgesia. Raised intrathoracic pressure may cause increased venous uptake of drug, with more drug reaching central structures (Cousins & Bridenbaugh, 1988). Iatrogenic causes of respiratory depression occur when parenteral doses of opioids or sedatives are administered without regard for the type of spinal opioid being used or when opioids already had been given a few hours before. Respiratory depression appears to result from sufficient quantities or concentrations of the drug reaching the respiratory centers in the brainstem.

Respiratory Depression Associated with Intrathecal Opioids

The onset of respiratory depression from intrathecal opioids is quite variable and is most often associated with their use in postoperative analgesia. Respiratory depression is usually evident within 6 to 10 hours (late). It is dose dependent and may be position or dilution-volume dependent as well. It is recommended that dilution volume not exceed 10% of spinal CSF volume (approximately 7.5 mL) (Cuocolo et al., 1987).

Respiratory Depression Associated with Epidural Opioids

Respiratory depression associated with epidural administration of opioids can occur early or late. Early respiratory depression is seen within 1 hour of injection. It is most often associated with catheter migration resulting in dural penetration or vascular penetration and with the drug obtaining intrathecal or blood access. It is also postulated that high doses of lipid soluble drugs may cause early respiratory depression at least partly by their rapid penetration of dural structures and achievement of peak concentrations near the brainstem in about 30 minutes (Cousins & Bridenbaugh, 1988).

Late respiratory depression is defined as decreased respiratory rate (i.e., <8/min) occurring 3 to 12 hours after an initial bolus is given or an infusion is started. Respiratory depression is most often associated with progressive signs of decreased level of consciousness and concomitant decreased respiratory rate rather than abrupt cessation of respiration. It occurs most often with morphine because of its longer duration of action and hydrophilicity. It is also frequently associated with large doses of preoperative or intraoperative narcotics or sedatives given concurrently with spinal opioid. At some institutions, no additional sedatives or narcotics are given without orders from the pain specialist.

Patients in critical care (e.g., from vascular surgery or abdominal aortic aneurysm repair) frequently remain on the ventilator for several hours or days after returning from the operating room. For these patients, after they are awake but while they are still on the ventilator, it is occasionally necessary to administer small doses of sedatives to enable them to cope with the interventions.

Postoperative pain, like all other pain, is multifactoral. For example, when wound pain is removed other discomforts become intolerable, e.g., nasogastric tube, backache. For some patients, the critical care environment is exceptionally stressful. No amount of analgesic is enough to cover their entire scope of needs. Their anxiety is overwhelming. Sleep deprivation may have additive effects on perceived pain (Aurell & Elmquist, 1985). These patients will need some sedative as well as spinal opioid. A small dose of a short-acting drug given intravenously and titrated to their needs frequently is necessary.

As always, care must be taken when administering sedatives with spinal opioids. Continuous ventilator support minimizes concern for the deleterious effects of respiratory depression. When weaning from mechanical ventilation is about to start, sedatives are cut to the merest fractional doses or stopped altogether.

Current nursing guidelines for care include the monitoring of respiratory rate and pattern as frequently as every ½ to 1 hour for the first 24 hours. Pulse oximetry or apnea monitors are used at some institutions in lieu of frequent nursing assessments. As with all mechanical devices, these monitors are not without inherent operating problems, which can be annoying for patients and nurses alike. In two large studies, the incidence of respiratory depression was 3.3:1,000 in

6,000 patients and 1:1,000 in 14,000 patients (Gustafsson, Schildt, Jackobsen, 1982; Rawal, Arneri, Gustafsson, and Allvin, 1987).

The current treatment for respiratory depression is rapid intravenous administration of naloxone (0.1 to 0.4 mg, repeated as often as necessary) if respiratory depression is severe (i.e., <8/min). In postoperative patients and in patients with preexisting cardiovascular disease, abrupt reversal of narcotic depression may result in tachycardia, increased blood pressure, and pulmonary edema. Therefore, it is important to titrate to the patient's need the dose of naloxone administered. To prevent the recurrence of respiratory depression, a continuous infusion of naloxone (5 µg/kg/hour) is suggested (Cousins & Bridenbaugh, 1988). Nalbuphine (5 to 10 mg intravenously, repeated twice if necessary) also has proven beneficial to treat mild to moderate respiratory depression (Latasch, Probst, & Dudziak, 1984).

Pruritis

Various studies have shown that the frequency of pruritis is from 1% to 100% (Bromage, Camporesi, & Chestnut, 1980; Cousins & Bridenbaugh, 1988). It appears most often with morphine but has been seen with nearly all spinal opioids. Morphine alkaloids are known to release histamine, but the exact cause of this phenomenon is not known.

Personal experience has shown that patients will report pruritis more often when questioned specifically regarding its occurrence. The itching appears to be scattered randomly over all body parts as opposed to being predominantly about the face and neck. Most patients do not appear to be extremely bothered by it; many are seen to be scratching "here and there." Allergies to tape and harsh detergents, diaphoresis, and dry skin are as frequently the causes of the pruritis.

It is obviously important to determine the actual cause(s) of pruritis. One patient who was receiving blood products and spinal opioid therapy concurrently began complaining of severe itching. Benadryl was administered intramuscularly to relieve his symptoms. It was later learned that he had a severe allergy to wheat. His physician postulated that the donated blood from a person who had recently ingested wheat may have been the culprit because the patient did not respond to the opioid antagonists that were used as treatment. In this particular case there was no increase in sedation level from the administration of Benadryl, even though the patient was receiving a continuous infusion of epidural hydromorphone.

Both low-dose naloxone and nalbuphine (5 to 10 mg intravenously; Henderson & Cohen, 1986) have been effective in treating pruritis secondary to spinal opioids. In most patients, analgesia is not reversed.

Nausea and Vomiting

Nausea and vomiting have been reported in 17% to 50% of patients receiving spinal opioid analgesia (Cousins & Bridenbaugh, 1988). Vomiting has been reported to occur without prior incidence of nausea. The rostral spread of opioid to intracerebral structures and the subsequent suppression of the vomiting center may be caused by the drug administration (Cousins & Bridenbaugh, 1988). Vomiting also is a frequent postoperative occurrence in patients not being treated with spinal opioids and may be indicative of new or unresolved surgical problems. A prior history of drug sensitivities or predisposition to nausea and vomiting (e.g., motion sickness) is helpful in determining the cause of the postoperative nausea and vomiting and in instituting accurate and timely treatment. It can be especially challenging in patients after abdominal surgery. Frequently, drugs that assist in gastric emptying are helpful in relieving nausea and vomiting in the postsurgical patient. It may be necessary to give antiemetics, however, even though most antiemetics have some sedative effect. A nonfunctioning nasogastric (NG) tube also has been the culprit on some occasions, and the NG tube itself may irritate the back of the throat and lead to vomiting.

When patients are out of bed or sitting up, it is helpful to determine whether the nausea is preceded by vertigo and to assess whether the cause may be orthostatic in nature. Inadequate fluid balance, as often is seen in critically ill patients, may lead to hemodynamic problems that are most apparent when the patient's position is changed (i.e., orthostatic hypotension). Hypotension may lead to vertigo, which then may lead to nausea.

The incidence of nausea and vomiting is reported to be much lower in patients who are treated with lipophilic opioids as well as those who require long-term therapy with opioids (e.g., cancer patients). Intravenous low-dose naloxone and antiemetics have been used successfully to treat this problem. Lowering the dose of spinal opioid also may help alleviate the severity of these symptoms. Supportive nursing measures such as applying cool cloths to the forehead, coaching in slow breathing, instituting temporary bedrest, monitoring vital signs when initial advancements in activity are started, and correlating activity with occurrence are helpful.

Urinary Retention

Several hypotheses have been suggested as cause for this side effect of spinal opioid administration. The most reasonable cause seems to be related to detrusor muscle relaxation and increased bladder capacity, so that urinary retention occurs (Cuocolo et al., 1987). This is not a problem when a urinary catheter is in place or in cancer patients. If there is no catheter in place, if the bladder is distended and/or there is no urine output for eight hours, IV naloxone in doses of 0.1 mg-0.4 mg, has been effective in inducing urination. Straight bladder catheterization to assess residual volume or to empty the bladder may have to be undertaken in some patients, especially when an indwelling catheter may increase risk for infection for particular populations (e.g., total joint replacements).

The incidence of urinary retention is reported as being from 15%-90% (Cousins & Bridenbaugh, 1988). It is not yet known if this incidence varies with the opioid used, the duration of use, or among males or females, but it does not seem to be related to amount of drug given. Other factors, such as anatomic site of surgery, supine position, and volume status are important assessment parameters to consider when evaluating the patient. Many patients confined to bed may be unable to void for that reason alone. Most patients in critical care units have indwelling catheters, so urinary retention does not usually pose a problem for them.

Other Side Effects

Other side effects of spinal opioid administration that may be potential problems include sedation, neurotoxicity, infection, opioid withdrawal syndrome, miosis, dysphoria, hypersensitivity, and neurologic dysfunction, e.g., parasthesia, palsies, and paralysis. Of these, sedation is much less in opioid naive patients, if the minimal effective dose is used and the patient does not have undiagnosed sleep apnea.

Neurotoxicity is avoided by using only preservative-free narcotics (opioids) and PFNS as a diluent. Also, when continuous opioid infusions are used, frequently the same kind of mechanical pump is used for this as for IV administration. With the usual high level of activity and acuity of most ICUs, it is conceivable that a mistake would not be hard to make. Therefore, the catheter and tubing should be marked distinctly so that other drugs are not inadvertently administered through this system. This includes, for the inexperienced, not giving drugs such as naloxone for treatment of side effects through the spinal catheter.

Infection always looms as a dreaded potential complication of spinal opioid administration. The best preventive measure is not to utilize this technique of pain control in patients with preexisting sepsis or those who are especially at risk for rapid development of sepsis. Maintaining aseptic conditions is of paramount importance during the catheter and analgesic insertion technique and the management phase. Most catheters are placed in the operating room, but consultation for pain management for the difficult to wean patient or for the patient at increased risk for respiratory disease may be indications for placement after surgery. In such cases the catheter frequently is inserted at the bedside. Maintaining as aseptic an environment as possible is crucial. An occlusive dressing is placed over the insertion site and should extend at least two-thirds of the way up the back. Hospital infection control guidelines should be used as the basis for frequency of changing the dressing, the infusion tubing (for continuous infusion), and the catheter.

In the acute care environment, the length of time for which the indwelling catheter is in place is usually 3 to 5 days; after this time patients should be evaluated closely for need and risk. A new catheter may need to be inserted at a different interspace. Care also is taken whenever the catheter integrity is broken for administration of spinal opioid. Nurses monitor temperature, vital signs, and neurological status as indicators of potential development of infection. They also observe the insertion site for any inflammation or drainage when dressing changes are done.

Catheter-Related Technical Problems

Catheter-related technical problems also may occur. Catheter migration through blood vessels or dura may result from the semirigid catheter construction material or from excessive pressures generated from bolus administration technique. It is recommended that a 3- or 5-mL syringe be used for checking catheter placement before a bolus injection is administered. At least a 12-mL syringe is then used to deliver the ordered opioid into the epidural space. This larger size also facilitates mixture of the opioid with the appropriate amount of PFNS to a total volume adequate to spread over the necessary dermatomes to provide analgesia. Larger sizes may be necessary for administration of larger amounts.

Other problems include kinking, breaking, shearing, or slipping out of place. The risk of catheter shearing is highest when the catheter is removed. It is important to remove it slowly from the insertion site and to check that it is removed intact. Having the patient flex forward slightly when the catheter is removed opens interspaces more and allows easier removal. Slipping out of place can be due to an unsutured catheter, a nonocclusive and loose dressing, or patient moving techniques. Observing the dressing at least every 8 hours and reinforcing or changing it as needed helps prevent this problem. Using additional tape placed strategically to prevent direct pulling pressure on the catheter also helps. Using lift sheets helps decrease drag on the back. An ounce of prevention goes a long way in maintaining integrity of the catheter.

Inadequate Analgesia

Nearly all patient complaints of excessive recurrence of pain in an otherwise comfortable analgesic state have been related to technical catheter problems. One patient had been comfortable nearly all day after his cardiovascular surgery when he suddenly started to complain of unrelieved pain. On examination of the cap connection, the tape on his back, and the sheet on the bed, it was obvious that the catheter had several small breaks in it, allowing the spinal opioid to escape.

Other pathophysiological events not related to the catheter may occur as well. Pain of increased intensity or from other locations than the treatment site is a symptom not to be ignored. For example, another patient in the cardiovascular unit began complaining of left lower leg pain after a thoracic surgery procedure. When she was examined by the pain service it was evident that one leg was much cooler than the other, and peripheral pulses in that extremity were faint to absent. She was taken back to surgery for an embolectomy and a fasciotomy of the leg. These examples are relatively rare but worth consideration and assessment time for all patients.

As with nearly all forms of analgesic therapy for pain management, sometimes the dose may be inadequate. A ''rescue dose'' of supplemental analgesia should be included to cover ''breakthrough pain'' or an inadequate infusion rate.

CASE STUDY

R.M., a 66-year-old native American man, was admitted to the hospital for the scheduled repair of an abdominal aortic aneurysm. The aneurysm was detected on physical examination several months before admission. The patient's past medical history included the following:

- 1960—intractable ulcer disease, antrectomy, and Billroth II operation
- 1981—coronary artery bypass surgery
- 1987—myocardial infarction (probably there was another one before this)
- 1988—pancolonoscopy with removal of several polyps; removal of basal cell cancer under left eye; occurrence of multiple renal cysts
  A temporal artery bypass operation because of frequent severe headaches
  A recent positive VDRL lab test which might be a result of latent syphilis
  Smoking history which was 1 pack per day prior to 1987

After an extensive medical work-up and preoperative optimization of his antianginal medications, R.M. was brought to the operating room. An epidural catheter was placed by the anesthesiologist at the beginning of the case and tested. The patient's previous midline incision was opened and continued down to the pubis. During surgery there was some difficulty dissecting the aneurysm from the duodenum. A 16 cm × 60 cm Dacron graft was inserted from just below the renal arteries to the bifurcation of the iliacs.

The patient was admitted to the critical care unit directly after the procedure (about 3 hours later). On admission (11:00) he was intubated, in ventricular bigeminy, and receiving both vasoactive and antidysrhythmic intravenous medications. Vessel access was maintained by both peripheral and central lines, including a thermodilution catheter. Just after the weaning process was begun, the patient was started on a continuous infusion of epidural hydromorphone at 0.3 mg/hour (14:00). Supplemental pain medication (fentanyl, 100 μg) was given per epidural catheter at 13:00, 16:00, 17:20, 21:00, and 00:15.

On the next day all vasoactive IV drip medications had been weaned to off, extubation was accomplished, and the patient was on nasal oxygen. He was able to move in bed, could raise three balls 10 times on the incentive spirometer, and had a productive cough. Only one supplemental dose each of fentanyl (100 μg) and hydromorphone (0.7 mg) was given for breakthrough pain (09:00), and the infusion rate was increased to 0.35 mg/hour. The patient was transferred to the step-down unit on the next day, and at 10:00 the continuous infusion was decreased to 0.2 mg/hour and the indwelling urinary catheter removed. He continued to do well, ambulating in the hallway, taking a full-liquid to regular diet, and voiding spontaneously. Pain scores at rest were 0 to 1 on a visual analog scale.

On the following day at 09:30, the epidural infusion was stopped, the catheter was pulled out intact, and the patient was ordered oral pain medication. When questioned, he said that he was ''very satisfied'' with his pain relief and would not hesitate to use epidural analgesia again. The patient continued his stay without incident and was discharged to home 1 week after admission.

CONCLUSION

Although the first patients with whom spinal opioid analgesia was used were always in the critical care units, currently at many large teaching hospitals noncritically ill patients who are using spinal opioids are all on the general care units. Other advances or uses for spinal opioids encompass patient-controlled devices for administration of epidural opioids (Marlowe, Engstrom, & White, 1989) as well as implanted epidural and intrathecal catheters. Access to these implanted catheters usually is gained via either a Port-a-Cath system or an infusion pump (Paice, 1986). Implanted systems are currently reserved for severe cancer pain, chemotherapy, or neurological spasticity. Patients may continue to receive therapy in a home care setting (Smith, 1986).

In conclusion, this chapter has presented a review of physiological mechanisms of pain, differentiation of local anesthetics from spinal opioids, characteristics of spinal opioids, and side effects associated with the administration of these drugs. Also discussed were the incidence and nursing/medical measures for assessment and treatment of these side effects of spinal opioid administration. When this technique is used by skilled physicians and nurses, it provides safe and effective pain management. A comprehensive nursing and medical education program is necessary to assure this. The nursing program should include both a didactic and/ or self-learning module theory portion and a clinical application portion. This ensures that nurses have an adequate knowledge base to integrate into patient care.

As with all interventions that are invasive, need versus risk or efficacy of use issues should be evaluated on an individual basis for each patient. There is still much to study about spinal opioids in human application, but their use in selected critical care patients is extremely valuable in alleviating pain.

REFERENCES

Albright, G.A., Ferguson, J.E., Joyce, T.E., & Stevenson, D.K. (1986). *Anesthesia in obstetrics: Maternal, fetal and neonatal aspects* (2nd ed.). Woburn, MA: Butterworth.

Aurell, J., & Elmquist, D. (1985). Sleep in the surgical intensive care unit: Continuous polygraphic recording of sleep in nine patients receiving postoperative care. *British Medical Journal, 290*, 1029–1031.

Behar, M., Olshwang, H., Magorai, F., & Davidson, J.T. (1979). Epidural morphine in treatment of pain. *Lancet, 1*, 527–529.

Boas, R.A. (1980). Hazards of epidural morphine. *Clinics in Critical Care Medicine, 8*, 377–378.

Brodsky, J.B. (1985). *Spinal Narcotics*. Unpublished manuscript, Stanford University School of Medicine, Stanford, CA.

Bromage, P.R., Camporesi, E., & Chestnut, D. (1980). Epidural narcotics for postoperative analgesia. *Anesthesia and Analgesia, 59*, 473.

Cousins, M.J., & Bridenbaugh, P.O. (Eds.). (1988). *Neural blockade in clinical anesthesia and management of pain* (2nd ed.). Philadelphia: Lippincott.

Cousins, M.J., & Mather, L.E. (1984). Intrathecal and epidural administration of opioids. *Anesthesiology, 61*, 276–310.

Cousins, M.J., Mather, L.E., & Glynn, C.J. (1979). Selective spinal analgesia. *Lancet, 1*, 1141.

Cousins, M.J., & Phillips, G.D. (1986). Acute pain management. *Clinics in Critical Care Medicine, 8*.

Cuocolo, R., Amantea, B., Savoia, G., Esposito, C., Befiore, F., Formicola, G., Savanelli, A., & Acampora, B. (1987). Which opioids are indicated for spinal anesthesia? *Advances in Pain Research and Therapy, 10*, 111–122.

Fine, P.G., & Hare, B.D. (1985). Pathways and mechanisms of pain and analgesia: A review and clinical perspective. *Hospital Formulary, 20*, 972–985.

Foley, K. (1985). The treatment of cancer pain. *New England Journal of Medicine, 313*, 84–95.

Gustafsson, L.L., Johannisson, J., & Garle, M. (1986). Extradural and parenteral pethidine as analgesia after total hip replacement: Effects and kinetics. A controlled clinical study. *European Journal of Clinical Pharmacology, 29*, 529.

Gustafsson, L.L., Schildt, B., & Jackobsen, P.T. (1982). Adverse effects of epidural and intraspinal opiates: Report of a nationwide survey in Sweden. *British Journal of Anesthesia, 54*, 479–486.

Henderson, S.K., & Cohen, H.J. (1986). Nalbuphine augmentation of analgesia and reversal of side effects following epidural hydromorphone. *Anesthesiology, 65*, 216–218.

International Association for the Study of Pain. (1979). Pain terms: A list with definitions and notes on usage. *Pain, 6*, 249–252.

Latasch, L., Probst, S., & Dudziak, R. (1984). Reversal by nalbuphine of respiratory depression caused by fentanyl. *Anesthesia Analogues, 63*, 814–816.

Marlowe, S., Engstrom, R., & White, P. (1989). Epidural patient-controlled analgesia (PCA): An alternative to continuous epidural infusions. *Pain, 37*, 97–101.

Max, M.B., Inturrisi, C.E., Kaiko, R.F. Grabinski, P.Y., Li, C.H., & Foley, K. (1985). Epidural and intrathecal opiates: Cerebral fluid and plasma profiles in patients with chronic cancer pain. *Clinical Pharmacology and Therapeutics, 38*, 631–641.

Orkin, F.K., & Cooperman, L.H. (1983). *Complications in anesthesia*. Philadelphia: Lippincott.

Paice, J.A. (1986). Intrathecal morphine infusion for intractable cancer pain: A new use for implanted pumps. *Oncology Nursing Forum, 13*, 41–47.

Rawal, M., Arneri, S., Gustafsson, L.L., & Allvin, R. (1987). Present state of extradural and intrathecal opioid analgesia: A nationwide follow-up survey. *British Journal of Anesthesia, 59*, 791–799.

Rawal, M., Sjostrand, U., Christoffersson, E., Dahlstrom, B., Arvill, A., & Rydman, H. (1984). Comparison of intramuscular and epidural morphine for postoperative analgesia in the grossly obese: Influence on postoperative ambulation and pulmonary function. *Anesthesia and Analgesia, 63*, 583.

Smith, K.A. (1986). Teaching family members intrathecal morphine administration. *Journal of Neuroscience Nursing, 18*, 95–97.

Wang, J.K., Nauss, L.E., & Thomas, J.E. (1979). Pain relief by intrathecally applied morphine in man. *Anesthesiology, 50*, 149.

RECOMMENDED READING

Etches, R., Sandler, A.N., & Daley, M.D. (1989). Respiratory depression and spinal opioids. *Canadian Journal of Anesthesia, 36*, 165–185.

Lieb, R.A., & Hurtig, J.B. (1985). Epidural and intrathecal narcotics for pain management. *Heart & Lung, 14*, 164–174.

Olsson, G.L., Leddo, C.C., & Wild, L. (1989). Nursing management of patients receiving epidural narcotics. *Heart & Lung, 18*, 130–138.

Wall, P.D., & Melzack, R. (Eds.). (1984). *Textbook of pain*. New York: Churchill Livingstone.

Chapter 8

Care of the Critically Ill Patient in Pain: The Importance of Nursing

Julia Faucett

Nursing as a profession is committed to the amelioration of pain and discomfort and the promotion of patients' health (American Nurses' Association, 1980; Meinhart & McCaffery, 1983). Despite nursing's professional standards, however, the management of pain in the critically ill has been shown to be inconsistent (Bondestam, Hovgren, Gaston-Johansson, Jern, Herlitz, & Holmberg, 1987; Cohen, 1980; Fagerhaugh & Strauss, 1977; Graffam, 1981; Meinhart & McCaffery, 1983; Teske, Daut, & Cleeland, 1983). Professional accountability for the management of pain involves assessing the need for and appropriateness of a nursing response to patients with pain in addition to performing, evaluating, and documenting nursing interventions (Graffam, 1979). The quality of pain management can be improved by identifying the unique aspects of nursing care, recognizing the diversity of interventions that nurses provide for patients in pain, and integrating those interventions into critical care. This chapter presents a perspective on the nursing care of critically ill patients in pain and then discusses cognitive-behavioral interventions that can broaden the nurse's pain management repertoire. The final section in the chapter discusses the application of these nursing interventions given the unique demands of severely ill patients and of the critical care unit.

THE NURSING FOCUS OF CARE

Nursing care of the patient in pain differs in perspective from care provided by other health care professionals. Although we share many principles of pain management with medicine and psychology, for example, nursing pain management focuses on the functional abilities of the patient in addition to underlying pathological processes. Because of the emphasis on promoting function, nurses monitor and attend to the psychological as well as the physiological needs and responses of the patient in pain (McCaffery, 1979). In the critical care unit, nurses continuously compensate for the inability of patients to self-regulate air exchange, food and fluid intake, elimination, hygiene, rest and activity; to communicate; and to manage the environment. They call on multiple skills to assist the patient to prevent, reduce, or endure pain that accompanies the most basic tasks of daily living.

The Need for Nursing Care

Life, health, and well-being are dependent on human functioning in specific areas called the universal requisites (Exhibit 8-1 Orem, 1985; Underwood, 1990). The learned activities that we perform to meet these universal requisites constitute self-care (Orem, 1985). Nursing is required when self-care ability is insufficient to meet these basic functional requisites, that is when there are self-care deficits due to physical or cognitive impairments or to lack of knowledge and expertise (Orem, 1985).

In critical care, nurses compensate for complex deficits in all the functional areas to sustain the life and well-being of their patients. For example, they monitor mechanical ventilation and cardiovascular function; the provision and intake of fluid and hyperalimentation; bowel, kidney, and bladder function; needs for rest, sleep, and repositioning; skin and wound condition; and the interpersonal communication related to emotional well-being. Persistent pain or its treatment may compromise nurse or patient attempts to meet functional care requirements. The critically ill patient who is in pain needs nurses to perform these basic life-sustaining activities and to assist them with managing pain that threatens functional ability as well as comfort.

Exhibit 8-1 Universal Self-Care Requisites

Maintenance of adequate air exchange
Maintenance of adequate intake of food and fluid
Provision of care associated with processes of elimination
Maintenance of personal hygiene and temperature
Maintenance of balance between activity and rest
Maintenance of balance between solitude and social interaction

Source: From *Nursing Concepts of Practice*, 3rd ed., by D. Orem, 1985, San Francisco, CA: McGraw-Hill, and from P. Underwood, "Orem's Self-Care Model: Principles and General Applications" in *Psychiatric and Mental Health Nursing Theory and Practice* by B. Reynolds and D. Cormack (Eds.), 1990, London: Chapman and Hall.

Pain or its treatment may affect care requirements in any of the universal requisite areas (Table 8-1). For example, full expansion and clearing of the lungs may be restricted by the pain of thoracic or upper abdominal incisions. Pain curtails or prevents restorative sleep. It increases sympathetic activity, adding to the effects of stress on the cardiovascular system. It may restrict positioning, compromising both skin condition and pulmonary drainage. Social withdrawal often accompanies severe pain, and concomitant irritability, anxiety, or depression may disrupt vital communication and emotionally sustaining social interactions. Pharmacological treatment for pain such as narcotic analgesics can cause respiratory depression, nausea, vomiting, appetite suppression, constipation, and increased somnolence. Mechanical devices such as transcutaneous nerve stimulators (TNSs) or patient-controlled analgesia pumps (PCAs) may restrict mobility and positioning.

Accountability for the nursing care of patients in pain requires that the nursing actions undertaken to minimize patient pain and its effects be deliberately performed, evaluated, and documented. Routine nursing care includes techniques to minimize or prevent pain, for example, that are rarely acknowledged as interventions. Such nursing actions in critical care include planning and teamwork in repositioning; bracing the patient while encouraging coughing; timing attention-diverting conversation; and preventing or managing painful skin breakdown, analgesia-related constipation, and gas pains. What nurses call "comfort meas-

Table 8-1 Examples of the Effects of Pain and Pain Therapy on the Universal Self-Care Requisites

Universal Self-Care Requisites	Pain may be Related to Problems with:	Pain Therapy and its Side Effects may be Related to:
Adequate exchange of air	Breathing, coughing	Respiratory depression
Adequate intake of food/ fluid	Nausea, vomiting, cramping	Nausea, vomiting, dry mouth
Elimination processes	Diarrhea, constipation, urination, gas	Diarrhea, constipation, urinary retention
Hygiene and body temperature	Skin condition and sensitivity, wound care	Intravenous line care, allergic reactions
Balance of rest and activity	Sleep deprivation, mobility, hypotension, range of motion	Somnolence and sedation, hypotension, decreased activity
Balance of solitude and social interaction	Social withdrawal, anxiety and depression, irritability	Emotional lability, dysphoria, concentration

ures'' are essential to the management of pain in the critically ill patient, for whom the smallest additional problem may be overwhelming.

Nursing care focuses on attaining results from two types of interventions: compensating for the inability of patients to care for themselves, and promoting and supporting the self-care ability of patients (Orem, 1985). In the critical care setting, compensatory care often means that nurses take over the entire responsibility of meeting the functional care requirements of the patient. Nursing forethought in critical care also is essential, however, to promote the patient's self-esteem and confidence necessary for the patient to reestablish or reappraise his or her role in self-care after transfer from the critical care unit.

Identifying opportunities to reinforce even simple decision-making skills, acknowledging the patient's role in enduring painful or difficult treatments, and providing information about procedures and sensations associated with treatments support confidence or self-efficacy and positive self-appraisal. Such nursing approaches promote a sense of perceived control for the patient coping with the potentially overwhelming environment of the critical care unit. In this way, nurses can help curb the onset of anxiety and depression, reduce the contribution of emotional distress to pain, and increase pain endurance (see Chapter 3).

Pain Work in Nursing

Pain management is commonly considered pain relief. Health care providers are not always able to provide total relief from pain, whether acute or chronic (McCaffery, 1979). More often the goals of pain management are to modulate pain, to increase the endurance of it, or to sustain patients emotionally while they endure it. *Pain work* is a more accurate and multidimensional term than *pain relief*, and signifies the many ways in which nurses interact with patients in pain (Fagerhaugh & Strauss, 1977). Exhibit 8-2 lists an expanded version of the dimensions of pain work described by Fagerhaugh & Strauss (1977).

Wound debridement of a ventilated patient provides examples of the many dimensions of pain work. Debridement may involve premedication to minimize pain and ongoing monitoring of potential analgesia-related side effects. Pain endurance and management of anxiety during the procedure may be extended by providing preparatory information and guided deep breathing and discussing how the patient will indicate to the nurse that the pain is too severe to continue and that a rest break is needed. Demonstrations by the nurse of concerned caring before or after the treatment may help prevent the resentment and communication breakdown that may ensue from the necessary and repeated infliction of pain. Furthermore, repeated experiences observing patients cope with debridement may be draining and may lead to desensitization among health care professionals. There-

Exhibit 8-2 Dimensions of Pain Work in Nursing

Minimizing or preventing pain
Assisting the patient to endure pain
Coping with pain expression
Diagnosing or assessing causes of pain
Inflicting pain
Managing side effects of pain therapies

Source: From *Politics of Pain Management: Staff-Patient Interaction* by S. Fagerhaugh and A. Strauss, 1977, Menlo Park, CA: Addison-Wesley.

---

fore, attention to one's own reaction as well as to the patient's may be an important adjunct to pain work.

Nursing Roles in Pain Work

In working with individual patients, nurses have developed interventions that assist patients in preventing, reducing, and enduring pain and in managing the expression of pain (Table 8-2). By preventing the occurrence of noxious stimuli, by modifying their noxious quality, and by altering sensory transmission, nurses help patients prevent or reduce pain. Premedication, counterirritation (e.g., rubbing an intramuscular injection site), and the performance for patients of potentially painful tasks are common examples.

Critical care nurses psychologically and physically support, comfort, and sustain patients who must endure procedure-related or task-related pain. Often simply staying with the patient who is suffering contributes to pain endurance (Gardner, 1985; McCaffery, 1979). Nursing interventions, for example, that take into account the cognitive and emotional as well as the physiological nature of the patient have been found to be more successful in alleviating pain than physiologically based interventions alone (Diers, Schmidt, McBride, & Davis, 1972; McBride, 1967; Moss & Meyer, 1966). Early intervention to bolster the self-confidence of the patient with, for example, mechanical ventilation, severe burns, or myocardial infarction may circumvent the exacerbation of pain by lessening anxiety or a debilitating sense of helplessness (Thompson, 1989) (see also Chapter 3).

Critical care nurses assist patients with the display or expression of pain by providing information and alternative methods of communication and by managing the intensive care environment. Chest tube removal, dressing changes, Foley catheter insertion, central or Swan-Ganz line insertion, and computerized

Table 8-2 Examples of Nursing Pain Work Interventions

Dimensions of Pain Work	Goals of Nursing Interventions	Examples
Pain reduction and prevention	To block or modify transmission	• Analgesia administration • Splinting of incisional pain during coughing or suctioning • Repositioning based on nursing knowledge of body alignment • Light slapping of site before injections • Handing objects to bed-bound patients to avoid pain exacerbation from movements • Application of cold, heat, vibration, massage, TNS • Use of relaxation-induction methods • Use of attention-distraction methods
Pain expression and communication	To promote appropriate pain expression and communication	• Providing communication devices • Discussing meaning and management of pain with patient • Providing sensory and procedural information • Providing alternative forms of expression: breathing techniques, gripping side rails, hand-holding
	To provide safe and secure environment	• Providing information and emotional support for patient • Monitoring staff movement and equipment • Closing curtains/doors for privacy
Pain endurance	To promote tolerance of pain during tasks and procedures	• Premedication administration • Providing hands-on support during activities • Monitoring, guiding, and teaching • Scheduling and pacing activities, rest periods, or visitors • Use of relaxation or diversion techniques • Practiced use of voice and touch • Hand-holding • Staying with patient

tomography are only some of the potentially threatening procedures that patients must endure. The timely provision of information about such procedures and equipment reduces threat and allows patients to prepare psychologically to cope with them. The resulting perception of increased personal control reduces the need for overt expressions of pain by reducing associated emotional distress. Providing a milieu that is perceived by patients as physically safe and psychologically secure also helps to circumvent the affective distress that can complicate the communication and assessment of pain (McCaffery, 1979). Accepting uncontrollable expressions of pain and providing privacy during painful procedures helps to convey the impression of a secure environment. As part of that environment, devices or special signals to call the nurse or indicate increases in pain must be provided for patients who are on respirators or otherwise impaired in their communication.

Patient Roles in Pain Work

Role expectations of patients and care-givers in pain work are often unspoken, and the types of pain work that patients do in relation to their critical illness and its treatment frequently go unnoticed (Fagerhaugh & Strauss, 1977). Patients typically are unfamiliar with the critical care environment and its standards and may be reluctant or unable to ask questions or to actively participate in certain procedures. Because their minimal functional capacity generally renders them extremely dependent, team members may overlook the capability of an individual patient to contribute to selected aspects of care (Walton, 1985).

Acknowledgment of what individual patients are able to do and promotion of their participation in self-care may affect their endurance of pain in the critical care setting. For example, Moss and Meyer (1966) demonstrated that patients who could participate by choosing which method of pain relief to try were more likely to obtain relief than patients who were not given choices.

Able patients are minimally expected to collaborate in pain work by communicating to care-givers that they have pain. They are expected to apprise care-givers of the location, intensity, and nature of the pain and about the efficacy of pain relief measures. Care-givers expect patients to cooperate during routine care and procedures and to attempt to control the expression of pain and distress to within the tolerance of the staff on the unit, even when procedures involve inflicted pain. Such expectations are rarely discussed with patients, particularly with the compromised patient in critical care. Nevertheless, misapprehension of roles, disagreements about pain management, and unnecessary pain and distress may be prevented by clarifying behavioral expectations and acknowledging the work that patients do (McCaffery, 1979).

Summary of the Nursing Focus of Care

Nursing interactions and interventions with patients who have pain in critical care settings are multifaceted, reflecting the complexity of pain work. Nursing care must take the affective components of pain into account as well as the sensory components as they work with patients in the potentially overwhelming environment of critical care. Easing pain, handling the expression of pain, and sustaining patients during the necessary procedures or functional daily tasks of critical care require that nurses broaden their perspectives of pain management beyond simply the administration of analgesics. The nursing care of patients in pain requires a comprehensive plan that integrates pain work into all other aspects of patient care.

NURSING INTERVENTIONS FOR PATIENTS IN PAIN

Important Considerations in Performing Nursing Interventions

The appropriateness of an intervention for a desired outcome and an individual patient and the way in which the intervention is presented to the patient and performed will influence its effectiveness. The following considerations, therefore, are important to the effectiveness of nursing interventions for patients in pain. First, clarity about the proposed outcome of an intervention is important to both its execution and the evaluation of its effectiveness and may forestall unrealistic expectations of results. Given the multidimensional nature of pain work, pain reduction may not be the preliminary goal (Cohen, 1980). Instead, promoting endurance of procedural pain, reducing anxiety, or supporting patient self-efficacy for pain management may be the intervention target. Each of these targets may contribute to pain management, but they require different approaches.

Second, effectiveness of interventions may vary with the patient's coping style. If the patient copes through denial or by relinquishing control to clinical experts, efforts to teach breathing and relaxation skills to be performed independently may lead to increases in anxiety and, thus, in pain (Scott & Clum, 1984; see also Chapter 3). If, however, the patient copes by vigilance and by seeking information and control, giving procedural and sensory information before painful critical care treatments and giving simple choices about the timing of treatments may facilitate coping and pain endurance (Johnson, Fuller, Endress, & Rice, 1978a; Thompson, 1989; Turk & Genest, 1979).

Third, the effectiveness of an intervention may be enhanced by the nurse's presentation of it. Fully 30% to 40% of patients respond to placebo medication with pain reduction (Levine, Gordon, Bornstein, & Fields, 1979; Melzack, 1974). The placebo effect is influenced by the beliefs of both provider and patient and is potentially a component of all active medications and treatments as well as of inactive medications (placebos). Although the placebo effect is not fully understood, it has been shown to involve activation of the endogenous opiate system (Levine, Gordon, & Fields, 1978). Therefore, response to a placebo should be taken as a measure not of feigned pain but of activation of the body's natural defenses. Any pain-relieving treatment, including analgesics, physical therapies, or cognitive-behavioral techniques, has the potential to have its natural effectiveness enhanced via the placebo effect, especially for severe pain. Therefore, the more the critical care practitioner can convey belief and confidence in a treatment's effectiveness in reducing pain, the more potential the treatment will have for helping the patient.

Finally, because critical care patients are so severely impaired, they must be assisted in performing pain management techniques, such as relaxation or imagery exercises, that they might otherwise perform independently. Pain treatments that are taught to patients who are unable to perform them consistently and with confidence during threatening procedures not only may be ineffective but may add to feelings of anxiety and helplessness (Bandura, Taylor, Gauthier, & Gossard, 1987; Miller, 1980; Rice, Caldwell, Butler, & Robinson, 1986). The efficacy of cognitive-behavioral treatments may be enhanced for patients if the critical care nurse or the clinical nurse specialist guides the performance of the intervention personally rather than teaches the patient or sets up a tape recorder. It is likely that the personal administration of relaxation, imagery, or breathing exercises by the nurse or specialist will increase the attention and concentration that the severely impaired patient is able to give to the therapy and thus will improve treatment effectiveness (Tamez, Moore, & Brown, 1978).

Cognitive-Behavioral Interventions for Pain

Information

Johnson and colleagues have shown that the effect of preprocedural information on coping and recovery depends on both the type of information provided and the patient's style of coping (Johnson et al., 1978a, 1978b). Providing information about procedures and the sensations associated with them to presurgical patients with low levels of fear increases anxiety but decreases anxiety in patients with higher levels of fear. Low-level fear in critical care patients may be indicative of denial or minimizing as a coping style (Lazarus & Folkman, 1984; Miller, 1980), so that attention-diversion techniques may be more effective. Providing procedural information to anxious patients or to patients who wish increased control also reduces the use of analgesic medication (Johnson et al., 1978a; Padilla et al., 1981). Thus detailed information provided in critical care units before such events as dressing changes, coughing exercises, catheter or nasogastric (NG) tube insertion, chest tube removal, or electrocardiography may be best utilized by patients who are anxious, vigilant over their care, and seeking information to extend personal control.

Providing sensory information about procedures (such as throat irritation or gagging from NG tube insertion, aching from incisions, tugging from suture removal, or stinging from topical medication) allows patients to compare their experience with their expectations, thus decreasing anxiety. Information about the temporal sequencing of events and accompanying sensations diminishes feelings of helplessness, possibly by reducing the threat from unfamiliar treatments and disorders (Johnson et al., 1978b; Thompson, 1989; Wells, 1984). Repetition at appropriate intervals of temporal and sensory information associated with such procedures as chest tube removal, suctioning, barium enemas, NG intubation, or repositioning also potentially lowers analgesic requirements for severely ill patients (Johnson et al., 1978b). Simple preprocedural instructions on how to move or guard to minimize pain related to repositioning or coughing also reduce subjective evaluations of pain and distress (Egbert, Battit, Welch, & Bartlett, 1964; Johnson et al., 1978b; Padilla et al., 1981).

Guiding Deep Breathing

Directing attention to the regulation of breathing pace and depth is a simple, useful focusing technique that is especially helpful for the pain of brief procedures. Such attention serves to minimize anxiety and tension related to pain or anticipation of its exacerbation by supplanting fearful images and thoughts and by encouraging relaxation (Miller, 1987). One version of this technique is offered in Exhibit 8-3.

The technique is initiated by watching the patient's chest rise and fall while he or she is breathing and becoming acquainted with the rhythm. Awareness of rhythm is an important component of many of the cognitive-behavioral methods. The normal respiratory rhythm is even, with a pause after expiration. With pain the expiration phase shortens, and there is no pause. Narcotics regularize the breathing pattern and restore the pause (Poznak, 1987).

Usually two or three deep breaths are enough to accomplish the goal of attention distraction and relaxation of superficial muscle tension. Variations on this deep breathing technique can be integrated into numerous procedures. The nurse can give the breathing instructions while preparing for or performing the procedure.

Basic Relaxation Inductions

The technique of guiding deep breathing can be used as a method of initiating a deeper relaxation induction. Just before the patient begins to exhale on the second or third deep breath, the nurse adds ''now begin to relax, from the top of your head to the tips of your toes.'' The pitch of the voice should be higher for ''top of your head'' and lower for ''tips of your toes,'' and the final phrase should be timed to coincide with the last half of the exhalation phase. The body naturally relaxes muscles during the exhalation phase, so that again the instruction corresponds to the physiological sensations of the body, promoting an association between the nurse's voice and the patient's physical sensations of relaxation. The changes in pitch capture and maintain attention and reinforce full exhalation and relaxation.

Exhibit 8-3 A Technique for Guiding Deep Breathing

Guiding begins as the chest starts to fall with exhalation. The nurse says:

"I want you to take a couple of *deep* breaths *in* now."

Vocal tone and emphasis draw attention to the nurse's voice and engage the patient in following directions. The word "deep" is timed to occur right before the end of the falling motion of the chest and the word "in" right at the beginning of the rise of the chest. The word "in," by coinciding with the actual physiological sensation of air intake, reinforces the association of the nurse's voice and words with changes in breathing.

As the chest continues to rise, full expansion is encouraged by repeating the words:

"Deep, deep, deep."

At the peak of expansion, as expulsion of the breath occurs, full exhalation is encouraged by saying:

"And then let your breath out slowly, slowly, slowly."

As the breath turns again to inhaling, the nurse retains control over the breathing rate and depth by saying:

"Take another *deep* breath *in* now."

Usually two or three breaths in this manner are enough to divert attention and to promote relaxation without hyperventilation.

Relaxation training reduces distress and may decrease pain and analgesic consumption (Flaherty & Fitzpatrick, 1978; Mogan, Wells, & Robertson, 1985; Wells, 1982). There are three major variations of basic relaxation induction: autogenics (Schultz & Luthe, 1969), simple progressive muscle relaxation, and tensing-relaxing inductions (Jacobsen, 1934). All involve the repetition of key phrases that are enhanced by variations in vocal tone, pitch, and tempo.

Autogenics involves the slow repetition of phrases such as "my arms and legs are heavy and warm," "my heart rate is regular and even," and "my forehead is cool." These call the patient's attention to the physiological sensations that are concomitant with deep muscle relaxation. The phrases are repeated two or three times each in an even pitch and a regular, slow tempo with 30 seconds or longer between phrases. This type of tempo and repetition encourages a steady increase in relaxation or deepening of the induction and permits the patient time to focus on each sensation as it is presented.

Simple progressive muscle relaxation relies on listing the muscle groups consecutively that the patient should focus on relaxing. Like the other variations, it serves to direct attention away from anxiety-provoking thoughts and to focus it on benign physical sensations. A rhythmic and repetitive tempo facilitates regular, slow breathing and the maintenance of concentration on the task of relaxing and letting go of tension. It is important to allow patients ample time to relax the requested muscle groups but not so much time that their attention wanders or that they actually lapse into sleep.

Sample phrases that may be used after introducing the guided deep-breathing technique described above are as follows: "Now, relax the muscles in your face. Think about relaxing and letting go of all the tension in your face. Let your jaw drop slightly. Take a deep breath in and relax the muscles of your face." Different muscle groups may then be selected. Relaxation may be deepened by saying "Relax your shoulders and your neck muscles now. Think about relaxing and letting go of all the tension in your shoulders and neck. Let your shoulders drop down a little, and let your head sink down comfortably into the pillow." Similar phrases may be introduced serially to suggest relaxation for the upper back, lower back, chest and abdomen, hips and legs, and finally the feet. Suggesting taking a deep breath periodically will help enhance the effect: "Take a deep breath in now and begin to relax all the muscles in your chest."

The tensing-relaxing technique is especially useful for patients who are having a hard time even beginning to relax. First tensing muscle groups and then relaxing them serves to reacquaint patients with the difference in sensation between tense muscles and relaxed ones and helps them realize that they have control over their ability to relax. The tensing-relaxing technique is similar to a simple progressive muscle relaxation in the serial listing of various groups of muscles. The difference is that the nurse suggests first that the patient tense all the muscles in a group and then that those same muscles be relaxed: "Now I want you to tense up all the muscles in your face. Tighten every one of them very tight. Hold that for a second or two, and then begin to relax all the muscles in your face. Let go of all the tension in your face. Let your jaw drop slightly. Take a deep breath and relax all the muscles of your face." The alternating of tensing and relaxing muscles group by group proceeds through all the muscle groups of the body as before. A quick version is to have the patient tense up the entire body and then relax the body muscles all at once.

After any relaxation induction is done with patients, it is important to get feedback from them about the success of the intervention and to ascertain how deeply they felt they were able to relax. A numerical scale ranging from 0, completely relaxed, to 10, extremely tense, is useful before and after the treatment. Some patients cannot tolerate tensing and relaxing alternately; some will relax better with imagery or breathing techniques, and some will respond negatively to particular phrases. Such feedback helps improve skills and personalize the treatment. With any of the attention-diversion or relaxing techniques presented in this chapter, practice also improves the nurse's skills in observation, timing, and delivery.

Basic Guided Imagery

Nurses use images frequently in their work. Descriptions of procedures and associated sensations are replete with images, similes, or metaphors that may or may not comfort patients and may even confuse and frighten them: "We're going to have to stick him again"; "Let's log-roll him"; "It gives your heart a little kick"; "T cells are like soldiers that go in and kill the bad-guy cells"; "The transplanted bone marrow sort of sets up housekeeping in your own bones"; "The incision is stapled"; "He's third-spacing." Clearly, awareness of everyday word selection is important in conveying the assurance of a safe and secure environment to the patient. In addition, nurses can help patients who are in pain or under stress develop pleasant images to facilitate relaxation and distraction.

Reminding patients of past pleasant and relaxing experiences is a simple way to introduce the idea of imagery: "Do you like going to the beach? Remember the last time you were in Hawaii, how nice the beach was, warm and relaxing?" Pleasant memories automatically begin to induce relaxation. Reminiscence can then be embellished by selectively focusing on the sensory elements of the experience, leading the patient to recall more and more detail.

Although imagery generally involves the evocation of sensations, it need not be confined to visual "pictures." Suggestions about soothing changes in temperature, relaxing tension, music or quiet breezes, and familiar fragrances evoke kinesthetic, auditory, and olfactory images. Visual images of the sun at the beach may not be as pleasant as the sun's imagined warmth on the skin. Imagery for the patient with sensory impairments may be quite effective if suggestions correspond to the patient's intact senses. Nurses helping patients ease pain and distress by creating distracting and calming images can enrich these images by using several sensory channels. The visual image of the beach becomes more accessible and realistic when the soothing sound of the surf, gentle warm breezes, and the warmth of the sand under back and legs are recalled.

Images can also serve as a benign rehearsal of a potentially threatening procedure, such as sitting up for the first time to dangle the legs, removal of a chest tube, or weaning from the respirator. Leading patients step by step through imaginary procedures provides them with procedural, sensory, and temporal information while enabling them to develop a sense of control and confidence. As noted above, the amount of detail that the nurse provides must be judged from the typical coping style of the patient as well as from the patient's own richness and skill in imagination. Some patients have limited access to imaging in certain senses or may need more assistance to develop detail.

As with relaxation induction, it is important to get feedback from the patient when possible. For example, comparing relaxation to melting butter may create pleasant images for some patients and repellant ones for others. With feedback, adjustments can be made in the amount of detail provided, the selection of the images suggested, and the relative emphasis on the various senses.

Music

Music can be a pleasant and relaxing distraction for patients in the critical care units, helping to divert their attention from the ongoing cacaphony of the unit and the busy interactions of staff for prolonged periods of time. Music has been shown to lower pain and anxiety in critical care patients (Stone, Rusk, Chambers, & Chafin, 1989) and to lower pain scores during wound repacking (Angus & Faux, 1989). With the availability of small personal cassette recorders and tiny earphones, equipment need not interfere with critical care technology. A small "listening library," including both music selections and books on tape, can be built up on the nursing unit over time. The patient's music preferences should be assessed with the patient or family.

Pacing and Leading

Distraction and relaxation techniques such as the ones discussed above are maximized by adopting and then subtly influencing the rhythm of the patient. In other words, by attending to the anxious and tense patient's breathing, the nurse can slow the breathing rate and promote relaxation. Matching the patient's rhythm by phrasing sentences or stroking the foot, hand, or shoulder in rhythm with the patient's breathing is called pacing (Bandler & Grinder, 1979). Leading is accomplished after the patient is paced for a while; gradually and subtly the nurse slows the rhythm, watching to see if the patient begins to adopt the nurse's rhythm and lead.

Pacing and leading require practice as well as close concentration by the nurse, who must monitor carefully not only patients' breath rates but also his or her own actions. As skill develops with practice, nurses can use pacing and leading in various activities to calm patients or to direct their attention. For example, for the dressing change of an anxious patient, the nurse can begin to describe the activities involved in the procedure while gently squeezing the patient's hand in rhythm to his breath. Giving one final firm and sustained squeeze, the nurse can suggest a deep breath to the patient and then begin the treatment: "Now take a deep breath in for me, and begin to relax." During the treatment, the nurse can continue phrasing or breathing at a rate slightly slower than the patient's breathing. Because the nurse gained the patient's attention earlier, the change in rhythm should maintain attention on the nurse rather than on physical sensations and keep the breathing rate slower throughout the treatment. A deep breath also can be suggested at the completion of the treatment.

Cues and Anchoring

When physical gestures, key words, or phrasing patterns accompany a particular suggestion or relaxation technique over and over again, they come to act as cues that trigger deep breathing and relaxation more and more easily for the patient (Bandler & Grinder, 1979). If exactly the same phrase is used to begin a relaxation treatment each time, that phrase will begin to trigger the physiological responses of relaxation.

Special cues can be established during relaxation exercises that can be used later during difficult procedures or activities to relax the patient. For example, when the patient is deeply relaxed from a particular relaxation technique, the nurse can put the palm of his or her hand lightly on the patient's upper arm and gently squeeze the arm while saying "Now take a deep breath in and relax more and more deeply, very deeply now." The nurse then removes the hand. With practice, the gentle touch and squeeze of the hand on the shoulder will serve to initiate relaxation apart from the entire relaxation script. The hand on the shoulder becomes an anchor or a reminder of the deeply relaxed state.

TAILORING PAIN INTERVENTIONS FOR USE IN CRITICAL CARE

Integrating Nursing Work and Pain Work in Critical Care

The regulation of nursing care for the critically ill patient in pain requires a comprehensive around-the-clock design that takes into account physiological, psychological, and environmental components. The work of understanding the causes and exacerbations of pain, of preventing or minimizing it, and of promoting and sustaining coping must be incorporated into nursing care designed to meet the patient's functional care requisites.

Thus scheduling pain reduction interventions throughout the day on the basis of the type of activities and treatment procedures in which patients must engage, the typical course of the pain, and the coping capability of the patient will optimize pain management. For example, analgesics, TNS devices, information, and relaxation techniques can be timed to help the patient prepare for, participate in, or recover from painful activities such as the removal of chest tubes or dressing changes. Massage, relaxation, and imagery can be incorporated into hygiene and skin care or preparation for sleep. Attention distraction or guided breathing may accompany the repositioning or lifting of the trauma or burn patient onto the bedpan. When increased muscle tension and anxiety exacerbate distress related to flatus, guided imagery or deep breathing may assist the patient in remaining relaxed while the waves of pain peak and pass.

Beginning a relaxation induction while injecting intravenous analgesia will combine relaxation, pain relief, and the cues or anchors that the nurse wishes to establish. The drug naturally will create increasing relaxation and pain relief, reinforcing the induction and anchors. In this way, the efficacy of the anchors or relaxation inductions performed later will be enhanced. The relaxation induction also may help facilitate the placebo effect of the active medication.

The cognitive-behavioral interventions recommended in this chapter may be tailored to the pace of critical care nursing and the patient's changing condition. Often a full 15- or 20-minute imagery script is not possible in this setting. The timing and modulation of the nurse's voice while he or she is repeating a brief series of selected phrases, however, may cue relaxation of tension or suggest pleasant images during routine care or procedures. Discussions about pain and expectations about its treatment or communication are best timed for periods of the day when levels of activities as well as pain and anxiety are relatively low and attention is unimpaired. Music may be used to reduce hypervigilance or to promote sleep in the busy unit. Visits with family members that are assessed as beneficial because they provide distraction or relieve depressive thinking may be encouraged and scheduled. On the other hand, the nurse may intervene to shorten visits that are tiring or result in increases in pain behavior. Thus nursing pain work in critical care reflects physiological, psychological, and environmental components.

Specific Patient Impairments and Interventions

Critically ill patients frequently have more than one type of impairment that requires nursing care. Such impairments may be related to physiological regulation, perceptual disturbances, physical coordination and strength, attention, memory, emotional lability, or knowledge and skill level (Nursing Development Conference Group, 1979). These impairments interfere with patient abilities to make the decisions or to perform the activities required by their care and to cope with pain.

Likewise, pain creates predictable impairments that require nursing intervention. Severe pain or its treatment, for example, may limit the concentration and attention that the patient can muster for problem solving or for coping with a treatment. Irritability, anxiety, or depression related to pain may decrease the patient's ability to make decisions, to tolerate various interventions, or to control the expression of pain and emotion. Fatigue, weakness, or lack of coordination secondary to severe pain and illness may limit the ability to bathe, to reposition for comfort, to self-massage, or sometimes even to ask for help.

In a wide variety of disorders seen in critical care, such as trauma, surgery, burns, neuropathies, and inflammation, pain produces limitations of movement. Patients with pain-limited physical mobility may be restricted in the ability to feed, toilet, and bathe themselves. Critical care nurses, who must ensure that functional care requirements related to food intake, elimination, and hygiene are met, typically physically assist the patient for whom such activities exacerbate pain. Providing information as well as premedication or attaching a TNS unit before painful tasks such as repositioning also will minimize exacerbations of pain. PCA pumps make pain reduction possible with a minimum of movement. Distraction in the form of a breathing exercise, diverting conversation, music, or a brief imagery intervention may modify potentially painful stimuli during movement and may reduce related anxiety. Interventions for skin irritation, ischemia, edema, and constipation also are essential components of pain work for the patient whose pain leads to immobility.

The critically ill patient in pain who is highly anxious or emotionally labile may benefit from simple relaxation therapy, including progressive muscle relaxation, deep-breathing exercises, and the modulated use of touch, rhythm, and voice in addition to appropriate analgesia. The degree to which anxiety and pain interfere with attention and concentration will determine how intensive or long the cognitive-behavioral intervention should be. Relaxation interventions can be repeated at regular intervals, increasing in length or intensity as the patient learns to respond. Regular scheduling of interventions will reinforce perceptions of control over the environment. Nurses may feel that their presence is beneficial to the anxious patient even when other health care providers are performing procedures. Interventions such as clarifying the patient's concerns, decreasing environmental stimuli, providing information and reassurance, and offering opportunities for simple decision making will reinforce the patient's sense of security in the environment and perceptions of control. Such interventions are brief and easily applied in critical care settings.

Meeting the care needs of the patient in pain who has an attention impairment requires a slightly different approach. Attention impairments in critical care occur commonly with severe anxiety or pain or with acute confusional states such as drug- or illness-related delirium. Such a severely impaired patient may not be able, for example, to concentrate on relaxation scripts, to decide among analgesic medications, or to follow directions for repositioning that are designed to minimize pain. By modulating vocal tone and rhythm and coordinating voice and touch, the nurse may be able to relax and reassure the patient while redirecting the patient's attention as necessary to the tasks required to meet functional care requirements. For the patient with a persistent attention problem, maintaining a regular schedule of interventions and staffing with the same nurse as much as possible may help the patient recognize or adapt to patterns of care. The primary nurse can begin to develop cues and anchors and to reinforce patient responses to promote relaxation, attention, or cooperation during procedures. Simple breathing exercises, counting, or brief imagery descriptions may help the patient sustain concentration or relaxation during tasks and procedures. Music also may help sustain the attention of these patients during mildly difficult tasks.

The patient who has a communication impairment requires careful nursing assessment and creative intervention to determine the characteristics of pain and its course. When communication by writing or even simple codes is precluded, such as with the aphasic, delirious, sedated, or comatose patient, team collaboration on the signs and symptoms presumptive of pain and pain relief for that individual is crucial. Documenting observations related to pain work becomes essential to team communication and effective pain management. Nonverbal interventions may be successful for some patients in mildly modulating pain and distress; thus the use of rhythm and the modulation of touch and voice may be soothing. Light stroking, rocking, or humming in rhythm with the patient's breathing or movements may minimize disorganized responses to the overstimulating environment and may create a sense of presence and protection.

The Critical Care Unit As a Hospital Subculture

The hospital can be viewed as a culture in its own right with specialized social roles, a unique language, rules, and sanctions for behavior (Fagerhaugh & Strauss, 1977; Meinhart &(McCaffery, 1983). Each unit develops as a subculture in relation to the patients seen and the type of care delivered. Thus an atmosphere that is quiet and serene is promoted in coronary care units to decrease stress for the patient with an impaired cardiovascular system. Unnecessary transgressions of the general calm are discouraged. In contrast, a surgical intensive care unit often is dynamic because concerns for peace and quiet are set aside in response to rapidly changing patient conditions.

Each critical care unit develops standard approaches to working with the types of pain commonly seen in patients on that unit (Fagerhaugh & Strauss, 1977). Priorities associated with pain management vary from one unit to another. Each staff member develops expectations and methods of working with the predominant types of pain seen on the unit. For example, postoperative pain follows a course that peaks several days after surgery and then declines. Such pain is generally improved by the administration of narcotic analgesics. The trajectories of pain due to myocardial infarction, severe burns, or malignancies each have expected patterns of progression, intensity, and response to treatment. Thus the staff on a burn unit may develop multiple skills for coping with the necessity of inflicting pain during wound debridement, whereas on another intensive care unit staff frequently may need to suspend attention to pain inflicted in the course of emergency procedures to focus on saving the patient's life.

Alterations in expected patterns of pain can be disruptive and distressing for the health care team. The lack of a clear-cut cause for the pain or unexpected variations in intensity, persistence, location, or radiation potentially unsettle the typical order of work on the unit. Patients with unexpected or atypical pain may come to be labeled as difficult or problem patients. As work disruption and staff as well as patient distress increase, patient-staff relations may progressively worsen (Fagerhaugh & Strauss, 1977; Graffam, 1981). Because each staff member may devise unique approaches to pain work with such a patient, the continuity of care and the efficacy of pain management may be threatened.

To work effectively with patients in pain, the critical care team needs to develop comprehensive and coordinated approaches. The skill of the individual critical care nurse in pain work is clearly essential to the comfort and well-being of the patient. Discrepancies in pain management philosophies, role expectations, or communication, however, reduce the capability of a team to assist patients. Variations in beliefs about narcotic analgesia use (Cohen, 1980; Graffam, 1979), cultural differences among staff or patients (Davitz & Pendleton, 1969; see also Chapter 5), various levels of professional expertise (Mason, 1981), and the personal pain experiences of staff contribute to differing perspectives on pain management. The development of team approaches to care involves recognizing and addressing such individual differences in care provider perspectives. Multidisciplinary or intershift case reviews, which allow for discussion of beliefs, expectations, and communication systems related to pain management, promote more integrated pain work by the entire team.

CONCLUSION

A diversity of approaches that are physiologically, psychologically, and environmentally focused is required in nursing critically ill patients in pain. McCaffery (1979) also admonishes that if one approach does not work, the nurse must keep trying. In addition to diversity in intervention and persistence in endeavor, integration of the multiple dimensions of pain work into routine nursing care is crucial to achieve continuity and quality of pain management. Professional accountability for the nursing care of the critically ill patient in pain depends on assessing, treating, and evaluating pain and associated distress in relation to the functional care requirements that nurses meet for patients around the clock.

The nurse plays an essential role in designing and monitoring a comprehensive pain management plan for the critically ill patient. It is often the critical care nurse who has the most current understanding of the individual patient's impairments, expected treatment course, and hour-to-hour capability for participation in care, and of pharmacological, cognitive-behavioral, and other pain management techniques that are appropriate and effective for that patient. In a sense, the critical care nurse acts as conductor, bringing together the many themes of pain work, modulating the pace and tempo of the work, determining the appropriate timing of specific interventions, and blending the work of the individual practitioners into the best harmony for the patient.

REFERENCES

American Nurses' Association. (1980). *Nursing: A social policy statement*. Kansas City: Author.

Angus, J., & Faux, S. (1989). The effect of music on adult postoperative patients' pain during a nursing procedure. In S. Funk (Eds.), *Key aspects of comfort* (pp. 166–172). New York: Springer.

Bandler, R., & Grinder, J. (1979). *Frogs into princes*. Moab, UT: Real People Press.

Bandura, A., Taylor, C.B., Gauthier, J., & Gossard, D. (1987). Perceived self-efficacy and pain control: Opioid and nonopioid mechanisms. *Journal of Personality and Social Psychology, 53*, 563–571.

Bondestam, E., Hovgren, K., Gaston-Johansson, F., Jern, S., Herlitz, J., & Holmberg, S. (1987). Pain assessment by patients and nurses in the early phase of acute myocardial infarction. *Journal of Advanced Nursing, 12*, 677–682.

Cohen, F. (1980). Postsurgical pain relief: Patients' status and nurses' medication choices. *Pain, 9*, 265–274.

Davitz, L.J., & Pendleton, S.H. (1969). Nurses' inferences of suffering. *Nursing Research, 18*, 100–107.

Diers, D., Schmidt, R., McBride, A., & Davis, B. (1972). The effect of nursing interaction on patients in pain. *Nursing Research, 21*, 419–428.

Egbert, L., Battit, G., Welch, C., & Bartlett, M. (1964). Reduction of postoperative pain by encouragement and instruction of patients. *New England Journal of Medicine, 270*, 825–827.

Fagerhaugh, S., & Strauss, A. (1977). *Politics of pain management: Staff-patient interaction*. Menlo Park, CA: Addison-Wesley.

Flaherty, G., & Fitzpatrick, J. (1978). Relaxation technique to increase comfort level of postoperative patients. *Nursing Research, 27*, 352–355.

Gardner, D. (1985). Presence. In G. Bulechek & J. McCloskey (Eds.), *Nursing interventions* (pp. 316–324). Philadelphia: Saunders.

Graffam, S. (1979). Nurse response to patients in pain: An analysis and an imperative for action. *Nursing Leadership, 2*, 23–25.

Graffam, S. (1981). Congruence of nurse-patient expectations regarding nursing intervention in pain. *Nursing Leadership, 4*, 12–15.

Jacobsen, E. (1934). *Progressive relaxation*. Chicago: University of Chicago.

Johnson, J., Fuller, S., Endress, J., & Rice, V. (1978a). Sensory information, instruction in a coping strategy, and recovery from surgery. *Research in Nursing and Health, 1*, 4–17.

Johnson, J., Fuller, S., Endress, J., & Rice, V. (1978b). Altering patients' responses to surgery: An extension and replication. *Research in Nursing and Health, 1*, 111–121.

Lazarus, R.S., & Folkman, S. (1984). *Stress, appraisal, and coping*. New York: Springer.

Levine, J., Gordon, N., Bornstein, J., & Fields, H. (1979). Role of pain in placebo analgesia. *Proceedings of the National Academy of Sciences, 76*, 3528–3531.

Levine, J., Gordon, N., & Fields, H. (1978). The mechanism of placebo analgesia. *Lancet, 2*, 654–657.

Mason, D. (1981). An investigation of the influences of selected factors on nurses' inferences of patient suffering. *International Journal of Nursing Studies, 18*, 251–259.

McBride, M.A. (1967). Nursing approach, pain, and relief: An exploratory experiment. *Nursing Research, 16*, 337–341.

McCaffery, M. (1979). *Nursing management of the patient with pain.* Philadelphia: Lippincott.

Meinhart, N., & McCaffery, M. (1983). *Pain: A nursing approach to assessment and analysis.* Norwalk, CT: Appleton-Century-Crofts.

Melzack, R. (1974). Psychological concepts and methods for the control of pain. *Advances in Neurology, 4*, 275–280.

Miller, K. (1987). Deep breathing relaxation. *AORN Journal, 45*, 484–488.

Miller, S. (1980). Why having control reduces stress: Why if I can stop the roller coaster, I don't want to get off. In J. Garber & M. Seligman (Eds.), *Human helplessness: Theory and research* (pp. 71–95). New York: Academic Press.

Mogan, J., Wells, N., & Robertson, E. (1985). Effects of preoperative teaching on postoperative pain: A replication and expansion. *International Journal of Nursing Studies, 22*, 267–280.

Moss, F., & Meyer, B. (1966). The effects of nursing interaction upon pain relief in patients. *Nursing Research, 15*, 303–306.

Nursing Development Conference Group. (1979). *Concept formalization in nursing: Process and product.* Boston: Little, Brown.

Orem, D. (1985). *Nursing: Concepts of practice* (3rd ed.). San Francisco: McGraw-Hill.

Padilla, G., Grant, M., Rains, B., Hansen, B., Bergstrom, N., Wong, H., Hanson, R., & Kubo, W. (1981). Distress education and the effects of preparatory teaching films and patient control. *Research in Nursing and Health, 4*, 375–387.

Poznak, A. (1987). The role of respiratory patterns in the treatment of pain and anxiety. *Journal of Post-Anesthesia Nursing, 2*, 189–191.

Rice, V., Caldwell, M., Butler, S., & Robinson, J. (1986). Relaxation training and response to cardiac catheterization: A pilot study. *Nursing Research, 35*, 39–43.

Schultz, J., & Luthe, W. (1969). *Autogenic therapy* (Vol. 1). New York: Grune & Stratton.

Scott, L., & Clum, G. (1984). Examining the interaction effects of coping style and brief interventions in the treatment of postsurgical pain. *Pain, 20*, 279–291.

Stone, S., Rusk, F., Chambers, A., & Chafin, S. (1989). The effects of music therapy on critically ill patients in the intensive care setting. *Heart & Lung, 18*, 291.

Tamez, E., Moore, M., & Brown, P. (1978). Relaxation training as a nursing intervention versus pro nata medication. *Nursing Research, 27*, 160–165.

Teske, K., Daut, R., & Cleeland, C. (1983). Relationships between nurses' observations and patients' self-reports of pain. *Pain, 16*, 289–296.

Thompson, D. (1989). A randomized controlled trial of in-hospital nursing support for first time myocardial infarction patients and their partners: Effects on anxiety and depression. *Journal of Advanced Nursing, 14*, 291–297.

Turk, D., & Genest, M. (1979). Regulation of pain: The application of cognitive and behavioral techniques for prevention and remediation. In P. Kendall & S. Hollon (Eds.), *Cognitive-behavioral interventions* (pp. 287–318). San Francisco: Academic Press.

Underwood, P. (1990). Orem's self-care model: Principles and general applications. In S. Reynolds and D. Cormack (Eds.), *Psychiatric and mental health nursing: Theory and practice.* London: Chapman and Hall.

Walton, J. (1985). Orem's self-care deficit theory of nursing. *Focus on Critical Care, 12*, 54–58.

Wells, N. (1982). The effect of relaxation on postoperative muscle tension and pain. *Nursing Research, 31*, 236–238.

Wells, N. (1984). Responses to acute pain and the nursing implications. *Journal of Advanced Nursing, 9*, 51–58.

RECOMMENDED READING

Bulechek, G., & McCloskey, J. (1985). *Nursing interventions: Treatments for nursing diagnoses.* Philadelphia: Saunders.

Dimotto, J. (1984). Relaxation. *American Journal of Nursing, 6*, 754–758.

Dossey, B. (1984). A wonderful prerequisite. *Nursing 84, 1*, 42–46.

Mast, D., Meyers, J., & Urbanski, A. (1987). Relaxation techniques: A self-learning module for nurses, unit I. *Cancer Nursing, 10*, 141–147.

Mast, D., Meyers, J., & Urbanski, A. (1987). Relaxation techniques: A self-learning module for nurses, unit II. *Cancer Nursing, 10*, 217–225.

Mast, D., Meyers, J., & Urbanski, A. (1987). Relaxation techniques: A self-learning module for nurses, unit III. *Cancer Nursing, 10*, 279–285.

Part III

Special Critically Ill Patient Populations and Their Pain

Chapter 9

Pain in the Critically Ill Neonate

Linda Sturla Franck

THE NEONATE'S PERCEPTION AND RESPONSE TO PAIN

How does the full-term or premature newborn perceive and respond to pain? What are the short-term and long-term effects of pain experienced in the neonatal period? Despite major advances in our understanding of pain, these basic questions remain to be answered definitively.

Historically, newborn infants were believed to be reflexive, decorticate beings without the capacity to feel or be affected by pain like the adult human (McGraw, 1969; Peiper, 1963). Infants were compared with semianesthetized adults, and it was believed that pain in infants was of no consequence (Swafford & Allan, 1968). Those who were concerned about infant pain found the phenomenon almost impossible to study because of the lack of objective methods with which to measure the responses of preverbal infants.

Recent advances in the understanding of adult pain physiology have provided a theoretical base for exploration of the nature of infant pain. The increasing population of neonates surviving numerous painful experiences in the intensive care nursery (ICN) and the increased awareness of both the advanced capabilities and the fragility of the immature brain have provided compelling reasons for renewed investigation. In this chapter, current knowledge regarding the physiology and management of pain in the critically ill premature and term infant during the first several months of life is explored.

Infant Pain: The Beginning of a Physiological Model

Infants have the neurological "equipment" to feel pain before birth, even before premature birth. Peripheral nerve endings are present and functional by 14 weeks of gestation and myelination has progressed rapidly by 16 weeks of

139

gestation (Gamble, 1966; Okado & Kojima, 1984). The neuronal structure of the spinal cord subserves motor function as early as the eighth week of gestation (Okado & Kojima, 1984) and is complete between the 18th and 26th week of fetal life (Volpe, 1987). By 20 to 24 weeks of gestation the cortex has its full complement of neurons and cortical synapses, and dendritic branching begins (Vaughan, 1975). Infants have a well-developed pituitary-adrenal axis and can mount a fight-or-flight stress response with production of catacholamines, just like the adult human (Anand, Brown, Causon, Christofides, Bloom, & Aynsley-Green, 1985; Lagerkrantz & Bistoletti, 1977; Williamson & Evans, 1986).

The intrinsic opiate analgesic system also is functional before birth. The fetus produces endorphins in response to asphyxia and acidosis (Burnard, John, Todd, & Hindmarsh, 1985; Gautray, Jolivet, Vielh, & Guillemin, 1977; Ramanathan, Puig, Lovitz, & Turndorf, 1987). There is speculation that endorphins provide protection to the central nervous system (CNS) during delivery, and the benefit of using the opiate antagonist nalaxone for infants with mild to moderate CNS depression at birth has been questioned (Facchinetti, Bagnoli, Bracci, & Genazzani, 1982; Goodlin, 1981). Increased endorphin levels may contribute to cardiorespiratory depression in asphyxiated infants, however (Davidson, Gil-Ad, Rogovin, Laron, & Reisner, 1987).

The erroneous belief that myelination is necessary for nerve function has contributed to misconceptions about the infant's experience of pain. Myelin serves to insulate the nerve fiber, and its presence affects only the speed of conduction along the nerve (Sarnat, 1984) and does not alter the quality of nerve conduction. In fact, a large number of nerve fibers that transmit pain impulses remain unmyelinated in the adult (Price & Dubner, 1977).

Healthy infants respond to painful cutaneous stimulation by withdrawal of the affected body part, gross motor movement, facial grimacing, and crying (Franck, 1986; Owens & Todt, 1984; Rich, Marshall, & Volpe, 1974). The cry of the infant experiencing pain has distinctive spectrographic characteristics that can be distinguished from other cries even by untrained adults (Porter, Miller, & Marshall, 1986). Behavioral responses are accompanied by changes in heart rate, blood pressure, and oxygenation (Brown, 1987; Norris, Campbell, & Brenkert, 1982). The timing of initial movements and crying in response to heel stick appears similar to the sequence of first and second pain experienced by adults (Franck, 1986). Noxious stimuli trigger a flexion reflex that moves the affected limb away from the stimulus. As with the adult, however, direct relationships between tissue insult and overt pain response cannot be inferred (Craig & Prkachin, 1983).

Possible Differences between Infant and Adult Pain

In theory, the perception of and response to pain in the adult and infant human probably differ, although the differences have yet to be described. Because of incomplete myelination, the infant may experience second pain concurrently with or before first pain (refer to Chapter 2 for a review of adult nociception). Infants have no previous experience or cognitive-affective coping mechanisms to mobilize in response to painful events and may experience pain more intensely than the adult. On the other hand, infants at birth cannot anticipate pain and, therefore, do not experience fear and anxiety, which tend to increase pain perception in the adult (Phillips & Cousins, 1986). Infants, especially premature infants, do not have the muscle tone of an adult and may not experience the increased pain produced by muscle tension or spasm. Further research will be needed to identify actual differences between adult and infant pain perception.

Pain in the Neonatal Period: Actual and Potential Consequences

There are two major reasons for concern about the effects of pain experienced by critically ill infants. First, pain causes many adverse physiological consequences. Second, the developing CNS is extremely vulnerable to environmental influences, and it has been shown that the structure and function of the brain can be altered by external events. Currently, acute and chronic pain cannot be differentiated in the infant; therefore, immediate and long-term effects of pain experienced by newborn infants are discussed here without attempt to distinguish between acute and chronic pain.

Pain causes adverse physiological effects in all major organ systems that can be life threatening in the acutely ill patient. These effects include reduced tidal volume and vital capacity in the lungs, increased demands of the cardiovascular system, and hypermetabolism resulting in neuroendocrine imbalances (Kehlet, 1986). The sympathetic response to pain of the infant's immature CNS is less predictable than the adult's. The mobilization of endocrine and metabolic resources results in changes in blood pressure (either increased or decreased) as well as changes in skin color, perfusion, and temperature. The immature cerebral vascular bed is particularly vulnerable to injury as a result of lack of autoregulation, and stimuli that increase cerebral vascular congestion or result in hypoxemia, such as crying, may increase the risk for intraventricular hemorrhage (Brazy, 1988). The infant in pain also experiences a flood of endorphins, which may jeopardize the ability to maintain blood pressure and breathing. These changes may be dramatic or subtle depending on the level of maturity of the infant's CNS and the amount of sympathetic stress to which the infant is subjected. Depletion of the infant's stress hormones will result in the absence of any overt behavioral or physiological response to painful events. Perception, however, remains intact despite lack of response. The physiological cost of maintaining heart rate, blood pressure, and oxygenation during painful events in terms of expended energy that would otherwise be used for tissue growth and repair is not currently known.

The stress response of preterm infants to surgical trauma has been reported (Anand, Sippell, & Aynsley-Green, 1987). Premature infants who underwent ligation of the patent ductus arteriosus while receiving nitrous oxide alone demonstrated substantial and prolonged catabolic reactions and had more circulatory and metabolic complications after surgery compared with infants who received nitrous oxide and fentanyl for anesthesia. This study suggested that the use of anesthesia and analgesia to mediate the metabolic and endocrine response to surgery is of benefit and may decrease postoperative morbidity and mortality, as has been shown in adults.

Studies of both animal and human neonates have demonstrated that environmental manipulations can permanently alter behavior, brain function, and even brain structure, particularly when the event occurs during critical periods of development (Duffy, Mower, Jensen, & Als, 1984). The developing human brain is most vulnerable to environmental influences during periods of rapid growth, which occur in the human infant between 10 to 18 weeks of gestation and again between 30 weeks gestation and 3 months postnatal age (Dobbing & Smart, 1974). Although the infant brain undergoes a tremendous period of growth, the process of neuronal competition for synaptic connections (particularly during the third trimester) results in a large amount of cell death and remodeling of the neuronal structure (Volpe, 1987). It is on this process that environmental influences can have the most profound effects. Patterned neuronal activity serves to select those cell populations that will proliferate from those that will degenerate (Janowsky & Finlay, 1986; Prechtl, 1984). It is of concern that the amount and frequency of painful stimuli inflicted on the infant receiving intensive care could possibly result in a reallocation of cortical resources and permanent alterations in cerebral neuroanatomy.

Animal research suggests that pain and stress in the neonatal period can profoundly influence adult behavior, resulting in an insensitivity to pain, decreased ability to learn mazes, body temperature instability, and even immunosuppression (Sandman, McGivern, Berka, Walker, Coy, & Kastin, 1979; Vorhees, 1981). Studies of human neonates have revealed marked differences in cortex of healthy term infants compared with cortex of preterm infants (Duffy, 1985). The constantly stressful environment (pain is a major stressor) of the ICN and the concomitant release of endorphins may create a situation of sensory deprivation in which brain development, particularly of the right hemisphere, is inhibited.

The arousal resulting from a painful event may be overwhelming for the infant, causing him or her to shut out all stimuli and to develop altered sleep patterns and interactions with care-givers (Als, 1983; Emde, Harmon, Metcalf, Koenig, & Wagonfeld, 1971; Marshall, Porter, Rogers, Moore, Anderson, & Boxerman, 1982). It has been suggested that a mismatch between the environmental demands of the ICN and the infant's neurobehavioral maturity can result in aberrant patterns of social interaction that may persist beyond infancy (Als, 1983).

Infants at birth have the capacity to learn (Lippsitt, 1977); and it is probable that some degree of behavioral conditioning occurs in infants who undergo multiple painful procedures. It is possible that difficulty in establishing nipple feedings in infants with chronic lung disease is at least in part the result of associations formed between oral stimulation and noxious events, such as when a pacifier is placed in the infant's mouth while a venipuncture is performed or during endotracheal suctioning. In one case report, an auditory stimulus was used to assist an infant in distinguishing between painful and nonpainful human contact (Sexson, Schneider, Chamberlin, Hicks, & Sexson, 1986) and thus allowed for development of more appropriate social interaction.

It has been well documented that the premature infant who spends the neonatal period in the ICN is at risk for developmental delays, permanent CNS handicap, and emotional disorders (Sell, 1986). Although at this time the contribution of painful procedures to these risks is unknown, the possibility of such a contribution should not be disregarded. The neonatal CNS must be considered an organ system at risk that is as important as the cardiovascular or pulmonary system and must be protected from adverse environmental events, including pain.

OPTIONS FOR MANAGEMENT OF PAIN IN THE NEONATE

Given that infants have the capacity to perceive and respond to pain, what are the options for pain management of the critically ill newborn infant when painful procedures must be performed?

Nonpharmacological Techniques for Management of Infant Pain

Noninvasive, nonpharmacological techniques used in management of pain provide support for the infant's own intrinsic coping mechanisms. The more immature the infant, the more external support is required. Preparation of the infant for a painful procedure should include careful planning and coordination such that the infant has time for rest and recovery between procedures. Swaddling and positioning comfortably will provide containment of behavioral responses for the immature infant who cannot control gross motor response to external stimulation. The infant also may be distracted with visual, oral, auditory, or tactile stimuli (Field & Goldson, 1984).

In adults, techniques that provide counterirritation (i.e., any peripheral, non-painful nerve input) are helpful in blocking pain sensation. One small study of infants did not demonstrate any decrease in behavioral distress with massage of the leg during a heel-stick procedure (Beaver, 1987). Nevertheless, counterirritation may be effective when applied contralaterally, that is on the limb opposite the one on which the procedure is being performed (McCaffery, 1979). Further investigation of the use of this technique in infants is warranted.

Providing assistance to the infant in regaining behavioral control will minimize energy expended in coping with the experience. Providing a pacifier, swaddling, and reducing all extraneous stimulation are ways to help the infant regain behavioral control after painful procedures.

Pharmacological Agents Used to Manage Infant Pain

The frequency and intensity of painful procedures in the care of critically ill newborns is such that nonpharmacological interventions provide limited analgesia. Pharmacological support may be required to prevent potentially life-threatening physiological compromise. Little is known about the effects of drugs used for analgesia or sedation on the developing CNS. Therefore, before psychoactive drugs are administered to infants, the unknown long-term risks of pharmacological therapy must be weighed against the immediate known and long-term unknown risks of pain.

Information regarding the effects of psychoactive drugs in infants is sparse. Nevertheless, these agents are being administered to infants (Franck, 1987), and their use should be guided by the general principles of pharmacology as highlighted in the following discussion.

Local Anesthetics

The use of a local anesthetic can minimize pain and reduce behavioral distress during invasive but relatively superficial procedures performed on the infant. Local anesthesia has been used successfully to achieve dorsal root nerve block of sensory nerves in the penis before circumcision (Maxwell, Yaster, Wetzel, & Niebyl, 1987). Lidocaine (1%) is the local anesthetic commonly used in the ICN (Roberts, 1984). A preparation without epinephrine is recommended because of the potential cardiovascular effects of epinephrine. A small amount (0.05 to 0.1 mL) of lidocaine can be injected subcutaneously at the site immediately before the procedure. Lidocaine use should be monitored closely in the infant who is undergoing multiple procedures because repeated administration can result in significant blood levels of the drug. To avoid systemic toxicity, CNS system and cardiovascular effects, no more than 0.5 mL of a 1% solution per kilogram body weight should be injected (Roberts, 1984). It has been suggested that a 0.5% solution is more appropriate in situations in which repeated injection is required (Bashein, 1980). The mean duration of effect shortened (to 75 minutes compared to 127 minutes in the adult), however, and more frequent instillation may be necessary during lengthy procedures.

The use of local anesthetics for nerve block and regional anesthesia (i.e., epidural and spinal anesthesia) also has been reported in neonates (Dohi & Seino, 1986; Harnik, Hoy, Potolicchio, Stewart, & Siegelman, 1986). Premature infants appear to be somewhat resistant to the effects of spinal anesthesia and require larger doses and more frequent instillation. Inadvertent injection of the anesthetic into the circulation can cause profound systemic effects.

The skin of a neonate is extremely permeable and could provide an effective vehicle for superficial local anesthesia, particularly for procedures such as arterial puncture or intravenous catheter insertion (Rutter, 1987). Although topical application of local anesthetic preparations has been studied in children (Jacobson & Koren, 1990) no studies of topical administration of local anesthetics in neonates have appeared in the literature to date.

Nonnarcotic Analgesics

Nonnarcotic analgesics are effective against mild to moderate pain, especially pain due to inflammation. The mechanism of action is thought to be inhibition of prostaglandin production. Because of the serious side effects of salycilates, such as bleeding, gastrointestinal irritation, and hypersensitivity reaction (Flower, Moncada, & Vane, 1980), they are not used in newborns. Indomethacin, a nonsteroidal anti-inflammatory agent, has only been used in infants to promote closure of the patent ductus arteriosus. It does have analgesic as well as anti-inflammatory effects, however.

Acetaminophen is used in infants, especially if fever is present. It can be used effectively for older infants in the ICN, such as those with bronchopulmonary dysplasia, who are especially at risk for upper respiratory and ear infections.

Antihistamines have weak analgesic effects but can potentiate the effects of opioid analgesics, although the mechanism of action is not well understood (Rumore & Schlichting, 1986). The use of the antihistamines diphenhydramine and hydroxyzine has been documented in neonates. Hydroxyzine has been used primarily as a preanesthetic and is not effective when used alone (Roberts, 1984). Infants given diphenhydramine are at risk for withdrawal symptoms if the drug is discontinued abruptly, although the onset of symptoms may be related to the immaturity of hepatic enzyme processes (Parkin, 1984).

Narcotic Analgesics

Narcotic analgesics are effective agents for severe pain. Opioid analgesics can cause histamine release, resulting in respiratory depression or hypotension, and should be used with caution in the nonventilated patient (Mather & Phillips, 1986). Neonates appear to be somewhat more sensitive than adults to the respiratory depressant effects of opioids (Lynn & Slattery, 1987). These effects are reversible with naloxone.

Of the opioids, morphine and meperedine have been used most commonly in infants (Franck, 1987). Meperedine is metabolized to normeperedine, an active metabolite that may be responsible for the rebound respiratory depression that sometimes is seen in neonates (Kuhnert, Kuhnert, Tu, & Lin, 1979). Reaction to opioids is unique in each individual, and an infant who had an adverse reaction to one agent may be able to tolerate another without problem.

Fentanyl is a synthetic opiate commonly used during surgery on neonates (Yaster, 1985). Fentanyl is short acting compared with morphine or meperedine and causes less histamine release and concomitant hypotension (Rosow, Moss, Philbin, & Savarese, 1982). Therefore, it may be the drug of choice for use before procedures of relatively short duration, such as bronchoscopy. The successful use of fentanyl given as a slow continuous intravenous drip has been reported in the management of infants with diaphragmatic hernias during their postoperative course, when cardiovascular stability and adequate oxygenation are critical (Vacanti et al., 1984). Muscular rigidity of the trunk area (stiff-chest syndrome) is seen with large doses of fentanyl in the adult (Christian, Waller, & Moldenhauer, 1983).

Reports demonstrating the efficacy for infants of other analgesics that are standard therapy for adults are not currently available. Effective analgesia for infants may not lie in the discovery of new agents, however, but in scrutiny of methods for delivering currently available analgesics. For example, research in both adults and children has shown the effectiveness of continuous infusion of minute doses of opioids and of scheduled (as opposed to "as needed") administration of analgesics (Miser, Miser, & Clark, 1980; Portenoy & Foley, 1986). Exploration of these pharmacological principles in infants is warranted.

Other Psychoactive Drugs Given to Infants

Sedatives and Hypnotics

Sedatives and hypnotics are used appropriately for inducing sleep but have no analgesic effects and can even cause a hyperalgesic state with increased sensation of pain (Roberts, 1984). In addition, sedatives and hypnotics can cause paradoxical reactions in infants and children, resulting in excitation rather than sedation. If the infant is experiencing pain, administering a sedative or hypnotic will only suppress some of the expression of the pain and will not treat the underlying cause.

Anxiolytics

Antianxiety agents produce muscle relaxation and a state of calm. These drugs have minimal analgesic effects and also can produce respiratory depression. As with the sedatives and hypnotics, paradoxical reactions also can occur. Diazepam has been used primarily for seizure control in infants and is effective in calming frantic infants. Its use as a sedative in neonates has been questioned, however, because of its active metabolite and its long half-life (Roberts, 1984).

Lorazepam is a short-acting benzodiazepine that has been used successfully as a preanesthetic as well as for seizure control (Burtles & Ashley, 1983). Lorazepam may be an appropriate agent for use in the agitated, hypoxic infant to break the cycle of agitation–air hunger–agitation (in the absence of signs of pain). The risk of toxicity with repeated administration is reduced because of lorazepam's shorter half-life and lack of active metabolites (Kyriakopoulos, Greenblatt, & Shader, 1978). The onset of action when the drug is given orally is relatively slow, and scheduled rather than "as needed" administration should be considered.

Neuroleptics

In adults, phenothiazines are used sometimes to potentiate the effects of analgesics and anesthetics. Chlorpromazine use has been reported to be relatively safe for newborns (Roberts, 1984). Others, however, have advised against the use of chlorpromazine in infants younger than 6 months of age (Wade, 1978). Neuroleptic drugs have wide-ranging neurological and endocrine effects, including blockade of dopaminergic pathways. Neuroleptics can be epileptogenic. Therefore, the risks and benefits of use of these drugs to the developing CNS must be weighed carefully. Chlorpromazine is no longer recommended for treatment of narcotic withdrawal syndrome (American Academy of Pediatrics, 1983).

Physical Dependence Compared to Addiction

All psychoactive drugs, when given over a period of time, produce some degree of physical dependence and tolerance. Therefore, the dosage of psychoactive drugs should always be tapered before the drug is discontinued. Abruptly discontinuing any psychoactive drug can precipitate withdrawal symptoms because the brain is not able rapidly to reestablish neurochemical balance in the absence of the drug. The potential for withdrawal syndrome appears to be greater with short-acting rather than longer-acting agents and may occur even at relatively low doses (Perry & Alexander, 1986).

Addiction is defined as "a behavioral pattern of drug use characterized by overwhelming involvement with the use of a drug (compulsive use), the securing of its supply, and a high tendency to relapse after withdrawal" (Jaffe, 1980, p. 536). The development of addiction in hospitalized patients is rare (Porter & Jick, 1980). Therefore, although it is clear that infants given a psychoactive drug over a period of time may develop physical dependence on and tolerance to the drug, it is unlikely that infants are capable of becoming truly addicted.

Guidelines for effective weaning of infants from psychoactive drugs have not been established. Maguire and Maloney (1988) reported that in one ICN a continuous fentanyl drip is decreased by 10% every 6 hours, and intermittent morphine doses are decreased by 10% every day. The infants are monitored closely for signs of withdrawal, and the weaning schedule is modified accordingly. A retrospective chart review of 33 cases showed that infants sedated with fentanyl were more likely to demonstrate withdrawal symptoms than infants sedated with morphine (Norton, 1988). Further research is needed for a better understanding of the effects of psychoactive drugs on the infant's CNS and to determine optimal weaning practices.

The Paralyzed Infant

Sensation remains intact in the infant who receives a neuromuscular blocking agent (Taylor, 1980). The infant perceives and can still respond to pain, at least neurochemically. It has been demonstrated in neonates that there is a dramatic release of corticosteroids and norepinephrine after administration of pancuronium, and this extra neuroendocrine load may contribute to decreased cardiac function (Cabal, Siassi, Artal, Gonzalez, Hodgeman, & Plajstek, 1985). Infants who receive these agents often are the most critically ill and unstable patients, and it may be most important that these infants receive analgesia to minimize the further physiological compromise due to pain.

Assessing the Need for Pharmacological Intervention for Pain and Agitation

Pharmacological management of infant pain should be considered only after all attempts to manipulate environmental factors and all noninvasive methods of providing comfort have proved insufficient. The lack of a behavioral response to a stimulus known to cause severe pain in an adult should not be interpreted as lack of perception of pain in an infant. The failure of an infant to respond to painful stimulation is an indication of the immaturity of the infant's CNS or the amount of stress that the infant has endured. If the infant is unable to demonstrate behavioral responses to pain, pain should be presumed on the basis of the intensity of the stimuli and managed accordingly within the parameters allowed by the infant's condition.

Even if the infant can respond behaviorally, current methods of assessing the infant's behavior are such that it is difficult to distinguish between pain responses and other behavior. The questions listed in Exhibit 9-1 provide a guide for identifying infant pain and selecting appropriate interventions.

Exhibit 9-1 Questions to Ask Before Using Psychoactive Drugs in Neonates

What behavior is the infant displaying that is actually or potentially harmful?
Is the infant compromised physiologically? How?
Is the behavior periodic or continuous; brief or prolonged?
Can any precipitating factors be identified?
Is the infant adequately ventilated?

- Is the endotracheal tube properly positioned and patent?
- Is the infant's breathing synchronized with the ventilator?
- Is increased oxygen necessary?
- Does the infant need to be suctioned?

Have nonpharmacological comfort measures been attempted?

- Is the infant's temperature stable?
- Have wet diapers or bedding been removed?
- Has abdominal distention been relieved?
- Has the infant been repositioned or swaddled?
- Has a minimal handling protocol been implemented?

Could the infant be experiencing pain?

- Have procedures been performed recently?
- Have internal sources of discomfort (e.g., teething, otitis media, abdominal distress) been investigated?

What routes are available for delivery of medication?
How long is pharmacological support anticipated to last?
Did the drug achieve the desired effect?
Was the trial period long enough to achieve adequate blood levels?
Were any side effects noted?
Was the infant too sedated?
Are there any potential concerns regarding toxicity?
What is the plan for withdrawing pharmacological support (weaning) as the patient's condition improves?
If the drug was ineffective:

- What effects were not achieved?
- What agent will be tried next? For how long?

Source: Adapted from ''Behavioral Issues for Infants with BPD'' by K.A. VandenBerg and L.S. Franck in *Bronchopulmonary Dysplasia: Strategies for Total Patient Care* by C.H. Lund, 1990, Petaluma, CA: Neonatal Network. Copyright 1990 by Neonatal Network. Adapted by permission.

It is crucial that the choice of a particular agent be based on the pharmacological requirements of the situation. For brief painful procedures, a rapid-onset, short-acting agent is required. For prolonged episodes a long-acting agent with a short half-life and minimal toxicity is required to minimize physiological compromise. For example, if the infant is assessed as needing sedation during a nonpainful procedure (e.g., computed tomography), a rapidly acting hypnotic such as chloral hydrate would be appropriate. In contrast, if the infant has a chronic condition the treatment of which necessitates frequent invasive procedures, scheduled, round-the-clock administration of an opioid would be indicated.

Evaluating Pain Management

Pain management must be evaluated as carefully and systematically as other aspects of the infant's care and should be discussed daily by the health care team during patient rounds. Although achieving effective pain management may involve some trial and error, the agents and dosage schedules should not be changed randomly because the effectiveness of any one agent or regimen will be masked. The questions in Exhibit 9-1 should be considered after any psychoactive agent is administered to the infant. In addition, the use of a nursing care plan will help ensure a consistent approach to and evaluation of nursing care (Table 9-1).

Attitudes of Physicians and Nurses Regarding the Pharmacological Management of Pain in Infants

The appropriate use of analgesics in the management of pain in infants is dependent not only on adequate knowledge of analgesic pharmacology but also on the attitudes and beliefs of the physicians prescribing the drugs and the nurses administering them. It has been demonstrated clearly that misperceptions and myths about pain and the pharmacological treatment of pain seriously hamper efforts to provide pain relief to adult patients (Weis, Sriwatanakul, Alloza, Weintraub, & Lasagna, 1983). Many physicians and nurses are overly concerned with addiction (Beaver, 1980). They also express a disproportionate fear of side effects from opioid analgesics and a perception that total pain relief, although probably achievable, is not the goal of pain management. Similar studies of children and neonates have demonstrated an even greater disparity between therapy appropriate for the condition and what is actually received by the patient (Burokas, 1985; Beyer, DeGood, Ashley, & Russell, 1983; Maxwell et al., 1987; Schechter, Allen, & Hanson, 1986).

Education of physician and nursing staff regarding the pharmacological properties of analgesics is essential. When neonatal pain management is better under-

Table 9-1 Children's Hospital—Oakland, Intensive Care Nursery, Developmental Care Plan (Excerpted)

Date	Nursing Diagnosis/Problem	Expected Outcomes	Nursing Plan	Status of Nursing Diagnosis/Problem	Nurse Initials
	Collaborative problem: Actual or Potential 1. Altered comfort: Pain and anxiety related to essential medical and nursing interventions 2. Impaired gas exchange related to pain and agitation	1. To minimize the physiological and behavioral disruption that results from agitation 2. To minimize the potential risks of administration of psychoactive drugs to a developing CNS	1. Before using medication for pain relief, identify potential causes of pain and/or agitation such as: • recent procedures performed • internal source of discomfort (teething, otitis media, abdominal distress, colic, fractures) • respiratory compromise (i.e., broncho-spasm, inadequate ventilation) 2. Nonpharmacologic treatments used: • bagging • swaddling • pacifier • holding • singing • patting • rocking • _____ 3. Pharmacological treatment: Meds used _____ Date _____ 4. Results achieved? _____ Side effects noted? _____ Weaning plan: _____		

Source: "Pain in the nonverbal patient: Advocating for the critically ill infant" by L.S. Frank, 1989, *Pediatric Nursing*, 15(1), p. 67. Copyright 1989 by Anthony J. Jannetti, Inc. Reprinted by permission.

stood and becomes a priority in medical and nursing care of infants, methods used to treat pain, both nonpharmacological and pharmacological, will become increasingly effective, and the goal of complete pain relief for infants receiving intensive care will be attainable.

REFERENCES

Als, H. (1983). Infant individuality: Assessing patterns of very early development. In J. Calls, E. Galenson, & R. Tuson (Eds.), *Frontiers of infant psychiatry* (pp. 363–378). New York: Basic Books.

American Academy of Pediatrics Committee on Drugs. Neonatal drug withdrawal. *Pediatrics, 72*, 895–902.

Anand, K.J., Brown, M.J., Causon, R.C., Christofides, N.D., Bloom, S.R., & Aynsley-Green, A. (1985). Can the human neonate mount an endocrine and metabolic response to surgery? *Journal of Pediatric Surgery, 20*, 41–48.

Anand, K.J.S., Sippell, E.G., & Aynsley-Green, A. (1987). Randomized trial of fentanyl anesthesia in preterm neonates undergoing surgery: Effects on the stress response. *Lancet, 1*, 62–65.

Bashein, G. (1980). Use of excessive lidocaine concentrations for local anesthesia. *New England Journal of Medicine, 302*, 122.

Beaver, P.K. (1987). Premature infants' response to touch and pain: Can nurses make a difference? *Neonatal Network, 6*, 13–17.

Beaver, W.T. (1980). Management of cancer pain with parenteral medication. *Journal of the American Medical Association, 244*, 2653–2657.

Beyer, J.E., DeGood, D.E., Ashley, L.C., & Russell, G.A. (1983). Patterns of post-operative analgesic use with adults and children following cardiac surgery. *Pain, 17*, 71–81.

Brazy, J.E. (1988). Effects of crying on cerebral blood volume and cytochrome aa$_3$. *Journal of Pediatrics, 112*, 457–461.

Brown, L. (1987). The clinical inference of cutaneous pain in neonates. *Neonatal Network, 6*, 18–22.

Burnard, E.D., John, E., Todd, D.A., & Hindmarsh, K.W. (1985). Beta-endorphinlike immunoactivity in newborn cerebrospinal fluid. In L. Stern, M. Xanthou, & B. Firis-Hansen (Eds.), *Physiologic foundations of perinatal care* (pp. 334–342). New York: Praeger.

Burokas, L. (1985). Factors affecting nurses' decisions to medicate pediatric patients after surgery. *Heart & Lung, 14*, 373–379.

Burtles, R., & Ashley, B. (1983). Lorazepam in children. *British Journal of Anesthesia, 55*, 275–278.

Cabal, L.A., Siassi, B., Artal, R., Gonzalez, F., Hodgeman, J., & Plajstek, C. (1985). Cardiovascular and catecholamine changes after administration of pancuronium in distressed neonates. *Pediatrics, 75*(2), 284–287.

Christian, C.M., Waller, J.L., & Moldenhauer, C.C. (1983). Postoperative rigidity following fentanyl anesthesia. *Anesthesiology, 58*, 275, 277.

Craig, K.D., & Prkachin, K.M. (1983). Nonverbal measures of pain. In R. Melzack (Ed.), *Pain measurement and assessment* (pp. 173–179). New York: Raven.

Davidson, S., Gil-Ad, I., Rogovin, H., Laron, Z., & Reisner, S.H. (1987). Cardiorespiratory depression and plasma beta-endorphin levels in low birthweight infants during the first days of life. *American Journal of Diseases in Children, 141*, 145–148.

Dobbing, J., & Smart, J.L. (1974). Vulnerability of developing brain and behavior. *British Medical Bulletin, 30*, 164–168.

Dohi, S., & Seino, H. (1986). Spinal anesthesia in premature infants: Dosage and effects of sympathectomy. *Anesthesiology, 65*, 559–560.

Duffy, F.H. (1985). *Evidence for hemispheric differences between fullterms and preterms by electrophysiologic measures.* Society of Research in Child Development, Toronto, Canada, 1985. Abstract.

Duffy, F.H., Mower, G., Jensen, F., & Als, H. (1984). Neural plasticity: A new frontier in infant development. In H.E. Fitzgerald, B.M. Lester, & M.W. Yogman (Eds.), *Theory and research in behavioral pediatrics* (Vol. 2, pp. 67–96). New York: Plenum.

Emde, R.N., Harmon, R.J., Metcalf, D., Koenig, K.L., & Wagonfeld, S. (1971). Stress and neonatal sleep. *Psychosomatic Medicine, 33*, 491–497.

Facchinetti, F., Bagnoli, F., Bracci, R., & Genazzani, A.R. (1982). Plasma opioids in the first hours of life. *Pediatric Research, 16*, 95–98.

Field, T., & Goldson, R. (1984). Pacifying effects of nonnutritive sucking on term and preterm infants during heelstick procedures. *Pediatrics, 74*, 1012–1015.

Flower, R.J., Moncada, S., & Vane, J.R. (1980). Analgesic-antipyretics and anti-inflammatory agents; drugs employed in the treatment of gout. In A.G. Gilman, L.S. Goodman, & A. Gilman (Eds.), *The pharmacologic basis of therapeutics* (6th ed., pp. 682–728). New York: Macmillan.

Franck, L.S. (1986). A new method to quantitatively describe pain behavior in infants. *Nursing Research, 35*, 28–31.

Franck, L.S. (1987). A national survey of the assessment and treatment of pain and agitation in the neonatal intensive care unit. *Journal of Obstetric, Gynecologic and Neonatal Nursing, 16*, 387–393.

Gamble, H.J. (1966). Further electron microscope studies of human foetal peripheral nerves. *Journal of Anatomy, 100*, 487–502.

Gautray, J.P., Jolivet, A., Vielh, J.P., & Guillemin, R. (1977). Presence of immunoassayable beta-endorphin in human amniotic fluid: Elevation in cases of fetal distress. *American Journal of Obstetrics and Gynecology, 129*, 211–212.

Goodlin, R.C. (1981). Naloxone and its possible relationship to fetal endorphin levels and fetal distress. *American Journal of Obstetrics and Gynecology, 139*, 16–19.

Harnik, E.V., Hoy, G.R., Potolicchio, S., Stewart, D.R., & Siegelman, R.E. (1986). Spinal anesthesia in premature infants recovering from respiratory distress syndrome. *Anesthesiology, 64*, 95–99.

Jacobson, S., & Koren, G. (1990). New approaches to topical anesthesia in children. *Current Opinion in Pediatrics, 2*, 234–237.

Jaffe, J.H. (1980). Drug addiction and drug abuse. In A.G. Gilman, L.S. Goodman, & A. Gilman (Eds.), *The pharmacologic basis of therapeutics* (6th ed., pp. 535–584). New York: Macmillan.

Janowsky, J.S., & Finlay, B.L. (1986). The outcome of perinatal damage: The role of normal neuronal loss and axon retraction. *Developmental Medicine and Child Neurology, 28*, 375–389.

Kehlet, H. (1986). Pain relief and modification of the stress response. In M.J. Cousins & G.D. Phillips (Eds.), *Acute pain management* (pp. 49–75). New York: Churchill Livingstone.

Kuhnert, B.R., Kuhnert, P.M., Tu, A.L., & Lin, D.C. (1979). Meperidine and normeperidine levels following meperidine administration during labor. II: Fetus and neonate. *American Journal of Obstetrics and Gynecology, 133*, 909–914.

Kyriakopoulos, A.A., Greenblatt, D.J., & Shader, R.L. (1978). Clinical pharmacokinetics of lorazepam: A review. *Journal of Clinical Psychiatry, 34*, 16–23.

Lagerkrantz, H., & Bistoletti, P. (1977). Catecholamine release in the newborn. *Pediatric Research, 11*, 889–891.

Lippsitt, L.P. (1977). The study of sensory and learning processes of the newborn. *Clinics in Perinatology, xx*, 163–186.

Lynn, A.M., & Slattery, J.T. (1987). Morphine pharmacokinetics in early infancy. *Anesthesiology, 66*, 136–139.

Maguire, D.P., & Maloney, P. (1988). A comparison of fentanyl and morphine use in neonates. *Neonatal Network, 7*, 27–32.

Marshall, R.E., Porter, F.L., Rogers, A.G., Moore, J., Anderson, B., & Boxerman, S.B. (1982). Circumcision II: Effects upon mother-infant interaction. *Early Human Development, 7*, 367–374.

Mather, L.E., & Phillips, G.D. (1986). Opioids and adjuvants: Principles of use. In M.J. Cousins & G.D. Phillips (Eds.), *Acute pain management* (pp. 77–104). New York: Churchill Livingstone.

Maxwell, L.G., Yaster, M., Wetzel, R.C., & Niebyl, J.R. (1987). Penile nerve block for newborn circumcision. *Obstetrics and Gynecology, 70*, 415–419.

McCaffery, M. (1979). *Nursing management of the patient with pain* (2nd ed.). Philadelphia: Lippincott.

McGraw, M. (1969). *The neuromuscular maturation of the human infant*. New York: Hafner.

Miser, A., Miser, J., & Clark, B. (1980). Continuous intravenous infusion of morphine sulfate for control of severe pain in children with terminal malignancy. *Journal of Pediatrics, 96*, 930–932.

Norris, S., Campbell, L.A., & Brenkert, S. (1982). Nursing procedures and alterations in transcutaneous oxygen tension in premature infants. *Nursing Research, 31*, 330–338.

Norton, S.J. (1988). Aftereffects of morphine and fentanyl analgesia: A retrospective study. *Neonatal Network, 7*, 25–28.

Okado, N., & Kojima, T. (1984). Ontogeny of the central nervous system: Neurogenesis, fibre connection, synaptogenesis and myelination in the spinal cord. In H.F.R. Prechtl (Ed.), *Continuity of neural function from prenatal to postnatal life* (pp. 31–45). Philadelphia: Lippincott.

Owens, M.E., & Todt, E.H. (1984). Pain in infancy: Neonatal reaction to a heel lance. *Pain, 20*, 77–86.

Parkin, D.E. (1984). Probable Benadryl withdrawal manifestations in a newborn infant. *Journal of Pediatrics, 85*, 580.

Perry, P.J., & Alexander, B. (1986). Sedative/hypnotic dependence: Patient stabilization, tolerance testing, and withdrawal. *Drug Intelligence and Clinical Pharmacy, 20*, 532–537.

Peiper, A. (1963). *Cerebral function in infancy and childhood*. New York: Consultants Bureau.

Phillips, G.D., & Cousins, M.J. (1986). Neurological mechanisms of pain and the relationship of pain, anxiety and sleep. In M.J. Cousins & G.D. Phillips (Eds.), *Acute pain management* (pp. 21–48). New York: Churchill Livingstone.

Portenoy, R.K., & Foley, K.M. (1986). Chronic use of opioid analgesics in non-malignant pain: Report of 38 cases. *Pain, 25*, 171–186.

Porter, J., & Jick, H. (1980). Addiction rare in patients treated with narcotics. *New England Journal of Medicine, 302*, 123.

Porter, F.L., Miller, R.H., & Marshall, R.E. (1986). Neonatal pain cries: Effect of circumcision on acoustical features and perceived urgency. *Child Development, 57*, 790–802.

Prechtl, H.F.R. (1984). Continuity and change in early neural development. In H.F.R. Prechtl (Ed.), *Continuity of neural function from prenatal to postnatal life* (pp. 1–15). Philadelphia: Lippincott.

Price, D.D., & Dubner, R. (1977). Neurons that subserve the sensory-discriminative aspects of pain. *Pain, 3*, 307–338.

Ramanathan, S., Puig, M.M., Lovitz, M., & Turndorf, H. (1987). Plasma beta-endorphin levels in term and preterm neonates. *Anesthesia and Analgesia, 66*, S144.

Rich, E.C., Marshall, R.E., & Volpe, J.J. (1974). The normal neonatal response to pinprick. *Developmental Medicine and Child Neurology, 16*, 432–434.

Roberts, R.J. (1984). *Drug therapy in infants: Pharmacologic principles and clinical experience.* Philadelphia: Saunders.

Rosow, C.E., Moss, J., Philbin, D.M., & Savarese, J.J. (1982). Histamine release during morphine and fentanyl anesthesia. *Anesthesiology, 56*, 93–96.

Rumore, M.M., & Schlichting, D.A. (1986). Clinical efficacy of antihistamines as analgesics. *Pain, 25*, 7–22.

Rutter, N. (1987). Drug absorption through the skin: A mixed blessing. *Archive of Disease in Childhood, 62*, 220–221.

Sandman, C.A., McGivern, R.F., Berka, C., Walker, J.M., Coy, D.H., & Kastin, A. (1979). Neonatal administration of beta-endorphin produces "chronic" insensitivity to thermal stimuli. *Life Sciences, 25*, 1755–1760.

Sarnat, H.B. (1984). Anatomic and physiologic correlates of neurologic development in prematurity. In H.B. Sarnat (Ed.), *Topics in neonatal neurology* (pp. 1–25). Orlando: Grune & Stratton.

Schechter, N.L., Allen, D.A., & Hanson, K. Status of pediatric pain control: A comparison of hospital analgesic usage in children and adults. *Pediatrics, 77*, 11–15.

Sell, E.J. (1986). Outcome of very very low birth weight infants. *Clinics in Perinatology, 13*, 451–459.

Sexson, W.R., Schneider, P., Chamberlin, J.L., Hicks, M.K., & Sexson, S.B. (1986). Auditory conditioning in the critically ill neonate to enhance interpersonal relationships. *Journal of Perinatology, 6*, 20–23.

Swafford, L., & Allan, D. (1968). Pain relief in the pediatric patient. *Medical Clinics of North America, 52*, 131–136.

Taylor, P. (1980). Neuromuscular blocking agents. In A.G. Gilman, L.S. Goodman, & A. Gilman (Eds.), *The pharmacologic basis of therapeutics* (6th ed., pp. 220–234). New York: Macmillan.

Vacanti, J.P., Crone, R.K., Murphy, J.D., Smith, S.D., Black, P.R., Reid, L., & Hendren, W.H. (1984). The pulmonary hemodynamic response to perioperative anesthesia in the treatment of high-risk infants with congenital diaphragmatic hernia. *Journal of Pediatric Surgery, 19*, 672–679.

Vaughan, H.G. (1975). Electrophysiologic analysis of regional cortical maturation. *Biological Psychiatry, 10*, 513–526.

Volpe, J.J. (1987). Neuronal proliferation, migration, organization and myelination. *Neurology of the newborn* (2nd ed.) Philadelphia: Saunders.

Vorhees, C.V. (1981). Effects of prenatal nalaxone exposure on postnatal behavioral development of rats. *Neurobehavioral Toxicology and Teratology, 3*, 295–301.

Wade, A. (Ed.). (1978). *Martindale: The extra pharmacopeia* 27th (ed.). London: Pharmaceutical Press.

Weis, O.F., Sriwatanakul, K., Alloza, J.L., Weintraub, M., & Lasagna, L. (1983). Attitudes of patients, housestaff, and nurses toward postoperative analgesic care. *Anesthesia and Analgesia, 62*, 70–74.

Williamson, P.S., & Evans, N.D. (1986). Neonatal cortisol response to circumcision with anesthesia. *Clinical Pediatrics, 25*, 412–414.

Yaster, M. (1985). The dose response of fentanyl in neonatal surgery. *Anesthesiology, 63*, A471.

Chapter 10

Pain in the Critically Ill Child

Heidi M. Morrison

Disease can destroy the body, but pain can destroy the soul.

Lisson (1987, p. 649)

The experience of pain for the critically ill child in the pediatric intensive care unit (PICU) is a phenomenon shrouded in concern and confusion for the child, family, and health professional. Children with various critical conditions and of all ages are admitted to PICUs. Their pain may be caused by pathology, surgery, trauma, or invasive procedures. Because children in PICUs often are unable to communicate, nurses must anticipate pain, recognize subtle signs of pain, and provide relief. Pediatric critical care nurses already have acute perceptive abilities and an intuitive sense of the subtle changes in children's conditions. They can integrate these qualities with a multidimensional pain assessment by using their knowledge of child development, analgesics, and specific nursing actions to treat pediatric pain effectively. This chapter describes the pediatric patient's pain experience in the critical care environment and offers suggestions for nursing care and treatment.

DEVELOPMENTAL STAGES OF THE CHILD IN PAIN

The responses to pain are developmentally determined and influenced by experiences and ability to communicate. During the neonatal period (birth to 1 month), free epithelial nerve endings, sensory pathways, and the central nervous system are developing. Because the motor pathways are poorly developed, neonates respond to pain with generalized body movements and do not reflexively withdraw the affected limb (D'Apolito, 1984). At around 3 months of age, infants begin to localize pain (Hazinski, 1984). As infants reach 6 months of age they can remember past painful events because they can develop associations between past painful events and concurrent experiences (Levy, 1960). Consequently, they may anticipate pain when they see a nurse approach with a needle and respond by crying.

Older infants, (13 to 24 months) manifest anticipatory distress and voluntary goal-directed movements such as rubbing an infection site (Craig, McMahon, Morison, & Zaskow, 1984). Irritability, restlessness, rigidity, lethargy, poor feeding, disturbed sleep patterns, crying, tachycardia, and increased respiratory distress also may indicate pain in infants (Johnston & Strada, 1986; Lewandowski, 1984).

Toddlers cannot comprehend the meaning of hospitalization and pain. When confronted with a painful event, they react with intense emotions and resistance. Toddlers' responses to pain are influenced by memories of a stress event, attachment to their parents, and physical restraint. In addition, their poorly defined body boundary can make them feel as if intravenous (IV) line tubing is part of their body, so that when a nurse inserts a needle in the IV tubing toddlers react as if their body was stuck. Furthermore, because toddlers are in the preoperational stage, they lack expressive vocabulary. Therefore, they often react to pain through aggressive behaviors such as biting, hitting, and temper tantrums. Taylor (1983) reported that, during the first postoperative hours after inguinal herniorrhaphy, 18 month- to 4-year-olds exhibited various pain-related behaviors: guarding, bending the knees, resting the feet on the bed, touching the operative site, and grimacing.

Preschoolers' understanding of pain is affected by egocentric fantasy and magical thinking. These children have intense concerns about body injury; therefore, injections are perceived by them as threatening. They may believe that a puncture hole will cause all the body fluids to leak out. Furthermore, because of their egocentric beliefs, hospitalization and procedures that cause pain may be perceived as punishment. Statements such as "Just hold still like a good child" may lead to feelings of guilt afterward if the child was unable to cooperate. Nurses can help the preschooler by giving explanations before the procedure to dissociate goodness and badness and can assist the child in working out feelings of guilt, fear, and anger through therapeutic play.

Studies have shown that school-aged children are more able to communicate effectively about their pain than younger children (Savedra, Gibbons, Tesler, Ward, & Wegner, 1982; Ross & Ross, 1988). Younger school-aged children will describe pain such as stomach ache, headache, and cuts in concrete terms. As children develop reasoning and abstract thought, they use words describing intensity and feeling such as sickening, uncomfortable, horrible, tiring, throbbing, piercing, burning, and crushing (Savedra et al., 1982).

The school-aged child desires to master the abstract concept of pain. In one study, for example, when children were asked how they deal with pain their responses included "grit my teeth, make a tight fist, and take a deep breath"

(Tesler, Wegner, Savedra, Gibbons, & Ward, 1981). Because of the nature of the PICU environment, however, the child often may be denied these coping strategies. Nurses can modify the child's environment by providing periods of supervised unrestraint. In addition, they may help the child develop new strategies for pain coping such as relaxation and distraction.

Because adolescents strive for independence and value their appearance, they often display self-control when in pain; their ability to deal with underlying anxiety may be lacking, however (Broome, 1985). In one study, adolescents indicated that they felt more pain than independent observers reported (Hilgard & Le Baron, 1982). Older children attempt to conceal their pain because such behavior is more socially desirable.

Fear and anxiety play an integral role in the individual's experience of pain, so that nurses need to help the adolescent report these concerns and to teach effective coping mechanisms. By giving valid information, providing choices, displaying a sincere belief in their pain, showing warmth and respect, and providing pain relief, the nurse can assist teenagers in expressing real feelings and avoiding problems of repressed emotional energy, which can lead to acting-out behaviors (Favaloro, 1988). Because of adolescents' need for control, nurses may give control back to them by recommending patient-controlled analgesic (PCA) approaches and by teaching the use of guided imagery, relaxation, and distraction.

In conclusion, because children respond differently to pain as a result of changes in cognitive and emotional development, health professionals must consider the child's developmental stage when assessing pain.

NURSES CARING FOR CHILDREN IN PAIN

Nurses may not consider pain relief a high priority in nursing care. They may not recognize subtle symptoms of pain, or they may be afraid of the complications of narcotics (Burokas, 1985; Weis, Sriwatanakul, Alloza, Weintraub, & Lasagna, 1983).

In fact, several studies have demonstrated that pain is inadequately managed in the PICU. For example, Beyer, DeGood, Ashley, and Russel (1983) found that, on the average, postoperative pediatric cardiac patients received only one to two doses of analgesics per day. In addition, these children received only 30% of their prescribed analgesics, whereas a comparable adult group received 70%. Schechter, Allen, and Hanson (1986) compared the charts of 90 adults and 90 children. They found that adults received 2.2 doses of narcotics per day whereas children only received 1.1 doses per day. Likewise, Burokas (1985) reviewed the charts of 40 postsurgical children and found that analgesics were given an average of only 2 times per day. Only two patients in this group received all the doses ordered during their postoperative course. Of 99 neonatal intensive care and PICU nurses studied by Bradshaw and Zeanah (1986), only one-third chose to use the maximum analgesic dose ordered for pain relief.

It seems apparent from the above study findings that nurses need to acknowledge and investigate their attitudes about narcotics and pain relief before they can adequately assess and treat children's pain. Because nurses spend a great deal of time at the child's bedside, they have the opportunity to assess the child's individual needs. If the nurse concentrates only on the high-priority technical and physical aspects of the child's care, then the opportunity to diagnose pain and to provide support is missed. Nurses must incorporate pain assessment and management as part of their daily regime.

THE ENVIRONMENT OF THE CHILD IN PAIN

Being in a PICU can be a harrowing experience for a child. The adverse effect of the environment on a child's pain can originate from two sources: factors that increase anxiety and therapeutic interventions. Children are exposed to an assortment of irritating and frightening sights and sounds that may increase their anxiety. For example, beeping equipment, intermittent alarms, hissing oxygen, shouting voices, monstrous machines, and unfamiliar faces all contribute to the terrifying and disorienting atmosphere that produces anxiety, which may intensify the child's level of pain.

Frequently, life-sustaining therapeutic interventions produce pain and stress. For example, injections, intubation, restraints, restrictions on food and fluid intake, and changes in sleep and elimination patterns were identified as stressors and sources of pain by PICU patients 7 to 17 years of age and their parents (Tichy, Braam, Meyer, & Rattan, 1988). In addition, Wong and Baker (1988) reported that, according to children, venipunctures, IV insertions, and injections were the most frequent causes of pain. The pain associated with chest tube insertions, arterial punctures, spinal taps, and bone marrow tests as well as postoperative pain and pain when being moved had the highest pain intensities. Furthermore, children's sense of security is diminished by separation from their parents and their inability to comfort themselves (Ross & Ross, 1988).

Nurses can decrease the child's anxiety and potentially decrease the pain by conducting preadmission tours to acquaint the child with the PICU environment, explaining procedures and equipment to avoid surprises, using distraction and relaxation to modify pain, and modifying the physical environment to decrease stressors that may heighten pain (e.g., dimming lights, maintaining the daily routine, providing privacy, and encouraging parents to visit). Table 10-1 summarizes suggestions for making the environment less threatening.

Table 10-1 Suggestions for Modifying the PICU Environment

Environmental	Physical	Psychological	Social
Dim lights, especially at night	Allow for at least 2 hours of uninterrupted sleep	Provide privacy	Encourage parents to bring in transitional objects such as blanket, pillow, or favorite toy
Lower monitor tones when possible	Allow for supervised periods of unrestraint	Provide daily routines	
Coordinate IV pumps to alarm at same time		Encourage parents to stay with child and to provide care as feasible	Provide distraction through play and music

ASSESSMENT OF THE CHILD IN PAIN

Assessing children's pain in the PICU is extremely challenging. The child's communication of pain may be influenced by intubation, restraints, paralysis, altered level of consciousness, type of anesthesia, developmental level, cultural background, and the parents' presence or absence. In addition, physiological responses such as hypoxia, low cardiac output, fever, and increasing intracranial pressure may produce signs similar to pain (e.g., agitation, pallor, tachycardia, and tachypnea). Careful, individualized, and continuous pain assessment is mandatory. Nurses also must be alert to worsening conditions for which pain is a significant indicator, such as ruptured spleen, meningitis, and compartment syndrome.

Pain can be assessed behaviorally and physiologically and by patient self-report. Because children may not be able to verbalize their pain during part of their intensive care recovery, often the only methods to assess pain are behavioral and physiological.

Behavioral Measures of Pain

Two categories of behaviors commonly used to assess pain in children are body movements and facial expressions. Eland (1981a) divides body movements that are associated with pain into four categories of behaviors: protective, massaging or rubbing, immobilizing, and restless. Protective behaviors are the child's response to impending or present tissue damage. For example, the child may hit or bite the person appearing to cause pain. A child's rubbing, massaging, or holding the affected body part is a behavior that helps localize the site of the child's pain. In addition, these behaviors are thought to stimulate the large nonpain fibers that may block transmission of the pain message, thus decreasing discomfort (Melzack & Wall, 1983).

Body posturing or immobilization, in addition to being signs of pain, decrease pain by reducing stretch and pull on traumatized nerve endings. In fact, a common position of the child after abdominal surgery is lying on the back with the knees flexed and the feet flat on the bed, even when sleeping. Children also splint their chests after open heart surgery by taking shallow breaths.

Finally, restless or purposeless movements signal intense pain such as muscle spasm from a fractured femur, bowel obstruction, or bladder repair. Thrashing and frequent, abrupt position changes are observed. That is, children may appear calm and pain free one moment and are crying out and restless the next.

In addition to movements, children also display an assortment of oral and facial expressions indicative of pain. Vocalizations can range from moaning, crying, and screaming to specific statements such as "It hurts" or "My boo-boo." Infants and young children lack the maturity in language to convey pain in words; therefore, their sounds may be involuntary as the pain occurs. Facial expressions often reflect conscious or semiconscious feelings. Nurses often comment on how restful a child appears to be sleeping by their facial expression. Children in pain appear to have "troubled" facial expressions.

Specifically, the typical pain expression has been described as follows: brows drawn down and together, tightly closed eyes alternating with wide open eyes, and angular shaped mouth, clenching teeth and biting lower lip (Abu-Saad, 1984; Izard, Heubner, Risser, McGinnes, & Dougherty, 1980).

Nurses often rely on the above mentioned behavioral cues to detect pain. Each behavior alone may have no contextual validity. However, when taken within the context of a patient's particular clinical situation, current behaviors serve as strong indicators of pain.

The most comprehensive behavioral pain scale is the Children's Hospital of Eastern Ontario Pain Scale or CHEOPS, (see Table 10-2; McGrath et al., 1985). The scale is best suited for young children unable to give verbal reports or for those children emerging from anesthesia. The scale consists of six categories of behaviors: crying, facial expressions, verbalizations, torso movements, touch, and leg movements. Each category is assigned a number based on the following criteria: 0 = behavior that is the antithesis of pain, 1 = behavior indicating no pain, 2 = behavior indicating mild or moderate pain, and 3 = behavior indicative of severe pain. The authors report high interrater reliability and good evidence of construct and content validity. Although the authors tested children one to seven years old, the behaviors listed may also apply to older children who are conscious or semiconscious. Additional research is needed to support the reliability and validity for older children and children experiencing nonsurgical pain. Because CHEOPS is based on behavioral assessment parameters, however, it is particu-

Table 10-2 Behavioral Definitions and Scoring of CHEOPS

Item	Behavior	Score	Definition
Cry	No cry	1	Child is not crying.
	Moaning	2	Child is moaning or quietly vocalizing; silent cry.
	Crying	2	Child is crying, but the cry is gentle or whimpering.
	Scream	3	Child is in a full-lunged cry; sobbing, may be scored with complaint or without complaint.
Facial	Composed	1	Neutral facial expression.
	Grimace	2	Score only if definite negative facial expression.
	Smiling	0	Score only if definite positive facial expression.
Child verbal	None	1	Child is not talking.
	Other complaints	1	Child complains, but not about pain, e.g., "I want to see mommy" or "I am thirsty."
	Pain complaints	2	Child complains about pain.
	Both complaints	2	Child complains about pain and about other things, e.g., "It hurts; I want mommy."
	Positive	0	Child makes any positive statement or talks about other things without complaint.
Torso	Neutral	1	Body (not limbs) is at rest; torso is inactive.
	Shifting	2	Body is in motion in a shifting or serpentine fashion.
	Tense	2	Body is arched or rigid.
	Shivering	2	Body is shuddering or shaking involuntarily.
	Upright	2	Child is in a vertical or upright position.
	Restrained	2	Body is restrained.
Touch	Not touching	1	Child is not touching or grabbing at wound.
	Reach	2	Child is reaching for but not touching wound.
	Touch	2	Child is gently touching wound or wound area.
	Grab	2	Child is grabbing vigorously at wound.
	Restrained	2	Child's arms are restrained.
Legs	Neutral	1	Legs may be in any position but are relaxed; includes gentle swimming or serpentine-like movements.
	Squirming/kicking	2	Definitive uneasy or restless movements in the legs and/or striking out with foot or feet.
	Drawn up/tensed	2	Legs tensed and/or pulled up tightly to body and kept there.
	Standing	2	Standing, crouching, or kneeling.
	Restrained	2	Child's legs are being held down.

Source: From "CHEOPS: A Behavorial Scale for Rating Postoperative Pain in Children" by P. McGrath et al., 1985, *Advances in Pain Research and Therapy, 9.* p. 396. Copyright 1985 by Raven Press. Reprinted by permission.

larly suited for the PICU population. Research into its use for PICU patients should be encouraged.

Physiological Measures of Pain

The initial response to acute pain frequently is activation of the sympathetic nervous system (SNS), which causes dilated pupils, perspiration, and changes in vital signs such as increased heart rate, myocardial contractility, blood pressure, and respiration. In addition, the parasympathetic nervous system (PNS) may respond to pain by causing nausea and vomiting. Because anxiety, fever, and other body responses to illness may influence the SNS and PNS, however, these responses are not considered unequivocally valid indicators of pain. Even so, they may be the only parameters available to assess. Consequently, PICU nurses frequently list evaluation of the child's vital signs as a factor influencing their decision to medicate the patient (Bradshaw & Zeanah, 1986; Burokas, 1985; Hudson, Torowicz, Mills, & Barnsterner, 1988).

Changes in a child's vital signs are not absolute indicators of pain. A possible method to validate the presence of pain would be to administer a test dose of analgesic appropriate to the situation when two or more vital sign changes that indicate pain are present. If signs or symptoms of pain abate, the nurse may deduce that pain was present. Orders for more frequent medication may be needed in such cases.

Patient Self-Report

Although report of pain by the patient is the most reliable and valid assessment of pain (Beyer & Byers, 1985), it may not always be possible for a PICU patient to use this subjective method. There are a number of self-report instruments or tools that may be feasible for use with many PICU patients; however.

The most widely tested and refined tool, the Oucher (Fig. 10-1), was developed by Beyer (1984). This tool provides two measure options: a series of six pictures denoting increasing pain intensity and a vertical numerical visual analogue scale (VAS; see Chapter 4 for description of VAS). If children can count to 100, they can use the VAS; if not, they use the picture scale. The Oucher has good content, construct, convergent, and discriminant validity (Aradine, Beyer, & Tompkins, 1988; Beyer, 1984; Beyer & Aradine, 1986, 1987, 1988). The Oucher is not suggested for use with children who are cognitively underdeveloped or semi-conscious, however. The tool has been used with children from 3 to 12 years old and with patients in PICUs.

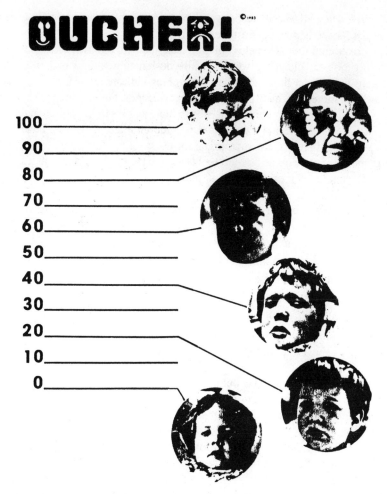

Figure 10-1 The Oucher. *Source:* Developed by Judith E. Beyer, RN, PhD. Copyright 1983 by The University of Virginia. Reprinted by permission.

Eland's (1985) color tool is another subjective, self-report pain tool that can be used in the PICU. The tool uses eight crayons and a body outline on which the child can report the location and, by the selection of color, the intensity of the hurt. When assessing pain, the child is asked to indicate the intensity and location of the pain by marking with the appropriate color on the area that hurts. The child develops this individual color scale by selecting different colors to represent increasing degrees of pain intensity (Eland, 1985). The nurse needs to question the child about whether the hurt is "right now" or from earlier in the day and why the area hurts. The child needs to be taught how to use this tool, preferably before surgery if its use is planned postoperatively.

The poker chip tool also helps children describe pain intensity (Hester, 1979). With this tool, the child is given four chips designating various pain intensities: One chip indicates a little bit of hurt, two chips indicate more hurt, three chips indicate still more hurt, and four chips indicate the most hurt possible. The child is instructed to use as many chips as needed to represent his or her present pain. The poker chip tool and Eland's color tool provide children something concrete to work with and therefore are appropriate for use with preschool children.

In conclusion, when a self-report tool is used in the PICU setting to assess pain, the nurse should keep in mind certain points:

- The child must be fully conscious, oriented, and recovered from the effects of anesthesia.
- Ideally, the child should be taught how to use the tool and practice using it before admission to the PICU.
- The child should be free of distraction while the tool is administered.
- No inferences should be given by adults.
- Terminology that the child can understand should be used.
- The results should be used in conjunction with parental impressions, the child's behaviors, and physiological signs of pain.

One caveat must be noted about use of these tools. Each of them assesses only one or two dimensions of pain (i.e., intensity and location). None addresses the qualitative characteristics of pain, that is the sensory, affective, and evaluative components of pain. Such a tool for children 8 to 17 years old has been developed and tested: The Pediatric Pain Questionnaire combines parts of the McGill Pain Questionnaire with child-oriented questions (Savedra, 1990).

Documentation of Pain in the PICU

As important as it is, documentation of pain and its management in the PICU appears to be difficult for nurses to incorporate into their charting (Davis, 1988). A feasible pain-management record that uses a flow sheet, which was developed from research findings (Craig et al., 1984; McGrath, Johnson, Goodman, Schillinger, Dunn, & Chapman, 1985) and empirical observations, is presented in Exhibit 10-1. This flow sheet consists of a simple checklist of assessment measures: behaviors, physiological parameters, self-reports, and analgesic administration and response record. In addition to improving documentation of the pain and the response to analgesics, this specific record can increase nurses' awareness of

Exhibit 10-1 Documentation Record

Date/POD# Time	Prior to Analgesic Administration					Analgesic Dose (AMT)	After Analgesic Adm. (During Peak Action)						Misc. Comments (LOC)
	Movement	Facial	Verbal	Physiologic HR BP R	Subjective Tool		Movement	Facial	Verbal	Physiologic HR BP R	Subjective Tool	

Movement

G = guarding
R = restless
Rb = rubbing

Facial

Gr = grimacing
Re = relaxed

Verbal

C = crying
M = moaning
S = screaming
C/O = complaining of pain

Physiological

HR
BP
R = respirations PaO$_2$
D = diaphoretic

Subjective Tools

CHEOPS
OUCHER
VAS
Poker Chip

if applicable
choose a tool
record the name
and score

children's pain. It is recommended that nurses facilitate the development of a pain flow sheet specifically designed for their units.

MANAGEMENT OF THE CHILD'S PAIN

Pharmacological Relief Measures

Because of the intensity of pain in PICU patients, narcotics are the most common analgesics administered. Mild analgesics have little use unless the child's stay has been prolonged beyond the normal recovery period and unless pain intensity is low to moderate. By far, IV administration of narcotics is superior to intramuscular administration because the onset of action is quicker and because problems associated with absorption are minimized. In addition, the fear of painful injections often leads children to deny pain; injections and IV insertions were identified as two of the most painful hospital experiences for children (Eland & Anderson, 1977; Tichy et al., 1988; Wong & Baker, 1988).

Morphine is probably the most common narcotic administered to children during the postoperative period. Meperidine also is commonly administered, but IV meperidine may cause central nervous system hyperirritability, seizures, and hallucinations from the accumulation of the active metabolite normeperidine (Foley, 1982).

Choosing the appropriate narcotic dosage for "as needed" use frequently is difficult. Dahlstrom, Bolme, Feychyting, Noack, and Paalzow (1979) found that the minimum morphine plasma concentration (in conjunction with nitrous oxide) necessary to suppress clinical signs of pain during surgery is 65 ng/mL. These investigators found no difference in morphine metabolism in children 1 month to 15 years of age. Because the initial distribution of morphine has a half-life of 2.5 minutes (meaning a rapid metabolism), attaining a constant blood concentration is nearly impossible. In addition, other investigators have found periodic IV morphine dosing to have only a 45-minute duration of effectiveness (Krane, Jacobson, Lynn, Parrot, & Tyler, 1987). Because morphine usually is prescribed every 2 to 4 hours, the patient cannot achieve continuous relief. For these reasons, continuous morphine infusions have gained popularity.

Bray (1983) and Lynn, Opheim, and Tyler (1984) studied the effects of continuous morphine infusion on postoperative pain in children and reported a significant reduction in pain with minimal side effects. Children 1 month to 15 years of age could be awakened easily and did not experience nausea nor itching. A few infants younger than 6 months developed irregular respiratory patterns that were reversed by decreasing the drip (Bray, 1983). Serum levels less than 30 ng/mL were not associated with increased carbon dioxide partial pressure, and weaning the children from the ventilators was not a problem (Lynn et al.,

1984). These findings challenge the appropriateness of withholding narcotics before extubation, which is a common practice. A suggested protocol for a morphine drip is to administer a bolus of 0.1 mg/kg and then to begin the infusion at 10 to 30 μg/kg/hour (Bray, 1983).

Another narcotic, fentanyl, is 50 to 100 times more potent than morphine and has fewer cardiovascular effects (Willis & Cousins, 1985). Hickey, Hansen, and Wessel (1984) found that a fentanyl dose of 25 μg/kg given to infants younger than 1 year blunted the stress responses of increasing pulmonary vascular resistance and increasing mean pulmonary artery pressure that often are seen with endotracheal suctioning. These investigators suggest that sudden death in PICUs associated with suctioning in this age group may be related to pulmonary stress response. In addition, because of its rapid distribution, fentanyl is best used as a continuous infusion (Willis & Cousins, 1985).

Respiratory depression is a major concern in pediatrics. All IV narcotics are capable of producing some degree of respiratory compromise, affecting the patient's respiratory rate, minute volume, and tidal volume. Respiratory depression with morphine is most likely to be seen within 7 minutes of IV, 30 minutes of intramuscular, and 90 minutes of subcutaneous injection (Schechter, 1985).

Epidural administration of narcotics can provide continuous, intense analgesia that is not usually associated with central nervous system depression. Several studies have shown that epidurally administered morphine can provide safe and reliable analgesia in pediatric postsurgical patients (Glenski, Warner, Dawson, & Kaufman, 1984; Krane et al., 1987; Shapiro, Jedeikin, Shalev, & Hoffman, 1984). Although drug dosages vary according to the type of drug and the size of the child, Glenski et al. (1984) found that morphine doses greater than 0.1 mg/kg do not increase the duration of analgesia but significantly increase the side effects. Onset of effect for epidural morphine is noted at 30 ± 12 minutes, and the duration of effect is 19.5 ± 8 hours (Attia, Ecoffey, Sandouk, Gross, & Samii, 1986).

Potential side effects of epidural analgesia include nausea, pruritis, urinary retention, and respiratory depression (Leib & Hurtig, 1985). Major benefits listed are improved quality of pain relief with lower total morphine requirements compared with IV administration, improved pulmonary function, and early ambulation (Glenski et al., 1984) (see Chapter 7 for a more detailed discussion of epidural analgesia).

Nonpharmacological Relief Measures

Various nonpharmacological techniques for pain management can be taught to children and parents to help reduce children's anxiety and pain. These include distraction, relaxation techniques, rhythmic breathing, and cutaneous stimulation.

Allowing the child to regain control by encouraging participation in these techniques may shift the focus from the pain and lead to a relaxed state.

Distraction for the young child can be accomplished through play or by providing a brightly colored mobile. Distraction tends to be more effective when all the senses are involved (McCaffery, 1977). For example, distraction in conjunction with topical anesthetic has been useful for injection pain (Eland, 1981b). Music has been shown to be both distracting and helpful in reducing pain and anxiety. Songs appropriate to the age group have been used to decrease distress during cardiac catheterization (Claire & Erickson, 1986).

Progressive relaxation, such as tensing and relaxing large muscle groups, in conjunction with rhythmic breathing is more suitable for the school-aged child who has the ability for increased concentration. Simple rhythmic breathing such as saying "he" on inspiration and "ho" on expiration can be taught to toddlers.

Cutaneous stimulation, such as by rubbing, is a technique used instinctively by children and parents. Fears that frequency of touch increases intracranial and blood pressures in critically ill children have been shown to be unfounded (Mitchell, Habermann-Little, Johnson, Van Inwegen-Scott, & Tyler, 1985); nurses therefore should not refrain from using touch to relieve pain. Changing the child's position every 2 hours relieves tense, tired muscles. In addition, supporting children in a comfortable position (e.g., on the side with hands crossed over the torso) enhances a feeling of security. Intubated infants may even be placed on their stomachs.

CASE STUDY AND CONCLUSION

In conclusion, to achieve an integrated approach for managing pain in the PICU, health professionals can construct a pain-management protocol applicable to their units. Such a protocol may be based on the following goals (Abu-Saad & Tesler, 1986): (1) clarification by health professionals of their beliefs about the reality and individuality of the patient's pain; (2) increased knowledge of pain in particular settings and situations, such as the PICU; (3) adoption or adaptation of appropriate assessment tools; (4) increased knowledge of pain-relief measures; and (5) implementation of pain management as an integral part of patient care. Additional goals may include implementation of nonpharmacological methods to relieve pain and anxiety, incorporation of preoperative teaching about assessment tools, and individualization of nursing care plans that reflect specific relief measures.

The following case study illustrates the challenge of appropriate pain management for a critically ill child.

K., an 18-month-old, 15-kg boy, was admitted to the PICU after repair of a ventricular septal defect. He was intubated and had a chest tube inserted during surgery. One hour after admission he became tachycardic. His blood pressure increased, and he was diaphoretic, wide-eyed, and thrashing. His capillary refill, liver margin, and hematocrit remained stable, however, suggesting adequate cardiac output and fluid balance. IV morphine (1.5 mg, 0.1 mg/kg) was given, whereupon his vital signs returned to normal. One hour later he again showed signs of pain. Nevertheless, the frequency of his pain medication order was 1.5 mg every 3 to 4 hours.

K.'s nurse obtained an order for diazepam, which sedated the child but did not relieve his restless movements. During the night the morphine and diazepam were given only when K. thrashed so much that there was concern that he would remove his tubes. In the morning the physician wrote an order to hold all K.'s sedative and narcotics in preparation for extubation. During the next 2 hours before extubation he was wide-eyed, thrashing, and tachycardic.

Immediately after K. was extubated, he fell asleep. The morphine order was resumed but at only 0.05 mg/kg every 4 hours as needed. During the next few days K. continued to have periods of increased respiration with splinting, extreme fussiness, crying, and refusing to drink. While sleeping, he remained in a guarded position.

This case clearly illustrates that K. had some observable signs of pain: thrashing, tachycardia, diaphoresis, wide-eyed expression, fussiness, and refusal to drink. The morphine order obviously was inadequate because the duration of action of IV morphine is about 45 minutes. The nurses incorrectly believed that, when sleeping, the child was not in pain. In reality, he probably was exhausted from the pain. In addition, the nurses medicated only when the child was extremely agitated; they did not anticipate pain and medicate before the pain became severe. A more prudent and physiologically safe as well as humane approach to pain management for K. certainly was indicated. This approach would have been an IV morphine drip tapered slowly or morphine administered via an epidural catheter.

REFERENCES

Abu-Saad, H. (1984). Assessing children's response to pain. *Pain, 19*, 163–171.

Abu-Saad, H., & Tesler, M. (1986). Pain. In V. Carrieri, A. Lindsey, & C. West (Eds.), *Pathophysiological phenomena in nursing: Human response to illness* (pp. 235–269). Philadelphia: Saunders.

Aradine C., Beyer, J., & Tompkins, J. (1988). Children's pain perception before and after analgesia: A study of instrument construct validity and related issues. *Journal of Pediatric Nursing, 3*, 11–23.

Attia, J., Ecoffey, C., Sandouk, P., Gross, J., & Samii, K. (1986). Epidural morphine in children: Pharmacokinetics and CO_2 sensitivity. *Anesthesiology, 65*, 590–594.

Beyer, J. (1984). *The Oucher: A user's manual and technical report.* Evanston, IL: Hospital Play Equipment.

Beyer, J., & Aradine, C. (1986). Content validity of an instrument to measure young children's perceptions of the intensity of their pain. *Journal of Pediatric Nursing, 1,* 386–395.

Beyer, J., & Aradine, C. (1987). Patterns of pediatric pain intensity: A methodological investigation of a self-report scale. *Clinical Journal of Pain, 3,* 130–141.

Beyer, J., & Aradine, C. (1988). The convergent and discriminant validity of a self-report measure of pain intensity for children. *Children's Health Care, 16,* 274–282.

Beyer, J., & Byers, M. (1985). Knowledge of pediatric pain: The state of the art. *Children's Health Care, 13,* 150–159.

Beyer, J., DeGood, D., Ashley, L., & Russel, G. (1983). Patterns of postoperative analgesic use with adults and children following cardiac surgery. *Pain, 17,* 71–81.

Bradshaw, C., & Zeanah, P. (1986). Pediatric nurses' assessment of pain in children. *Journal of Pediatric Nursing, 1,* 314–322.

Bray, R. (1983). Postoperative analgesia provided by morphine infusion in children. *Anesthesia, 38,* 1075–1078.

Broome, M. (1985). The child in pain: A model for assessment and intervention. *Critical Care Quarterly, 8,* 47–55.

Burokas, L. (1985). Factors affecting nurses' decisions to medicate pediatric patients after surgery. *Heart & Lung, 14,* 373–378.

Claire, J., & Erickson, S. (1986). Reducing distress in pediatric patients undergoing cardiac catheterization. *Children's Health Care, 14,* 146–152.

Craig, K., McMahon, R., Morison, J., & Zaskow, C. (1984). Development changes in infant pain expression during immunization injections. *Social Science Medicine, 19,* 1331–1337.

Dahlstrom, B., Bolme, P., Feychyting, H., Noack, G., & Paalzow, L. (1979). Morphine kinetics in children. *Clinical Pharmacology and Therapeutics, 26,* 354–365.

D'Apolito, J. (1984). The neonate's response to pain. *Maternal Child Nursing, 9,* 250–264.

Davis, K. (1988). *Postoperative pain in toddlers: Nurses' assessment and intervention.* Unpublished manuscript.

Eland, J. (1981a). Pain. In L. Hart, J. Reese, & M. Fearing (Eds.), *Concepts common to acute illness: Identification and management* (pp. 164–196). St. Louis, MO: Mosby.

Eland, J. (1981b). Minimizing pain associated with prekindergarten intramuscular injections. *Issues in Comprehensive Pediatric Nursing, 5,* 361–372.

Eland, J. (1985). The role of the nurse in children's pain. In L. Copp (Ed.), *Recent advances in nursing: Perspectives on pain* (pp. 29–45). London: Churchill Livingstone.

Eland, J., & Anderson, J. (1977). The experience of pain in children. In A. Jacox (Ed.), *Pain: A source book for nurses and other health professionals* (pp. 453–473). Boston: Little, Brown.

Favaloro, R. (1988). Adolescent development and implications for pain management. *Pediatric Nursing, 14,* 27–29.

Foley, K. (1982). The practical use of narcotic analgesics. *Medical Clinics of North America, 66,* 1091–1104.

Glenski, J., Warner, M., Dawson, B., & Kaufman, B. (1984). Postoperative use of epidurally administered morphine in children and adolescents. *Mayo Clinic Proceedings, 59,* 530–533.

Hazinski, M. (1984). Children are different. In M. Hazinski (Ed.), *Nursing care of the critically ill child* (pp. 1–11). St. Louis, MO: Mosby.

Hester, N. (1979). The preoperational child's reaction to immunization. *Nursing Research, 28,* 250–255.

Hickey, P., Hansen, D., & Wessel, D. (1984). Responses to high dose fentanyl in infants. *Anesthesiology, 61,* A445.

Hilgard, J., & Le Baron, S. (1982). Relief of anxiety and pain in children and adolescents with cancer. *International Journal of Clinical and Experimental Hypnosis, 30,* 417–442.

Hudson, D., Torowicz, D., Mills, B., & Barnsterner, J. (1988). *Assessment and intervention for pain in young children.* Manuscript submitted for publication.

Izard, C., Huebner, D., Risser, D., McGinnes, G., & Dougherty, (1980). The young infant's ability to produce discrete emotion expressions. *Developmental Psychology, 16*(2), 132–140.

Johnston, C., & Strada, M. (1986). Acute pain response in infants: A multidimensional description. *Pain, 24,* 373–382.

Krane, F., Jacobson, L., Lynn, A., Parrot, C., & Tyler, D. (1987). Caudal morphine for postoperative analgesia in children. *Anesthesia and Analgesia, 66,* 647–653.

Leib, R., & Hurtig, J. (1985). Epidural and intrathecal narcotics for pain management. *Heart & Lung, 14,* 164–173.

Levy, D. (1960). The infant's earliest memory in inoculation: A contribution to public health procedures. *Journal of Genetic Psychology, 96,* 3–46.

Lewandowski, L. (1984). Psychological aspect of pediatric critical care. In M. Hazinski (Ed.), *Nursing care of the critically ill child* (pp. 12–62), St. Louis, MO: Mosby.

Lisson, E. (1987). Ethical issues related to pain control. *Nursing Clinics of North America, 22,* 649.

Lynn, A., Opheim, K., & Tyler, D. (1984). Morphine infusion after pediatric cardiac surgery. *Critical Care Medicine, 12,* 863–866.

McCaffery, M. (1977). Pain relief for the child. *Pediatric Nursing,* July/August 11–17.

McGrath, P., Johnson, G., Goodman, J., Schillinger, J., Dunn, J., & Chapman, J. (1985). CHEOPS: A behavioral scale for rating postoperative pain in children. *Advances in Pain Research and Therapy, 9,* 395–402.

Melzack, R., & Wall, P. (1983). *The challenge of pain.* New York: Basic Books.

Mitchell, P., Habermann-Little, B., Johnson, F., VanInwegen-Scott, D., & Tyler, D. (1985). Critically ill children: The importance of touch in a high-technology environment. *Nursing Administration Quarterly, 9,* 38–46.

Ross, D., & Ross, S. (eds). (1988). Child's view. In *Childhood pain* (pp. 35–75). Baltimore: Urban & Schwarzenberg.

Savedra, M. (1990). *Pediatric pain questionnaire.* San Francisco: University of California, Department of Family Health Care Nursing.

Savedra, M., Gibbons, D., Tesler, M., Ward, J., & Wegner, C. (1982). How do children describe pain? A tentative assessment. *Pain, 14,* 95–104.

Schechter, N. (1985). Pain and pain control in children. *Current Problems in Pediatrics, 15,* 6–66.

Schechter, N., Allen, D., & Hanson, K. (1986). Status of pediatric pain control: A comparison of hospital analgesic usage in children and adults. *Pediatrics, 77,* 11–15.

Shapiro, L., Jedeikin, R., Shalev, D., & Hoffman, S. (1984). Epidural morphine analgesia in children. *Anesthesiology, 61,* 210–212.

Taylor, P. (1983). Post-operative pain in toddler and pre-school age children. *Maternal Child Nursing, 12,* 35–50.

Tesler, M., Wegner, C., Savedra, M., Gibbons, P., & Ward, J. (1981). Coping strategies of children in pain. *Issues in Comprehensive Pediatric Nursing, 5,* 351–359.

Tichy, A., Braam, C., Meyer, T., & Rattan, N. (1988). Stressors in pediatric intensive care units. *Pediatric Nursing, 14*, 40–42.

Weis, O., Sriwatanakul, K., Alloza, J., Weintraub, M., & Lasagna, L. (1983). Attitudes of patients, housestaff and nurses toward postoperative analgesic care. *Anesthesia and Analgesia, 62*, 70–74.

Willis, R., & Cousins, M. (1985). Pain relief in acute care. *Persistent Pain, 5*, 33–63.

Wong, D., & Baker, C. (1988). Pain in children: Comparison of assessment scales. *Pediatric Nursing, 14*, 9–16.

RECOMMENDED READING

Abu-Saad, H. (1984). Cultural group indicators of pain in children. *Children's Health Care, 13*, 187–196.

Beyer, J., & Levin, C. (1987). Issues and advances in pain control in children. *Nursing Clinics of North America, 22*, 601–676.

Ferguson, C. (1987). Childhood coping: Adaptive behavior during intensive care hospitalization. *Critical Care Quarterly, 4*, 81–93.

Rennick, J. (1980). Reestablishing the parental role in pediatric intensive care units. *Journal of Pediatric Nursing, 1*, 40–44.

Stevens, B., Hunsberger, M., & Browne, O. (1987). Pain in children: Theoretical, research and practice dilemmas. *Journal of Pediatric Nursing, 2*, 154–166.

Chapter 11

Pain in the Patient with Acute Myocardial Ischemia

Marilyn Kuhel Douglas

The pain of acute myocardial ischemia has two serious consequences. Not only does it affect the comfort and well-being of the patient, but it also causes the injured organ to work harder and faster as a result of the sympathetic response to pain in general. Both tachycardia and the rise in systemic blood pressure demand more oxygen of the already compromised heart. This increased demand for oxygen may exacerbate both the ischemia and its accompanying risks.

Because myocardial ischemia is associated with the risk of infarction, dysrhythmias, and sudden death, careful evaluation and timely, appropriate treatment of this pain are crucial. Whether in the emergency department, coronary care unit, or medical or surgical intensive care unit, the nurse as the health care team member most accessible to the patient ultimately is responsible for the continuous diagnosis and treatment of the patient's pain.

In recognition of this responsibility, this chapter describes the various clinical presentations of acute myocardial ischemia for use in assessment, traces the path of its pain stimulus to the central nervous system and back, and outlines nursing measures to manage this pain.

DEFINITIONS OF MYOCARDIAL ISCHEMIC PAIN

The pain of myocardial ischemia has been described in various ways, but it is identified primarily by a characteristic pattern of intensity, duration, and precipitating and relieving factors. This syndrome was first described as angina pectoris, or "strangling in the chest," by Heberden in 1772.

Stable Angina Pectoris

Today, the classic presentation of angina still contains the essential elements of this original description. Angina pectoris is now generally defined as a syndrome

175

characterized by the onset of episodes of dull, retrosternal pressure or pain that occasionally radiates to the left upper extremity or adjacent areas; usually it is initiated by exercise, emotion, or other causes and is relieved by rest or nitrates. If there have been no changes in its frequency, duration, or precipitating causes within the last 60 days, this type of angina is classified as stable (Hurst, 1982).

The location, radiation, intensity, character, and duration of anginal pain can have wide variability, although description of the pain in a given individual usually is consistent. The pain commonly is located at or behind the middle or upper third of the sternum and is centered at the level of the third or fourth rib. On occasion, the pain can occupy the entire precordium or even be localized on the right.

The pattern of radiation frequently extends to adjacent areas, especially when the pain is severe. These areas can include the neck, both arms, shoulders, jaw, throat, and teeth. Sometimes it may even be predominantly manifested between the scapulae. In its most characteristic form, however, the pain radiates across the precordium to the left shoulder and upper arm and frequently extends to the elbow, wrist, or fingers. The intensity of the pain also may vary from mild to moderate to severe. The pain of stable angina usually is rated as moderate.

The character of the pain also is described in many ways. Words frequently used to describe this sensation include squeezing, constricting, and choking; it may be likened to pressure, a vice or band around the chest, or a weight on the chest. Others have described it as discomfort, a dull pain, constant pain, or a sensation similar to heartburn. For many, especially when the pain is severe, this feeling is accompanied by a vague, indescribable feeling of distress.

The duration of the anginal episode is usually 1 to 3 minutes; it may persist for up to 30 minutes but rarely lasts longer. Although the character, radiation, and location of anginal pain can be diverse, precipitation by exercise or emotional stress and rapid relief by rest are the cardinal features of angina pectoris.

Unstable Angina

Unstable angina is the term used to describe various anginal symptoms, such as those that occur for the first time or have been present for less than 60 days, or when there is a change in the frequency, duration, or precipitating factors of previously stable angina. Other terms used to describe this situation are preinfarction angina, crescendo angina, and acute coronary insufficiency. The symptoms of unstable angina closely resemble those of acute myocardial infarction (AMI). The pain or discomfort usually lasts longer and is more severe than that of stable exertional angina and is difficult to relieve with nitroglycerin.

Variant (Prinzmetal's) Angina

A third subset of angina is Prinzmetal's or variant angina. In this case, the anginal symptoms typically occur at rest (rather than during exercise), at night, or at the same time each day. The electrocardiographic characteristics of Prinzmetal's angina include ST segment elevation, transient Q waves, and occasionally atrioventricular block (Prinzmetal, Kennamer, Merliss, Wada, & Bor, 1959). Angiographic studies have shown this syndrome to be due to coronary artery spasm both with and without fixed atherosclerotic lesions (Hurst, 1985).

Acute Myocardial Infarction

The pain of AMI is usually identical in nature to that of angina pectoris, but the pain lasts longer (i.e., for hours to days), is more intense, is unrelieved by rest or nitrates, and may be accompanied by nausea, vomiting, and diaphoresis. Serial electrocardiograms and serum creatine kinase levels are needed for the diagnosis of AMI to be substantiated.

Acute Compared to Chronic Pain

The distinction between acute and chronic pain is necessary not only to understand the progression of pathology but also for the recognition of psychological symptoms or disorders. This is particularly important in the case of myocardial ischemic pain because it has both acute and chronic elements.

Severe, acute pain, such as the type seen with an AMI, usually is accompanied by situational anxiety and the signs of sympathetic stimulation. In contrast, chronic pain, such as with stable angina, more often is accompanied by depression, increased somatization, and irritability (Merskey, 1986). These psychological symptoms are seen as consequences of the pain and usually abate with pain reduction. Neuroticism also is found to be elevated in chronic pain patients, but this too decreases with pain reduction (Sternbach & Timmermans, 1975). When the patient has an underlying depression or anxiety disorder, however, these symptoms may be exacerbated in the event of pain.

SENSATION OF MYOCARDIAL ISCHEMIC PAIN

When pain is described in terms of physiological concepts, it is defined as a sensory response to noxious stimuli or tissue damage (National Institutes of Health, 1986; Perl, 1984; Zimmerman, 1984). Nociception is the term used to describe the neural processes involved in the recognition of painful stimuli (Sherrington, 1906). Currently, an afferent sensory neuron is defined as nociceptive if it shows a strong response to stimuli that produce pain in humans and the equivalent reactions in animals (i.e., retreat, defense reflexes, and vocalization; Mense, 1983).

Peripheral Pain Receptors

In the viscera, the nociceptors lie in the organs themselves. Specifically, in the heart the sympathetic nervous system serves as the primary pathway for the afferent nociceptive impulses. Hence cardiac pain impulses originate at the terminal sympathetic receptor sites in the myocardium.

Nociceptive Stimuli

The nociceptors in visceral organs, such as the intestines and heart, respond to ischemia, spasm, distention, and stretching. They differ from cutaneous tissue nociceptors in that they are not sensitive to cutting, heat, and cold.

The most typical cardiac pain is due to acute irreversible ischemia (AMI) or recurrent reversible ischemia (angina pectoris). Its pathophysiology has been ascribed to at least two mechanisms: the action of chemically noxious stimuli on the myocardial nociceptors, and the mechanical stimulation of these receptors by increased diastolic pressure in the left ventricle during an anginal episode.

Chemical Stimuli

A wide variety of chemical substances have been implicated in the initiation of a nociceptive response. In vascular and myocardial ischemia, these include the following: increased concentrations of extracellular hydrogen and potassium ions, lactic acid, endogenous catecholamines, proteolytic enzymes, histamines, serotonin, and kinins such as bradykinin and prostaglandins (Afifi & Bergman, 1986; Chaudry, 1985; Mela, 1982; Sobel, 1985; Zimmerman, 1984).

Animal studies of myocardial ischemia show an accumulation of hydrogen ions and a significant reduction in intracellular stores of glycogen within 30 to 60 seconds of coronary ligation. In normal states, glucose and free fatty acids provide the heart with a source of energy in the form of adenosine triphosphate (ATP). Large amounts are used to provide metabolic energy for the contractile activity of the heart. In the event of ischemia, however, glucose delivery is reduced, and energy production is changed to the much less efficient mechanism of the anaerobic pathway, with severely reduced amounts of ATP being produced. Lactic acid accumulates as a by-product of anaerobic glycolysis, and the resultant acidosis contributes to further cell function depression, such as decreased myocardial contractility (Chaudry, 1983; Kubler & Spieckermann, 1970).

Within minutes of coronary occlusion, marked electrolyte imbalances also occur in the myocardium as a result of changes in cell membrane permeability. Animal experiments have demonstrated acute increases in the potassium levels of the coronary sinus blood draining the ischemic area (Jennings, Baum, & Herdson, 1965). The lack of ATP to drive the sodium-potassium pump causes large amounts of intracellular potassium to be lost.

Ischemia provokes a local activation of kinins and serotonin, both of which are powerful vasoactive and pain-producing substances. Serotonin, in particular, plays an important role in circulatory disorders such as myocardial thrombosis. In such states, serotonin is released from the platelets that are aggregated at the site of the thrombosis. Furthermore, both bradykinin and serotonin potentiate the pain-producing activity of histamines and potassium (Del Bianco, Del Bene, & Sicuteri, 1974).

The precise mechanism by which these noxious stimuli activate the nociceptors is not fully understood. It is hypothesized, however, that these substances accumulate during ischemia and cause capillary damage and pain. Because of the lack of an adequate blood flow, they are not diluted and removed from the ischemic zone. Subsequently, these accumulated substances cause a change in membrane permeability of the nociceptors. The resulting influx of positive ions raises the membrane potential to the threshold level, thus initiating an action potential along the neuron.

Mechanical Stimuli

Although cardiac afferent nerves contain both thinly myelinated and unmyelinated fibers, most of the cardiac sensory activity observed thus far arises from activity in the thinly myelinated Aδ fibers. These fibers also respond to direct mechanical pressure during the normal course of the cardiac cycle (Brown, 1967; Brown & Malliani, 1971; Uchida & Murao, 1974).

During coronary occlusion and myocardial ischemia, the activity of the cardiac mechanoreceptors reportedly increases significantly. It is postulated that dilation of the ventricles and the mechanical stimulation caused by increased left ventricular pressure account for this activity.

Summary

In summary, although the precise characteristics of the nociceptors involved in myocardial ischemic pain remain uncertain (Perl, 1984), strong chemical and

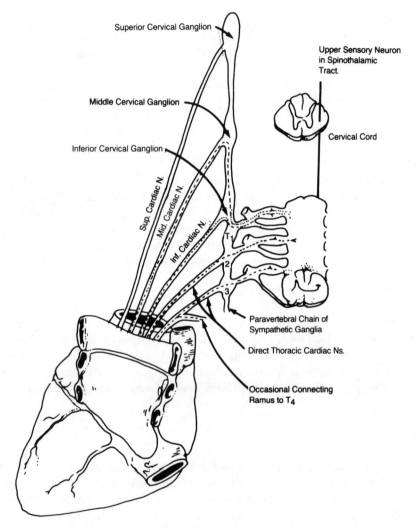

Figure 11-1 Diagrammatic representation of the cardiac pain pathways. Pain from coronary insufficiency in the left ventricle tends to follow this course, with a simple arrangement on the opposite side for conduction of pain from the right ventricle. *Source:* From "Cardiac Pain: Anatomic Pathways and Physiological Mechanisms," by J.C. White, 1957, *Circulation, 16*, p. 646. Copyright 1957 by Grune and Stratton, Inc. Reprinted by permission.

mechanical stimuli have been implicated as the initiators of the nociceptive activity in the myocardium. Much of the pain research devoted to peripheral nociception has focused on cutaneous tissue rather than the visceral organs and on peripheral vascular ischemic pain more than myocardial ischemic pain. The

Figure 11-1 continued

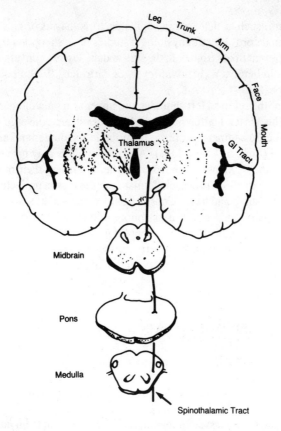

degree of similarity in the phenomena, however, has led to inferred similarities in their physiological mechanisms.

Central Transmission and Integration

After an action potential has been initiated at the terminal receptor sites, it travels toward the spinal cord by way of afferent sensory fibers. Cardiac afferent fibers pass through the sympathetic ganglia before terminating in the dorsal horn of the spinal cord at the level of T-1 through T-3 or T-4. From the dorsal horn the impulse travels up the spinothalamic tract until it reaches the thalamus. Figure 11-1 illustrates the pathway of the pain impulse from the heart to the brain (White, 1957).

Referred Pain

Referred pain, such as that seen in angina pectoris, has its origins in the dorsal horn of the spinal cord. Electrophysiologic studies have supported the hypothesis that sensory afferent fibers from both the skin and the viscera converge on the same spinal neurons in lamina V (Fields, Meyer, & Partridge, 1970; Pomeranz, Wall, & Weber, 1968).

In the case of the referred left shoulder and upper arm pain of angina, the axon terminals of the visceral afferent fibers from the heart converge at the same thoracic spinal cord segments as those from the left shoulder and arm and other thoracic viscera (Figs. 11-2 and 11-3). Also, these fibers may turn up or down a segment before they synapse in the cord, further confusing their origin.

The line of demarcation from each dermatome (the region projecting from each dorsal root) is not sharp and fixed. Considerable overlap exists among the regions. Such overlap explains the variable descriptions of referred anginal pain, such as to the jaw, arms, and shoulders. Because these dorsal cells are more often activated by cutaneous input, the brain misinterprets the discharge as arising from the cutaneous receptors, giving rise to the perception of pain in these areas (Carpenter, 1984).

AUTONOMIC RESPONSE TO PAIN

A major physiological response to pain is the activation of the autonomic nervous system. In the heart, this system serves as the conduit for afferent pain impulses from the heart as well as the efferent route for the sympathetic response back to the heart (Fig. 11-4).

The autonomic nervous system regulates cardiac function from numerous sites and has the ability to initiate a coordinated reaction, such as the fight-or-flight sympathetic response, when intense noxious stimuli are registered. Stimulation of the sympathetic response elicits multiple physiological changes, which contribute to many of the overt signs and symptoms observed during anginal ischemic pain.

Sites of Influence

The spinal autonomic reflex arc is an example of the first and simplest connection between the cardiac afferent and efferent neurons. Myocardial nociceptive impulses are transmitted through the afferent fibers to the dorsal horn of the spinal cord. There they synapse at two points: first with the interneurons and then with the preganglionic fibers of the efferent sympathetic neurons. Their axons exit by way of the ventral horn and terminate in the thoracic sympathetic ganglia. A third

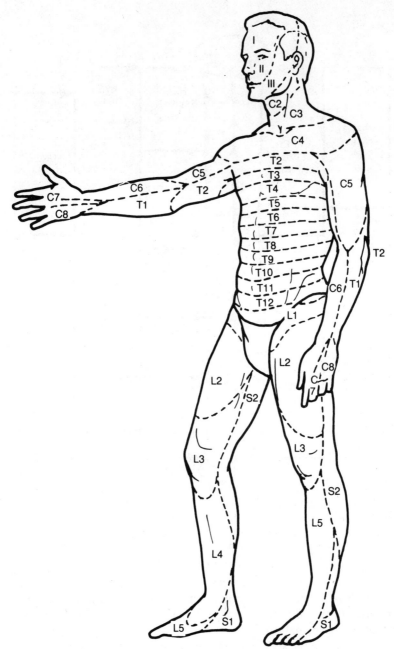

Figure 11-2 Segmental innervation of the skin dermatomes. Each dorsal (sensory) spinal root innervates one dermatome. *Source:* From *The Human Nervous System: Basic Principles of Neurobiology*, 3rd ed., (p. 156) by C.R. Noback and R.J. Demarest, 1981, New York, NY: McGraw-Hill, Inc. Copyright 1981 by McGraw-Hill, Inc. Reprinted by permission.

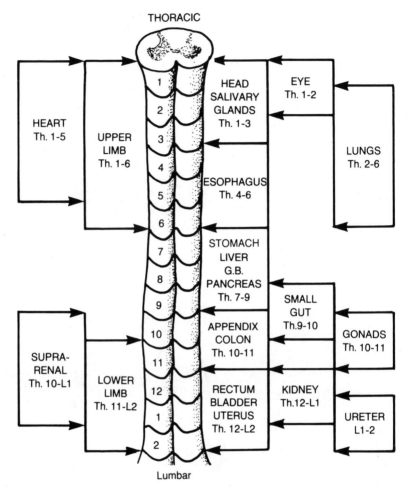

Figure 11-3 Relationships among the spinal levels of various sympathetic nervous system connector cells. Note that the sympathetic innervation of the heart overlaps with that of the upper limbs, head, lungs, and esophagus. *Source:* From *Anatomy, Regional and Applied*, 7th ed., (p. 35) by R.J. Last, 1984, Edinburgh, Scotland: Longman Group Ltd. Copyright 1984 by Longman Group Ltd. Reprinted by permission.

synapse in these autonomic ganglia transmits the impulse along the postganglionic sympathetic fibers, ultimately terminating in their effector sites, such as the sinoatrial node or myofibrils.

Four types of spinal reflex arcs are shown in Fig. 11-5. The route for the sympathetic response to myocardial pain is represented as the visceroautonomic reflex (example 4).

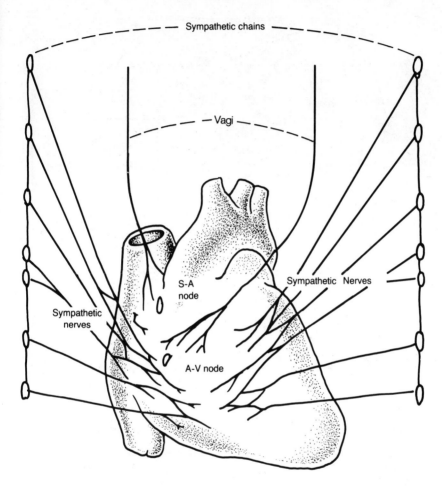

Figure 11-4 The cardiac nerves. *Source:* From *Basic Human Neurophysiology*, 3rd ed., (p. 66) by A.G. Guyton, 1981, Philadelphia, PA: W.B. Saunders Company. Copyright 1981 by W.B. Saunders Company. Reprinted by permission.

Autonomic influence on cardiac function also originates from the brainstem and higher centers. The vasomotor center, located in the lower third of the pons and upper two-thirds of the medulla, controls vascular tone, heart rate, and myocardial contractility. This center, in turn, is influenced by widespread areas in the cerebral cortex and the limbic system, where emotional behavior, memory, and the integration of homeostatic processes (such as the fight-or-flight sympathetic response) occur.

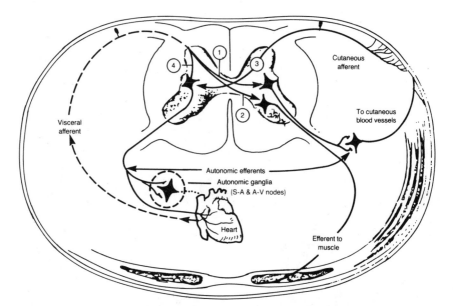

Figure 11-5 Synaptic connections joining autonomic and somatic efferents and somatic and visceral afferents in the spinal cord to form reflex arcs. (1) Viscerocutaneous reflex, (2) viscerosomatic reflex, (3) cutaneovisceral reflex, (4) visceroautonomic reflex. Interneurons in the spinal cord have been omitted. *Source:* From *Fundamentals of Neurophysiology*, 3rd ed., (p. 240) by R.F. Schmidt (Ed.), 1985, New York, NY: Springer-Verlag. Copyright 1985 by Springer-Verlag. Reprinted by permission.

The hypothalamus also plays a central role in integrating the autonomic response, although the exact mechanism of this integration remains unknown. The physiological explanation of how emotions, such as the fear and anxiety observed with acute myocardial ischemic pain, influence autonomic response has not been outlined.

Mechanism of Autonomic Influence

Stimulation of the sympathetic system results in the release of neurotransmitters from the terminal fibers of the postganglionic neurons. In the heart, these β-adrenergic receptors are stimulated by the catecholamine norepinephrine.

Catecholamines such as epinephrine and norepinephrine also are released from the adrenal medulla when sympathetic stimulation occurs. They act to reinforce the effects of the sympathetic neurons on the heart and other organs, but the primary function of adrenal catecholamines is the mobilization of glucose and fatty acids to provide the fuel for increased activity.

Autonomic Response Pattern

Sympathetic stimulation of the heart causes multiple effects: an increase in sinus node discharge rate, faster atrioventricular conduction, increased automaticity, greater myofibril shortening, and increased arterial constriction (Braunwald, 1980). These increase myocardial oxygen demand and aggravate the supply-demand imbalance present during myocardial ischemia and AMI.

Clinically, the cardiac response to sympathetic stimulation is reflected in an increase in heart rate, an increased tendency to ventricular ectopy, and an increase in systemic blood pressure. Additional physiological signs of sympathetic stimulation, which also often accompany the pain of AMI, include the following: increased respiratory rate and depth, diaphoresis, dilation of the pupils, decreased gastric motility, and increased skeletal muscle tension.

Many of these cardiovascular and other physiological changes observed after sympathetic stimulation also are evident during myocardial ischemic pain. Effective pain management aimed at decreasing the sympathetic input to the cardiovascular system results in a decrease in myocardial oxygen demand and restoration of a more optimal supply-demand ratio.

NURSING THERAPIES

"Nursing is the diagnosis and treatment of human responses to actual or potential health problems" (American Nurses' Association, 1980, p. 9). Pain, especially in the case of acute myocardial ischemia, most often is a warning to the individual that an actual or potential health problem exists. Therefore, the management of that pain is a nursing function.

Analgesia Administration

The pain of AMI, especially in the early stages, is usually considered severe. Morphine sulfate is the narcotic analgesic drug of choice for this pain. Doses of 2 to 10 mg given intravenously at 5- to 15-minute intervals are titrated until pain relief is achieved safely (Bergersen, 1979).

Besides its central effect on pain relief, morphine has the additional benefit of decreasing myocardial oxygen demand by lowering both preload and afterload. By increasing venous capacitance, morphine reduces venous return and thereby decreases preload. Left ventricular afterload is reduced because of morphine's effect on lowering systemic vascular resistance. Evidence of this effect is seen in the transient drop in blood pressure after administration and also in the toxic side effect of hypotension.

Sublingual nitroglycerin (glyceryl trinitrate) is another drug used for the relief of anginal pain. The effectiveness of nitroglycerin is attributed to two actions: peripheral and coronary vasodilation (Bernstein, Friesinger, & Lichtlen, 1966) and, probably more significant, a decrease in preload due to dilation of the peripheral venous system and reduced venous return. The resultant increased coronary blood flow, accompanied by decreased myocardial consumption, may contribute to reestablishing the balance between myocardial oxygen supply and demand and hence will relieve the pain.

Nitroglycerin also can be administered intravenously if the patient's pain is not alleviated after morphine sulfate and large doses of sublingual nitroglycerin. An infusion of 25 mg of nitroglycerin (Tridil, 5 mL) diluted in a 250-mL solution (100 μg/mL) is begun at 10 to 20 μg/min. The flow rate is increased by 5 μg/min every 5 minutes for the first 15 to 20 minutes until pain relief is achieved (Guzzetta & Dossey, 1984).

The onset of action of intravenous nitroglycerin occurs within 30 to 60 seconds. Therefore, each time the flow rate is changed, the patient's blood pressure, heart rate, and, if possible, pulmonary capillary wedge pressure and cardiac output should be measured. Frequent monitoring of these hemodynamic parameters should continue throughout the course of the infusion.

Anxiety Reduction

Anxiety frequently accompanies the pain of myocardial ischemia because of its meaning and significance. The fear of impending death as well as the alien intensive care or critical care environment significantly contribute to this anxious state.

Anxiety is detrimental in the situation of myocardial ischemia because it provokes the sympathetic response. Anxiety-reducing measures may offset this response, which places such a heavy demand on the heart.

During the initial, most acute phase of myocardial ischemic pain, anxiety may be decreased by utilizing such measures as reassurance, support, assistance with slow-breathing techniques, and teaching about angina. If the patient remains anxious, audio or visual tapes with music can be used in the critical care unit. Such therapies as imagery and relaxation techniques also may be useful if the nurse feels confident in his or her ability to instruct the patient in these techniques.

Control of the Environment

To reduce the sympathetic response to pain, stress-producing stimuli should be removed from the environment as much as possible. A quiet, dimly lit room is optimal for patients with acute myocardial ischemia. The number of family visits should be limited to achieve the best balance between the stimulation of the visitors and the anxiety-reducing effect that they may have on the patient.

The patients themselves need to be able to control their environment as much as possible. Placing sublingual nitroglycerin at the bedside may give patients a sense of control over their own pain relief. Involving the patient in the planning of daily routines and sleep periods is another means of allowing some control.

Sleep, a restorative process, is interrupted by the pain and anxiety of acute myocardial ischemia. The deprivation of sleep caused by the light, noise, and frequent interruptions in the critical care unit increases sensitivity to pain and irritability (Sebilia, 1981). Hence sleep periods should be incorporated into the plan of care as part of pain control.

To derive the benefit of sleep, the patient should not be awakened until a full cycle of 60 to 90 minutes has been completed. The best time to interrupt sleep is just after the completion of the rapid eye movement (REM) stage (Hayter, 1980). This stage can be recognized by rapid eye movements under closed lids; complete muscle relaxation, especially of the lower jaw; and slight muscle twitching. Interrupting REM sleep to check the vital signs is inappropriate because blood pressure and heart rate are variable and irregular during this stage (Guzzetta & Dossey, 1984; Landis, 1988).

CONCLUSION

The pain of acute myocardial ischemia is life threatening in itself. The reflexive sympathetic response to pain further exacerbates the imbalance between oxygen supply and demand in the compromised heart. Nursing measures to relieve pain and anxiety also serve to decrease myocardial oxygen demand by reducing the sympathetic response. Thus pain control is another way to decrease oxygen demand and to prevent such complications as dysrhythmias and extension of an infarction.

REFERENCES

Afifi, A.K., & Bergman, R.A. (1986). *Basic neuroscience*. (2nd ed.). Baltimore: Urban & Schwarzenberg.

American Nurses' Association. (1980). *Nursing: A social policy statement*. Kansas City, MO: Author.

Bergersen, B.S. (1979). *Pharmacology in nursing* (14th ed.). St. Louis, MO: Mosby.

Bernstein, L., Friesinger, G.C., & Lichtlen, P.R. (1966). The effect of nitroglycerin on the systemic and coronary circulation in man and dogs. *Circulation, 33*, 107–116.

Braunwald, E. (1980). *Heart disease: A textbook of cardiovascular medicine*. Philadelphia: Saunders.

Brown, A.M. (1967). Excitation of afferent cardiac sympathetic nerve fibres during myocardial ischemia. *Journal of Physiology, 190*, 35–53.

Brown, A.M., & Malliani, A. (1971). Spinal sympathetic reflexes initiated by coronary receptors. *Journal of Physiology (London), 212*, 685–705.

Carpenter, R.H.S. (1984). *Neurophysiology*. Baltimore: University Park Press.

Chaudry, I.H. (1983). Cellular mechanisms in shock and ischemia and their correction. *American Journal of Physiology, 245*, R117–R134.

Chaudry, I.H. (1985). Cellular alterations in shock and ischemia and their correction. *Physiologist, 28*, 109–117.

Del Bianco, D.L., Del Bene, E., & Sicuteri, F. (1974). Heart pain. *Advances in Neurology, 4*, 375–381.

Fields, H.L., Meyer, G.A., & Partridge, L.D. Jr. (1970). Convergence of visceral and somatic input onto spinal neurons. *Experimental Neurology, 26*, 36–52.

Guzzetta, C.E., & Dossey, B.M. (1984). *Cardiovascular nursing: Body-Mind Tapestry*. St. Louis, MO: Mosby.

Hayter, J. (1980). The rhythm of sleep. *American Journal of Nursing, 80*, 457.

Heberden, W. (1772). Some accounts of the disorders of the breast. *Medical Transcriptions of the Royal College of Physicians, 2*, 59.

Hurst, J.W. (Ed.). (1982). *The heart: Arteries and veins* (5th ed.). New York: McGraw-Hill.

Hurst, J.W. (Ed.). (1985). *The heart: Arteries and veins* (6th ed.). New York: McGraw-Hill.

Jennings, R.B., Baum, J.H., & Herdson, P.B. (1965). Fine structural changes in myocardial ischemic injury. *Archives of Pathology, 79*, 135–144.

Kubler, W., & Spieckermann, P.G. (1970). Regulation of glycolysis in the ischemic and anoxic myocardium. *Journal of Molecular Cell Cardiology, 1*, 351–355.

Landis, C.A. (1988). Arrhythmias and sleep pattern disturbances in cardiac patients. *Progress in Cardiovascular Nursing, 3*, 73–80.

Mela, L. (1982). Mitochondrial function in shock, ischemia and hypoxia. In R.A. Cowley & B.F. Trump (Eds.), *Pathophysiology of shock, anoxia and ischemia* (pp. 6–46). Baltimore: Williams & Wilkins.

Mense, S. (1983). Basic neurobiological mechanisms of pain and analgesia. *American Journal of Medicine, 76*, 4–14.

Merskey, H. (1986). Pain and psychiatry. In R.A. Sternbach (Ed.), *The psychology of pain* (2nd ed., pp. 97–120). New York: Raven Press.

National Institutes of Health. (1986). The integrated approach to the management of pain. *Consensus Development Conference Statement, 6*, 1–23.

Perl, E.R. (1984). Pain and nociception. In S.R. Geiger (Ed.), *Handbook of physiology. The nervous system* (Vol. III, Part 2, pp. 915–975). Bethesda, MD: American Physiological Society.

Pomeranz, B., Wall, P.D., & Weber, W.V. (1968). Cord cells responding to fine myelinated afferents from viscera, muscle and skin. *Journal of Physiology, 199*, 511–532.

Printzmetal, M., Kennamer, R., Merliss, R., Wada, T., & Bor, N. (1959). Angina pectoris: I. A variant form of angina pectoris. *American Journal of Medicine, 27*, 375–388.

Sebilia, A.J. (1981). Sleep deprivation of biological rhythms in the critical care unit. *Critical Care Nurse, 1*, 19.

Sherrington, C.S. (1906). *The integrative action of the nervous system*. London: Scribner.

Sobel, B.E. (1985). Cardiac enzymes and other macromolecular markers of myocardial injury. In J.W. Hurst (Ed.), *The heart: Arteries and veins* (6th ed., pp. 108–149). New York: McGraw-Hill.

Sternbach, R.A., & Timmermans, G. (1975). Personality changes associated with the reduction of pain. *Pain, 1*, 177–181.

Uchida, Y., & Murao, S. (1974). Excitation of afferent cardiac sympathetic nerve fibers during coronary occlusion. *American Journal of Physiology, 226*, 1094–1099.

White, J.C. (1957). Cardiac pain: Anatomic pathways and physiological mechanisms. *Circulation, 16*, 644–655.

Zimmerman, M. (1984). Neurobiological concepts of pain, its assessment and therapy. In B. Bromm (Ed.), *Pain measurement in man. Neurophysiological correlates of pain in man* (pp. xx–xx). Amsterdam: Elsevier Science.

RECOMMENDED READING

Guyton, A. (1981). *Basic human neurophysiology* (3rd ed.). Philadelphia: Saunders.

Janig, W. (1985). The autonomic nervous system. In R.F. Schmidt (Ed.), *Fundamentals of neurophysiology* (3rd ed., pp. 216–269). New York: Springer-Verlag.

Last, R.J. (1984). *Anatomy, regional and applied.* Edinburgh: Churchill-Livingstone.

Noback, C.R., & Demarest, R.J. (1981). The human nervous system. Basic principles of neurobiology (3rd ed.). New York: McGraw-Hill.

Schmidt, R.F. (1985). Motor systems. In R.F. Schmidt (Ed.), *Fundamentals of neurophysiology* (3rd ed., pp. 155–200). New York: Springer-Verlag.

Chapter 12

Pain in the Burn Patient

Nancy C. Molter

FRAMEWORK FOR PAIN MANAGEMENT IN THE BURN PATIENT

Critical care nurses make a crucial difference in patient outcomes, and nowhere is this more clearly evident than in the burn intensive care environment, where patients experience intense pain related to injury and treatment. The elimination of all or even some of the pain of burn injury has been shown to have a significant effect on a positive outcome for the patient, both physiologically and psychologically (Murray, 1972).

Although the goal of any pain management program is to eliminate pain, there is a necessity for a compromise among pain perception, the pain state, and safe medical practice (Loeser, 1987). This compromise helps prevent physiological complications. Psychological morbidity is a problem in burn patients, however, and presents as several syndromes with consistent patterns of symptoms. Such morbidity is significantly more likely to develop in patients with pain-management problems than in patients with controlled pain (Ehleben & Still, 1985).

There are four factors present in pain: nociception, pain perception by the individual, suffering, and pain behavior (Loeser, 1987). Of the four, nociception is the easiest to understand. It has been described as the perception by the system of potential tissue damage caused by thermal or mechanical energy that impinges on specialized nerve endings (A-delta and C fibers; Loeser, 1987).

Pain perception by the individual is best described as what the individual says the pain is like and when he or she says it occurs (McCaffery, 1979). At the National Institutes of Health (NIH) consensus conference, pain was described as

[a] subjective experience that can be perceived directly only by the sufferer. It is a multidimensional phenomenon that can be described by pain location, intensity, temporal aspects, quality, impact and meaning.

193

> Pain does not occur in isolation but in a specific human being in
> psychosocial, economic and cultural contexts that influence the mean-
> ing, experience, and verbal and non-verbal expression of pain. (NIH,
> 1987, p. 36)

Inherent in this definition is the concept of suffering, an affective response generated by pain at higher nervous centers (Loeser, 1987). Suffering is affected by stress, anxiety, fear, depression, and loss, all of which are exaggerated by the very nature of an acute burn injury. The language of pain is used to describe suffering. Therefore, "I hurt" may be an expression of an affective state rather than of actual pain stimuli.

Suffering leads to pain behavior. All behaviors are real and perceived by patients to be expressions of real pain; therefore, the care-giver must ask why the patient is exhibiting pain behavior rather than whether the pain is real. One group of investigators found that there were no significant relationships between variables such as total body surface area burned, depression, or days since burn injury and expressed pain behavior (Charlton, Klein, & Gagliardi, 1981). Nevertheless, environment strongly influences pain behavior, leading some clinicians to advocate controlling pain in the burn unit by modifying the environment to control manifestations of pain behavior (Fagerhaugh, 1974). The major environmental stressors in the critical care burn unit include temperature, noise, and fatigue from continuous monitoring.

There are a number of other stressors, both physiological and phychological, that lead to pain in the burn patient. As a result of damage to skin, exposed nerve endings, and the release of chemicals in response to injury, physical pain exists (Kibbee, 1984). Burn pain is acute in nature and most often subsides with healing (Merskey, 1986). It is often intermittent as a result of operative procedures and other painful treatment regimens, but it has an underlying persistent background component that contributes to an overall perception of nearly constant pain (Perry, Heidrich, & Ramos, 1981). Chronic pain can develop as a result of complications related to scar formation as well as functional deformities (Freund et al., 1981).

Major psychological stressors associated with burn injury involve the real threat to survival and fear of disfigurement (Davidson & Noyes, 1973; Noyes, Andreasen, & Hartford, 1971). Often, depression results from guilt related to the cause of the burns, forced dependency on others, and impaired emotional gratification as life plans are disrupted. Cultural influences, fatigue, repeated surgeries, painful procedures, and anxiety related to the ability to cope with pain are major influences on how pain is perceived. Such stressors, coupled with the need to interact with and depend on staff who both inflict and relieve pain, can be overwhelming to even the emotionally strongest of individuals.

There are three phases of burn care associated with pain-control requirements: resuscitative, acute, and rehabilitative (Marvin, 1987). All three phases require a combination of pharmacological and nonpharmacological therapy, but the balance between the two changes as physical healing takes place.

This chapter discusses the role of the critical care nurse in pain management of the adult burn patient. The nursing process provides the framework for the discussion of the applications and implications of research findings for nursing practice primarily in the resuscitative and acute phases, when patients are the most critically ill. Future research considerations are explored.

ASSESSMENT OF BURN PAIN

Pain in the burn patient is difficult to assess accurately. The perception of pain by the burn patient is multidimensional and varies considerably, as it does in all patients with acute pain (NIH, 1987). There will always be some manifestations of pain behavior unless the patient is pharmacologically paralyzed. The nurse may make some judgments of the amount of pain that the patient is experiencing on the basis of the extent of injury and previous experience of pain in other patients, but intensity and severity of injury are not adequate indicators of the severity of pain (Kibbee, 1984; Perry et al., 1981). Suffering obviously occurs, but its nature is unique to each patient's physiological and psychological stressors.

If the operational definition of pain in the clinical area is that it is whatever the patient says it is and occurs when the patient says it occurs, then theoretically the health care team should be able to base interventions on the patient's own assessment of his or her pain. In reality, even if the patient is well oriented, this is difficult to do while ensuring safe medical practice during burn therapy. Although pain management should be a cooperative effort among all health care team members, the patient, and the patient's family, often the nurses' subjective assessments of pain behaviors are the only assessments made (Kibbee, 1984). The assessment of burn pain has been the topic of a number of research studies focusing on the patients' perceptions, the nurses' assessments, or the correlation of the two.

In a comprehensive descriptive study of how patients assessed their burn pain, patients' descriptions of pain intensity varied little despite heterogeneity in the group related to extent of burn, age, ethnicity, and socioeconomic background (Perry et al., 1981). Background as well as procedural pain was evaluated, and findings indicated that most patients had extended periods of mild or no pain. Despite these periods, patients rated their overall pain as high because of its intensity during procedures and because the milder pain affected movement and sleep. Often the patients did not complain of pain or request more frequent medication administrations. Perry et al. (1981) were unable to correlate the severity of the patients' pain with dosage, type, and frequency of analgesics given, emphasizing a possible lack of accurate or thorough assessments as a basis for individualizing pain management.

A study of the pain experience of patients with posttraumatic stress disorder (PTSD) revealed that such patients reported higher levels of procedural and nonprocedural pain than other burn patients but had a tendency to manifest fewer behavioral cues (Perry, Cella, Falkenberg, Heidrich, & Goodwin, 1987). This patient population was drawn from a sample of 134 adult patients in a broader analgesic study. Of the 104 subjects whose records were complete enough for review, 43 (41%) had untreated PTSD. If these patients do give fewer cues, these findings indicate that there may be a significant group of undermedicated patients unless careful assessments are done on all patients.

Burn patients have demonstrated more positive than negative adaptive behaviors during painful treatments (Klein & Charlton, 1980). Observations of positive adaptive behaviors included patient discussions of progress and future plans, statements of well-being or ability to manage pain, and compliance with instructions. Negative behaviors most often were reflected in statements of physical discomfort rather than signs and symptoms of psychological problems such as depression. There was no correlation between differences in frequency of positive and negative adaptive behaviors related to burn variables such as extent of burn, days since onset of injury, and site of burn (Klein & Charlton, 1980).

There is a great deal of disparity in research findings concerning nurse characteristics and their influences on assessment of patient pain. Some research findings in this area are noteworthy, however. Amnad, Perry, and Genovese (1982) found that nurses significantly underestimated the intensity of nonprocedural pain compared to their patients. In contrast, Walkenstein (1982) reported a positive correlation between the nurses' and patients' overall perceptions of pain, although she could find no significant correlation when procedural pain assessment was analyzed. It has been shown that new graduates, new burn nurses, associate and bachelor degree graduates, and nurses older than 30 years of age tend to overestimate the patient's procedural pain, whereas veteran nurses, diploma graduates, and nurses younger than 25 underestimated pain (Iafrati, 1986). Although the difference was not statistically significant, Walkenstein (1982) found that nurses licensed for 3 to 5 years assessed pain more accurately than nurses with less than 2 years of experience or those with more than 6 years of experience. Fagerhaugh (1974), on the other hand, did not find that length of stay in nursing or burn nursing affected pain perception or intervention. Perry and Heidrich (1982) did find a statistically significant overestimation of pain perception by staff members who had spent less time in burn care. They found no discrepancy between how physicians and nurses assess pain, however.

In summary, the research findings indicate that pain assessment principles are difficult to generalize in the burn patient population but that application of such principles to the individual patient is essential to effective pain management. Findings conflict about correlations between patients' and nurses' assessments of pain. It may well be that only the patient can serve as the true control for assessing pain. The use of pain flow charts may be the only reliable way to determine the effectiveness of management through continuous assessment and analysis. The validity and reliability of pain assessment scales are well established, but nurses and other health care team members must have the knowledge and confidence to treat pain on the basis of assessed data.

Future research is needed to establish pain-assessment parameters for noncommunicative patients. Physiological signs may be the only factor available, but such parameters need to be evaluated closely in light of the maximal physiological stress that the burn patient undergoes.

The incidence of routine documentation of pain assessments is not reported in the literature. Empirical evidence indicates that usually only verbal expressions of pain with occasional general comments mentioning restlessness are documented. What criteria nurses use to document assessments, and the thoroughness of the documentations, need to be described. If patients and nurses are reporting undertreatment of pain, then perhaps assessments are not adequate, especially as they relate to evaluation of pain therapy. Nurses must be patient advocates for appropriate pain therapy. They cannot fulfill this responsibility, however, without accurate assessments based on knowledge of the patient's response to therapies.

PLANNING FOR INTERVENTION

There is no universally accepted treatment for the relief of pain and suffering (NIH, 1987), but five factors are essential to a plan of care for effective pain management: adequate assessment (already discussed), establishment of a therapeutic goal, knowledge of therapeutic modalities, documentation and communication of the plan, and evaluation of the plan.

Who is accountable for pain management? In determining the goal of therapy, the issue of accountability for pain management must be addressed. It is an integrated approach involving patient, family, physician, nurse, and allied health care professionals (NIH, 1987). It must be emphasized that each plan must be individualized on the basis of adequate assessment.

Nurses are able to predict which experiences will be painful. These are most commonly related to the following burn care procedures: debridement; dressing changes; occupational and physical therapy procedures such as ambulation, positioning, and immobilization of grafted limbs; care of donor sites; second-degree burns; regeneration of nervous tissue; underlying chronic discomfort without environmental stimuli; and emotional suffering (Heidrich, Perry, & Amnad, 1981). As previous discussion has indicated, correlations between nurses' and patients' perceptions of pain vary. Such discrepancies can lead to differences in goals and result in ineffective care plans.

Establishment of a Therapeutic Goal

Although the goal of total pain relief within safe parameters is verbalized by many, contemporary science cannot ensure the relief of all pain. This fact can, and does, lead to unclear goals for pain management in the critically burned patient.

Fagerhaugh (1974) undertook the study of pain expression and control with the premise that total relief of pain is not possible and, therefore, that patients must be helped to tolerate the pain. Pain was evaluated from an organizational–work–interactional perspective. The investigator believed that the primary aspects of management for both patients and staff are the endurance of pain and the controlling of pain expression. Several key assumptions were delineated that could affect the goal of therapy:

- The degree and duration of pain depend on the extent and location of the burn as well as other factors. (This assumption was not supported in other studies [Kibbee, 1984; Perry et al., 1981].)
- Expressions of pain such as crying out, moaning, and screaming are intolerable and devastating to patients and staff.
- Staff members must control their own responses to pain expression.

The investigator drew many interesting conclusions that could have a significant impact on determining the goal of therapy and thus interventions chosen to effect that goal:

- Staff give a high priority to technical competence, which prevents them from thinking about a patient's tragic future. Staff use pride in technical competencies and the reputation of the burn unit to control the patient's pain behavior.
- Patients with less severe and extensive burns feel that they have less right to complain.
- If staff neglect pain therapy, then patients feel that they have a right to complain.

Because the goal of therapy is the philosophical foundation for the plan of care, it must be clearly defined. Without a goal of total relief of pain, then such an outcome does not exist in the minds of the patients or the staff. If such a goal becomes the target, then adequate pain relief always becomes possible through effective cooperation between the critically ill patient and the critical care nurse in an environment conducive to achieving this mutual goal.

Knowledge of Therapeutic Modalities

The third step in planning for adequate pain control in the burn unit is selecting effective therapeutic modalities. This requires knowledge of the psychological and physiological changes in the three phases of burn care as well as how to implement the actual modalities.

The paradox of pain management in burn nursing is that nurses inflict pain and then must relieve it (Heidrich et al., 1981; Walkenstein, 1982). The paradox causes conflicting emotions that often lead nurses to minimize the severity of the patient's pain or to become outwardly unresponsive to the patient while inflicting pain. As one nurse stated, "If it's for long periods, I sometimes get headaches or stomach cramps. If it's when I'm behind schedule or my assignment is very difficult, or I'm finishing off a long work stretch, I get angry or intolerant," (Heidrich et al., 1981; p. 261).

Some nurses believe that the unsatisfactory management of burn patients' pain is due to burn patients' being a difficult group of patients with many personality problems (Heidrich et al., 1981). They stated that they would use placebos to see "how much pain the patient is really having," (Heidrich et al., 1981, p. 260). Although misconceptions related to the use of placebos is documented, one may hope that such punitive use is waning with increased education.

There are several other major reasons for undertreatment of pain in burn patients (Kibbee, 1984). The most common reasons are fear of addiction to drugs, fear of respiratory depression, fear of nutritional consequences of constipation, and lack of knowledge of the pharmacology of pain medication. Although these factors have been studied and reported in the general literature as well as in the burn pain-management literature, health care providers continue to have such fears, and they are reflected in clinical pain management. No studies could be found that evaluated the effectiveness of continuing education about pain therapies in terms of changing or improving staff interventions for pain management.

Documentation and Communication of the Plan

Documentation and communication of the plan is the fourth factor to be considered when establishing a plan for pain management. Such documentation and communication is often inadequate. This is inferred from the number of patients who complain about inadequate pain relief. No studies could be found in the literature that actually investigated the prevalence of a documented plan for pain management or what components of the nursing process most frequently are documented. The nursing diagnosis proposed by the North American Nursing Diagnosis Association for acute pain is unclear and not well researched. Burn pain is not addressed at all and should be investigated as a separate diagnosis because it has components of both acute and chronic pain syndromes (Merskey, 1986).

Evaluation of the Plan

Without adequate documentation and communication of the plan, evaluation cannot occur. This fifth and crucial component of the plan must be considered at the beginning of the planning process. Evaluation provides the feedback loop for the critical care nurse to reassess the patient and environment, in light of the observed responses to implemented therapies, and to determine whether the goal is being met.

Summary of Intervention Planning

There is clearly a need for individualized nursing care plans for acute pain management (NIH, 1987). Without adequate planning, consistent and effective pain management is not possible. Such planning is the foundation for the implementation and evaluation of this most crucial aspect of burn care.

IMPLEMENTATION OF THE PLAN OF CARE

There are three phases of burn care, all requiring analgesia therapy as well as other pain-management techniques (Marvin, 1987). Throughout all three phases, two components of the burn pain experience are present: background or non-procedural pain and procedural pain. Both these components must be addressed in each phase to achieve the goal of total pain relief. Both pharmacological and nonpharmacological pain relief measures must be considered.

Phase 1: The Resuscitation Phase

In this phase pain is generally injury related (i.e., thermal and associated injuries), acute, and often severe at first (Marvin, 1987). It is described as throbbing, stinging, and smarting and increases in intensity with movement or procedures (Merskey, 1986). Often this pain is continually present in some degree and is exacerbated by the application of antimicrobial topical creams.

Phase 1 lasts approximately 72 hours and is characterized by marked vascular instability and severe fluid shifts resulting in massive edema. Narcotic medication is universally used in this phase, but absorption of medication is unpredictable unless it is given intravenously.

There are three methods for administering intravenous narcotics: intermittent bolus, fixed-rate continuous infusion, and continuous modified variable-dose infusion (Wolman, 1988). The most common narcotics used in this phase are meperidine and morphine. The choice of narcotic used should reflect planning according to deposition factors described in studies with burn patients. Meperidine (Demerol) has widely varying peaks of effects that do not gradually decline predictably in the burn patient (Goodfellow, Bloedow, Marvin, & Heimbach,

1981). Morphine also has been shown to be more rapidly eliminated in burn patients even though it has a rapid and extensive distribution (Inturrisi, Perry, & Genovese, 1982; Perry & Inturrisi, 1983).

Although drug administration by intermittent bolus allows for increasing titration to control for adverse effects such as respiratory depression or cardiac instability, this method results in unstable blood levels of the drug and increased nursing time. Boluses usually begin at the equivalent of approximately 5 mg of morphine and are increased until background pain relief is obtained or significant respiratory depression occurs. Any respiratory depression that will occur usually does so within 7 minutes of intravenous administration (Jaffe, 1980).

Hypotension can be a significant consideration in this phase when evaluated in the context of the burn patient's altered capillary dynamics. If rapid adjustment of drug level becomes necessary as a result of overmedication, then naloxone can be used to control the side effects. The patient must be monitored closely after the administration of naloxone because of its short half-life compared to narcotics.

The fixed-rate continuous infusion method provides stable drug levels and consistent pain control with decreased nursing time. There is a delay in action onset and a risk of accumulation with resulting overdose as pain requirements change. Disadvantages of this method are negated with the use of a continuous variable-dose infusion, which allows the nurse to modify the dose of the infusion according to the patient's response (Wolman & Luterman, 1988).

A comparison study of continuous modified variable-dose infusion and intermittent boluses indicated that the continuous variable-dose infusion group required less morphine sulfate and fewer narcotic administrations per hour of hospitalization than the intermittent bolus group. Patients in both groups did receive supplemental intermittent boluses of narcotics, anxiolytics, and sedatives as needed. No significant differences were noted in the total amount or number of administrations of anxiolytics between groups (Wolman & Luterman, 1988).

In a study of continuous methadone infusion in patients, results indicated good pain control in the resuscitative phase (Miller, Denson, Concilus, & Warden, 1988). These findings were predicated on patient perception of pain relief. If the patient was unable to respond because of mental status changes, then subjective assessments of pain relief were made by the medical and nursing staff. Caution must be exercised with methadone because of its extended half-life and the difficulty in rapidly reversing its adverse effects.

The important concepts in administering narcotics in the resuscitative phase are related to the dynamics of capillary changes, sustained control of background pain, and recognition of additional requirements related to procedural pain. Intermittent bolus administration of narcotics to control nonprocedural pain is ineffective and reinforces negative pain behavior.

The critical care nurse's thorough knowledge of the pharmacokinetic properties of the drug chosen is essential to the safe implementation of the pain-management plan in this phase. As nurses gain knowledge in drug dosages and phar-macokinetics, fears about addiction, drug tolerance, and respiratory depression will not interfere with the implementation of a well-planned pain-management program titrated to the patient's specific response.

Phase 2: The Acute Phase

This phase ranges from 72 hours after the burn in patients with extensive burn injuries until healing or closure of the burn wound. Pain-management modalities begun in this phase often are the initial pain therapies for burn patients with less than 20% burns (Marvin, 1987). In phase 2, capillary dynamics are stabilized and analgesic medications can be given safely by intravenous, intramuscular, or oral routes, depending on the size of the burn and stage of healing.

Intravenous narcotic medications continue to be used in this phase for pain control because of the numerous operative and treatment procedures required at this time. As healing begins, other methods of narcotic administration can be used effectively and in combination with other therapies. There are a number of side effects that can result from narcotic analgesia, but they can be minimized with careful planning. Although development of tolerance poses a minimal risk, it can occur. To decrease this problem, medication can be titrated for effect and then weaned as need decreases (Kibbee, 1984). Fear of constipation in patients who have an increased need for nutritional intake can be managed effectively by the use of stool softeners and bulk laxatives (Kibbee, 1984). The method chosen to administer the narcotic and careful assessment of the patient can reduce the risk of respiratory depression.

Procedural and nonprocedural pain remains a problem until all wounds are healed and may continue after wound healing as a result of physical therapy, scar maturation, and psychological manifestations. Procedural pain related to wound management is severe and usually produces extreme anxiety, which exacerbates the pain.

Control of anxiety is acknowledged to be important in pain relief, but treating anxiety with medications increases pain behavior and physical tolerance to anal-gesics (Halpern, 1974). In addition, sedation can decrease the patient's ability to cooperate with treatment regimens while masking the symptoms of inadequate pain control. It therefore becomes important, even in the early stages of burn care, for nurses to use some form of nonpharmacological antianxiety measures along with pharmacological measures to mediate pain relief.

Stress reduction is beneficial in dealing with acute burn pain management. In a study by Wernick, Jaremko, and Taylor (1981), patients and nurses were given training in procedures for developing patients' cognitive coping skills, cognitive restructuring, and application. The treated subjects showed improvement in terms of decreased unauthorized pain medication requests, physical and emotional self-ratings, control of pain during hydrotherapy and wound debridement, compliance with hospital routine, and decreased anxiety.

In a second study, a patient group trained in three treatment methods (relaxation; imagery, desensitization, and sensory information; and biofeedback) was compared with a control group (Kenner & Achterberg, 1983). Significant improvement on measures of subjective pain, state anxiety, and peripheral temperature was seen in the imagery and biofeedback groups. There were no differences among measurements of these variables in the control group. Measurements in the relaxation group were inconsistent.

It was demonstrated in another experimental study that patients who received a standardized debriefing about burn care and pain and a short training program in relaxation and imagery techniques had better pain control than patients who did not receive such interventions (Tobiasen, Hove, Mani, & Hiebert, 1984). One hundred percent of the experimental group stated that their coping strategies reduced their pain, compared to only 50% of the control group's perceptions of pain relief. In addition, the nurses perceived that the experimental group patients were more compliant with the treatment regimen than the control group.

Such nonpharmacological methods appear to be effective for both background pain and procedural pain, particularly when combined with pharmacological pain management. More definitive studies related to relaxation techniques are indicated. The following case study illustrates my personal use of such procedures.

John was a 25-year-old man who attempted suicide by turning on the gas oven in his apartment. When he awoke the next morning, he was dismayed to find that he had been unable to kill himself and automatically lit his morning cigarette. The apartment exploded, and John received partial- and full-thickness burns over 70% of his body. In the burn unit, his anxiety precluded effective pain relief. He cried and yelled continuously.

One night I attempted to use imagery and relaxation techniques to assist John. I had never attempted these techniques and was very busy, but I felt that the effort would be worth it if John could be helped to relax. I asked John to imagine that he was on a cloud floating peacefully over the countryside. In approximately 20 minutes, he was relaxed and quiet.

John remained comfortable for almost an hour, when he suddenly started screaming for me (apparently he was falling off his cloud). Despite this setback, imagery and relaxation remained useful techniques to assist John as long as he was guided to a peaceful place that was on the ground.

204 PAIN IN THE CRITICALLY ILL

The question remains, How extensively are such techniques used by nurses in acute pain management? No studies could be found that describe the extent of use of such techniques or how to train nurses to use the techniques effectively. It may be a perception on the nurses' part that such methods are time consuming and produce inconsistent results or that they require extensive training to learn.

During phase 2 many procedures are carried out that can be extremely painful. In fact, procedural pain related to debridement is described by patients as being the most painful burn care experience (Perry et al., 1981). Perry and Heidrich (1982) surveyed 151 American burn units to determine how burn pain is assessed and managed during debridement. Table 12-1 indicates their findings related to analgesic preferences, dose, and administration route during debridement for adults.

Methods of controlling pain described in their study are still being evaluated. They include narcotics, nitrous oxide, ketamine, hypnosis, transcutaneous electrical nerve stimulation, variations in procedural techniques, and supportive psychotherapy and relaxation training. Many of these studies are being conducted by nurses as the primary investigators. Despite the volume of research, there

Table 12-1 Analgesic Preference, Dose, and Administration Route during Debridement in Adults

Route	Analgesic	N	Dose (mg, mean ± standard deviation)	Range (mg)
Intramuscular (IM)	Morphine	50	10.7 ± 4.5	2– 35
Intravenous (IV)	Morphine	32	8.9 ± 5.4	2– 25
IM	Meperidine	37	75.7 ± 52.9	25–375
IV	Meperidine	8	70.5 ± 14.1	50–100
Oral	Codeine	30	63.0 ± 22.7	30–130
IM	Codeine	3		
Oral	Oxycodone	5		
IM	Alphaprodine	2		
IV	Alphaprodine	1		
Oral	Pentazocine	2		
Oral	Methadone	1		
	None	6		

Source: From "Management of Pain during Debridement: A Survey of U.S. Burn Units" by S. Perry and G. Heidrich, 1982, *Pain, 13,* 269. Copyright 1982 by Elsevier Science Publishers BV. Reprinted by permission.

continues to be no documented definitive analgesic method for burn pain management.

In more recent years investigators have explored the role of β-endorphins and their relationship to pain management in burns. Goosen (1986) identified peaks and sudden elevations in β-endorphin levels associated with specific clinical events. She was not able to show any significant relationships between β-endorphin levels and the following variables: time interval after burn, burn severity, required analgesic dosage, or a combination of burn severity and the required analgesic dosage. In contrast, Osgood, Carr, Kazianis, & Kemp (1988) found that lowered plasma β-endorphin levels were even lower in burned rats 2 days after burn while the rats were receiving exogenous opioids. This finding was in agreement with their clinical findings. Although the data from the two studies appear to conflict, the possibility that narcotics may contribute to low plasma endorphin levels by competing with endorphin at μ receptor sites should continue to be explored carefully.

A new category of drugs, endorphin releasers, shows promise in the area of pain relief. One of these is Ceruletide, a synthetic decapeptide closely resembling cholecystokinin and gastrin. When this drug was administered intravenously over 30 minutes once or twice a day, powerful analgesia was obtained that lasted up to 12 hours (Doleček et al., 1983). It was accompanied (after several days of administration) by a euphoric mood and persistent increased elevations of β-endorphins in the blood.

Phase 3: The Rehabilitative Phase

This phase covers the period from closure of the wound to complete scar maturation (Marvin, 1987). It lasts approximately 6 to 12 months. Although this phase is rarely encountered by critical care nurses, it is helpful to understand the pain control issues that patients face to prepare them for the transition from acute burn care. Generally there are more behavioral manifestations of pain in this phase as patients begin to assimilate some of the life changes required as a result of their devastating injury.

Even after the burn wound has healed, pain can result from the return of nerve function. The return of nerve function can be accompanied by active vasodilation, vasoconstriction, and return of tactile sensation. The reflex neuronal function may be restored within 5–6 weeks of excision and grafting, or return may take up to 6 months in wounds healed by granulation and contracture or late grafting (Freund et al., 1981). It has been demonstrated that neuronal tissue can be trapped in the scar and cause pain in a wound that is completely healed (Ponten, 1960).

Scar tissue produced by an inflammatory process also may be painful because of persistent activity of tissue enzymes. As scar tissue matures, itching and pain with exercise occur. Itching in particular is a mentally and physiologically fatiguing symptom. When patients compared the effects of the three most commonly used medications to relieve the symptom of itching, hydroxyzine (Atarax) was perceived to be the most beneficial (Vitale & Luterman, 1988). The critical care nurse also will be required to assist patients with this annoying symptom when patients with extensive burns require grafting procedures over a period of several weeks. In this situation wound or donor sites in various stages of healing are present in different areas of the body.

Pharmacological management of pain in the rehabilitative phase usually consists of acetaminophen and nonsteroidal anti-inflammatory agents. Antidepressants or mild analgesics may be useful.

During the rehabilitative phase the patient faces many psychological problems, with depression and anxiety frequently manifested (Marvin, 1987). Pain perception is exacerbated by these emotions and complicates the diagnosis and management of pain symptoms. Group therapy and other psychological modalities may be necessary to prevent the extensive development of pain behaviors that may develop into a chronic problem. Such therapies often begin in the acute phase, and the critical care nurse must be cognizant of the influences of depression and anxiety on pain management even in the early stages of care of patients with extensive burns.

As many clinicians have often stated, the only safe way to administer narcotic analgesia is to titrate the dose to the patient's response. In burn care, this axiom can be extended to all forms of pain therapy. The pain involved is usually severe, continuous at some level of intensity, and associated with several confounding psychological and cultural variables. It is not possible to assume that one particular protocol will benefit most patients in a particular phase of care. It is the critical care nurse who must continually assess the patient's responses and then mobilize the entire health care team to modify the plan of care.

EVALUATING THE PLAN OF CARE

In evaluating the effectiveness of a pain-management plan for critically burned patients, several questions can be posed. First, is the patient satisfied with the level of pain management? If not, the nurse must assess the following:

- What does the pain mean to the patient? Is the goal of the care-giver the same as that of the patient?
- Is pain control ineffective for background pain? Procedural pain? Both? Is some other factor involved, such as an inflamed intravenous site or hidden injury?

- What is the balance between pharmacological and nonpharmacological pain relief modalities? Is the balance appropriate for the phase of burn care? Is anxiety a major factor, and is it being managed appropriately?
- How and when does the patient express pain? Does the pain correlate with inappropriate dosage intervals for the analgesic used? Is the dosage appropriate? What method of administration is used? Would a flow sheet be helpful to collate and analyze data (for example, to correlate symptoms with therapies and results)? What environmental factors may be affecting the patient?
- What does the patient think will control the pain better?

The nurse also must ascertain whether there are physiological side effects with the current medication plan. If so, he or she must reassess the type and method of delivery of analgesic and then weigh the benefits of the current analgesic therapy against the risks of side effects.

There is an obvious need to continue studies and to explore combinations of therapies for both procedural and background burn pain. Both physicians and nurses must examine their attitudes toward pain management and work collaboratively to develop safe and effective approaches to pain management in the critical care environment. Old myths and misconceptions must be replaced by personal accountability for continued education related to pharmacological and nonpharmacological pain therapy advances.

Much more patient, nursing, and physician education is needed to maintain sensitivity and to promote greater use of the full spectrum of pain-control modalities that have already been studied and found effective. The patient and family must be actively involved in the implementation of the plan of care through honest feedback as to the effects of medication and control of the medication dosage and by participating in nonpharmacological methods to reduce pain.

As Heidrich and colleagues (1981) write, burn pain is ''not a single entity but a kaleidoscopic experience, a series of discrete severely painful procedures punctuating the day and night and superimposed upon an underlying pervasive physical and psychologic discomfort,'' (p. 260). Nurses are at the bedside 24 hours a day; therefore, they must take the initiative to evaluate and ensure the adequacy of burn pain management. They are the only health care providers available continuously to evaluate the plan. The following guideline summarizes the responsibilities of the nurse regarding pain management:

P—place the patient in as much control as possible
A—assess and analyze continuously the response to pain therapy
I —individualize the approach to pain control for each patient
N—never give up

REFERENCES

Amnad, R., Perry, S., & Genovese, V. (1982). Non-procedural pain as perceived by burn patient and nurse. *Proceedings of the American Burn Association, 14*, 64.

Charlton, J.E., Klein, R., & Gagliardi, G. (1981, September). *Assessment of pain relief in patients with burn.* Paper presented at the third World Congress on Pain at the International Association for the Study of Pain, Edinburgh, Scotland.

Davidson, S.P., & Noyes, R. (1973). Psychiatric nursing consultation on a burn unit. *American Journal of Nursing, 73,* 1715–1718.

Doleček, R., Ježek, M., Adámková, M., Polivka, P., Kubis, M., Šajnar, J., Dolečková, D., Kurková, J., & Závada, M. (1983). Endorphin releasers: A new possible approach to the treatment of pain after burns—A preliminary report. *Burns, 10,* 41–44.

Ehleben, C., & Still, J. (1985). Psychological morbidity and pain. *Proceedings of the American Burn Association, 17.* (Abstract 104).

Fagerhaugh, S. (1974). Pain expression and control on a burn care unit. *Nursing Outlook, 22,* 645–650.

Freund, P.R., Brengelmann, G.L., Rowell, L.B., (1981). Vasomotor control in healed grafted skin in humans. *Journal of Applied Physiology, 51,* 168–171.

Goodfellow, L.C., Bloedow, D., Marvin, J., & Heimbach, D. (1981). Meperidine disposition following burn trauma. *Proceedings of the American Burn Association, 13,* 66.

Goosen, G. (1986). β-Endorphin levels in burned patients. *Proceedings of the American Burn Association, 18.* (Abstract 127).

Halpern, L. (1974). Treating pain with drugs. *Minnesota Medicine, 57,* 176–184.

Heidrich, G., Perry, S., & Amnad, R. (1981). Nursing staff attitudes about burn pain. *Journal of Burn Care and Rehabilitation, 2,* 259–261.

Iafrati, N. (1986). Pain on the burn unit: Patient vs nurse perceptions. *Journal of Burn Care and Rehabilitation, 7,* 413–416.

Inturrisi, C., Perry, S., & Genovese, V. (1982). Morphine: Pharmacokinetics and pain relief in burn patients. *Proceedings of the American Burn Association, 14,* 45.

Jaffe, J.H. (1980). Drug addiction and drug abuse. In A.G. Goodman, L.S. Goodman, & A. Gilman (Eds.), *The pharmacological basis of therapeutics,* (6th ed., pp. 535–584). New York: Macmillan.

Kenner, C., & Achterberg, J. (1983). Non-pharmaceutical pain relief for burn patients. *Proceedings of the American Burn Association, 15,* 100.

Kibbee, E. (1984). Burn pain management. *Critical Care Quarterly, 7,* 54–62.

Klein, R., & Charlton, J.E. (1980). Behavioral observation and analysis of pain behavior in critically burned patients. *Pain, 9,* 27–40.

Loeser, J. (1987). Conceptual framework for pain management. *Journal of Burn Care and Rehabilitation, 8,* 309–312.

Marvin, J. (1987). Pain management. *Topics in Acute Care Trauma Rehabilitation, 1,* 15–24.

McCaffery, M. (1979). *Nursing management of the patient with pain,* (2nd ed.). Philadelphia: Lippincott.

Merskey, D.M. (Ed.). (1986). Classification of chronic pain: Descriptions of chronic pain syndromes and definitions of pain terms. *Pain, 3,* s43–s44.

Miller, A., Denson, D., Concilus, R., & Warden, G. (1988). Continuous infusion of methadone in severely burned patients. *Proceedings of the American Burn Association, 20.* (Abstract 149).

Murray, J. (1972). The history of analgesia in burns. *Postgraduate Medical Journal, 48,* 124–127.

National Institutes of Health Consensus Development Conference. (1987). The integrated approach to the management of pain. *Journal of Pain and Symptom Management, 2,* 35–44.

Noyes, R., Andreasen, N.J.C., & Hartford, C.E. (1987). The psychological reaction to severe burns. *Psychosomatics, 12,* 416–442.

Osgood, P., Carr, D., Kazianis, A., & Kemp, J. (1988). Exogenous opioid analgesics may suppress β-endorphin release in the normal and burned rat. *Proceedings of the American Burn Association, 20.*

Perry, S., Cella, D., Falkenberg, J., Heidrich, G., & Goodwin, C. (1987). Pain perception in burn patients with stress disorders. *Journal of Pain and Symptom Management, 2,* 29–33.

Perry, S., & Heidrich, G. (1982). Management of pain during debridement: A survey of U.S. burn units. *Pain, 13,* 267–280.

Perry, S., Heidrich, G., & Ramos, E. (1981). Assessment of pain by burn patients. *Journal of Burn Care and Rehabilitation, 2,* 322–326.

Perry, S., & Inturrisi, C. (1983). Analgesia and morphine disposition in burn patients. *Journal of Burn Care and Rehabilitation, 4,* 276–279.

Ponten, B. (1960). Grafted skin: Observation on innervation and other qualities. *Acta Chirurgica Scandinavica 257*(Suppl.), 1–178.

Tobiasen, J., Hove, G., Mani, M., & Hiebert, J. (1984). Coping with pain: Training strategies for the burn-injured patient. *Proceedings of the American Burn Association, 16,* 38.

Vitale, M., & Luterman, A. (1988). Severe itching and the burn patient. *Proceedings of the American Burn Association, 20.* (Abstract 46).

Walkenstein, M. (1982). Comparison of burned patients' perception of pain with nurses' perception of patients' pain. *Journal of Burn Care and Rehabilitation, 3,* 233–236.

Wernick, R., Jaremko, M., & Taylor, P. (1981). Pain management in severely burned adults: A test of stress inoculation. *Journal of Behavioral Medicine, 4,* 103–109.

Wolman, R. (1988, March). *Concepts.* Paper presented at the 20th annual meeting of the American Burn Association, Seattle, WA.

Wolman, R., & Luterman, A. (1988). The continuous infusion of morphine sulfate for analgesia in burn patients: Extending the use of an established technique. *Proceedings of the American Burn Association, 20.* (Abstract 150).

Chapter 13

Pain in the Postoperative Patient

Susan B. Christoph

THE PROBLEM OF POSTOPERATIVE PAIN IN THE CRITICALLY ILL PATIENT

Although pain is most often considered a protective mechanism, postoperative pain serves no useful purpose and can be deleterious. The deleterious effects of postoperative pain are both physiological and psychological. Despite the knowledge that postoperative pain is deleterious it is frequently undertreated, and patients suffer.

Physiological Impact of Postoperative Pain

Critical care nurses are all too familiar with the decreased lung volume, increased oxygen consumption, immobility, and depletion of energy that occur when a patient must cope with pain (Christoph, 1988). Pain disrupts sleep, which further depletes the body's natural reserves for healing.

The postanesthesia patient has experienced some interference with his or her respiratory system; therefore, attention must be directed specifically toward maintaining adequate gas exchange. The major factor contributing to low lung volumes in the postanesthesia patient is a shallow, monotonous, sighless breathing pattern caused by anesthesia but added to by pain.

The ''stir-up'' regimen is the most important aspect of care for the postanesthesia patient. The stir-up regimen is aimed at prevention of complications, primarily atelectasis and venous stasis. It consists of five major activities:

Note: The opinions or assertions contained herein are the private views of the author and are not to be construed as official or as reflecting the views of the Department of the Army or the Department of Defense.

deep-breathing exercises, coughing, positioning, mobilization, and pain relief. The stir-up regimen must include adequate relief of pain so that the other required activities can be accomplished. The relief of pain is particularly important to maintaining adequate respiratory effort. Narcotics depress the cough reflex and ciliary activity and may lower alveolar ventilation by direct depression of the respiratory center; they must not be used indiscriminately. If breathing is painful and splinting occurs, however, or if the patient refuses to cough or move because of pain, nothing is gained by the stir-up regimen (Drain & Christoph, 1987).

Psychological Impact of Postoperative Pain

It is clear that pain is more than just a physiological experience; it is a psychological experience as well. Just as emotional and sociocultural factors influence the pain experience, the pain experience may influence the patient's general psychological responses.

It is generally accepted that a positive relationship between anxiety and the pain experience exists. Although the exact relationship has not been delineated, it is known not only that anxiety influences pain perception but that pain perception or the fear of pain stimulates anxiety.

For the critically ill or injured patient, the perceived and real lack of control over the environment and care may significantly augment anxiety levels. It is hoped that most patients will emerge from general anesthesia in a calm, tranquilized manner. Some patients, however, will emerge in a state of excitement, a condition characterized by restlessness, disorientation, crying, moaning, or irrational talking. In the extreme form of excitement, which is referred to as emergence delirium, the patient will scream, shout, and thrash about wildly. Postoperative pain or discomfort from prolonged maintenance of an abnormal position on the operating table as well as the fear of disfigurement, fear of cancer, and a feeling of suffocation contribute to the likelihood of emergence excitement.

The patient looks to the health care team, specifically the nurse, to manage and control pain. Unmanaged pain will contribute to the development of critical care psychosis and personality disorders. How well the patient's pain is managed can greatly influence the sense of trust that is central to the therapeutic nurse-patient relationship.

ASSESSMENT OF POSTOPERATIVE PAIN IN THE CRITICALLY ILL PATIENT

The development of an effective postoperative pain treatment plan depends on accurate assessment. Assessment of the postoperative patient's pain experience is often difficult because of the residual effects of anesthesia. The postoperative patient's responses to pain will vary according to the extent to which his or her level of consciousness is altered. Communication with the postanesthesia patient may be difficult owing to a clouded sensorium.

Influence of Surgical Site and Procedure

Postoperative pain perception is largely a physiological phenomenon that is influenced primarily by the tissue damage caused by incision, manipulation, retraction, and excision. The site and nature of the operative procedure performed influence the type and magnitude of the postoperative pain experienced. The site of the operative procedure influences the nature of the patient's response to postoperative pain.

Patients who have undergone abdominal and intrathoracic operations generally experience the most pain (Jaggard, Zager, & Wilkins, 1950; Keats, 1956; Loan & Dundee, 1967; Papper, Brodie, & Rovenstein, 1952). Thoracic surgery patients experience pain from the incision and from the insertion of chest tubes. Posterolateral incisions tend to be more painful than anterolateral ones. The incisions for major vascular surgery are long and painful. Large doses of narcotic analgesics may be required to keep the patient comfortable and to promote respiratory effort. Surgery on the joints, back, and anorectal area also generally is quite painful (Benedetti, Bonica, & Bellucci, 1984).

Pain is not common after most eye surgery. Even so, the fear and anxiety of having one's eyes operated on may evoke responses of pain. It is important that the nurse be armed with factual information from the surgeon about expectations for the patient so that reassurances offered are realistic.

The nurse must be prepared to provide significant support to the critical care patient through both verbal communication and touch.

Influence of Anesthetic Technique and Agents

The type of anesthetic technique and agents used will influence the postoperative pain experience. The inhalational agents, including enflurane (Ethrane), isoflurane (Forane), and halothane (Fluothane), are commonly used, short-acting drugs and provide little to no residual analgesia postoperatively. The intravenous agent sodium pentothal (Thiopental) is a poor analgesic and may even have an antianalgesic effect. Therefore, postoperative patients with pain may become irrational, restless, and hyperactive.

A balanced anesthetic technique that includes the administration of narcotics such as meperidine (Demerol), morphine, fentanyl (Sublimaze), sufentanil (Sufenta), or alfentanil commonly is used. When the patient has received meperidine, morphine, fentanyl, or sufentanil, some residual analgesia may be expected. These drugs may exacerbate respiratory depression, so that the patient should be monitored carefully. Alfentanil has an extremely short action time, and patients who receive this drug as the narcotic portion of a balanced anesthetic technique will probably experience pain in the immediate postoperative period and require additional analgesia.

Often, narcotics are reversed with a narcotic antagonist at the end of surgery. The nurse should be aware of any antagonist administered and be alert to signs and symptoms of increased blood pressure and pain. The nurse also must be alert to symptoms of withdrawal in patients who have a history of narcotic drug use. Withdrawal symptoms in the postanesthesia patient may include anxiety, jittery behavior, rhinorrhea, hypotension, muscle twitching, sweating, pupillary dilation, gooseflesh, and nausea and vomiting. Treatment for withdrawal should include the administration of narcotic analgesia.

The patient who receives regional anesthesia (local, spinal, or epidural blocks) may have residual analgesia during the postoperative recovery period, but the analgesia may be short lived. The nurse should assess the patient's level of sedation, including the amount of premedication and sedation during the surgical procedure, before administering pain medication.

Constellation of Pain Indicators

Pain draws attention to itself and can influence all physiological and psychological responses. The assessment of pain, therefore, involves the evaluation of a constellation of pain indicators. It is the grouping of associated symptoms that will be most helpful in assessing pain in the critically ill postoperative patient.

Verbalizations

The patient's own verbalizations are the most reliable indicators of pain. The postoperative patient may experience pain yet be unable to verbalize it accurately. Groaning, grunting, and crying are probable indicators that pain is present. Communication with the postoperative patient may be difficult owing to a clouded sensorium and the presence of apparatuses such as nasogastric tubes, artificial airways, and so forth. Nevertheless, the nurse must collaborate with the patient to identify the location, intensity, and quality of pain being experienced before implementing a plan for pain control. Pain or discomfort for the postoperative patient may be due to a number of factors other than incisional pain. Headache, sore throat, or muscular aches may be the result of anesthetic technique. Intravenous infusion sites and irritation from other associated apparatuses, such as nasogastric tubes, may be the source of complaint.

Physiological Indicators

The physiological indicators of pain result primarily from autonomic stimulation. Postoperative pain elicits primarily sympathetic responses including pallor, increased respirations, increased heart rate, increased blood pressure, dilated pupils, and increased muscle tension. The colon, rectum, and bladder are innervated through the sacral parasympathetic nerves, however, so that surgery involving these viscera may elicit parasympathetic pain responses including nausea and vomiting, decreased heart rate, and decreased blood pressure.

Behavioral Clues

Excitement, irritability, anger, hostility, depression, unusual quietness, or withdrawal may indicate that the patient is experiencing pain. The patient in pain may hold the body or the painful part rigid and immobile in an attempt to limit pain. On the other hand, activity may increase. The patient may rock, rub a painful body part, become restless, or exhibit purposeless activity. As the patient emerges from the first stage of anesthesia there may be enough residual anesthetic effect that he or she awakens, complains of pain, and then falls asleep again.

Respiratory status is the most important assessment when deciding whether or not to administer an analgesic to such a patient. The administration of a reduced dose of analgesic will prevent the development of significant pain and promote a quieter and more comfortable, albeit prolonged, emergence.

MANAGEMENT OF POSTOPERATIVE PAIN

Prevention

The first goals of pain management for the postoperative patient are to prevent pain and to promote comfort. Recent evidence demonstrates that opiate premedication and the use of local anesthetic blocks reduce postoperative pain (McQualy, Carroll, & Morroe, 1988). It is suggested that anesthetic blocks and small narcotic doses prevent the barrage of stimuli created by surgery on the central nervous system and thereby prevent the development of a hyperexcitable state. This evidence also provides a sound rationale for the prompt treatment of postoperative pain with appropriate analgesia, before the development of severe pain, because once severe pain exists much larger doses of narcotic analgesics are necessary to suppress the hyperexcitable state and to bring the pain response under control.

Once surgery is over, the prevention of pain requires attention to detail to reduce noxious stimuli. Positioning of the postoperative patient is particularly important. Careful attention to positioning body parts that may still be paralyzed by regional anesthesia is important in the prevention of discomfort later in the postoperative period. Good body alignment and frequent changing of position will help prevent muscle contractions and spasms. Injured parts should be supported to prevent muscular strain and fatigue.

Injured tissue must be handled carefully and further trauma avoided whenever possible. The patient often is the best judge of how to avoid stimulating pain. Incisions or operated sites should not be placed under tension or pressure. Sometimes, something as slight as the minimal pressure of a bedsheet may produce noxious stimuli.

Postoperative patients should have been taught preoperatively how to splint abdominal and thoracic incisions externally to minimize painful stimuli during ventilatory exercises. Patients in the postanesthesia care unit who are still under the influence of anesthesia often need assistance during the immediate postanesthesia period. Emergency surgery patients may not have been prepared at all for surgery and will need primary teaching and intensive coaching to manage respiratory maneuvers in the postanesthesia period. A semirigid splinting device such as a folded bath blanket or firm pillow is useful for splinting incisions.

Attention to comfort details can reduce sensory stimulation and support pain tolerance. A clean, dry, wrinkle-free bed in a quiet environment improves comfort. A dry mouth, which frequently is a problem after anesthesia, can be relieved with ice chips, moistened gauze, and petrolatum ointment applied to the lips. All drainage tubes should be checked frequently for patency to avoid distention of the drainage site. A common source of postoperative pain and restlessness is a distended bladder, and this possibility must not be overlooked. Any apparatus attached to the patient should be checked frequently to ensure that it is secure and will not cause irritation of the tissue from movement or create tension from pulling. The nurse must ensure that dressings and casts are not too tight and do not restrict circulation or create irritating friction.

Reassurance that surgery is over and that the patient is doing well, as well as explanations of what is going on and what sensations will be experienced, do much to allay anxiety. The nurse should allow the patient as much decisional control as is realistic. The preferred site for an intravenous route, the timing of treatments, and the adjunctive pain relief modalities to be used are decisions into which the critical care patient can have input.

Pharmacological Management

Analgesics

A number of modalities are available for the management of postoperative pain, but first and foremost is the administration of appropriate analgesics. Concern for the side effects of narcotic analgesics has drastically limited treatment with narcotics that could be effective if used properly. Although it is true that use of narcotics eventually leads to addiction, this has never been a significant problem when they are used to treat acute pain from surgical procedures (Porter & Jick, 1980).

The goal for narcotic analgesic administration is to produce the highest and most constant concentration of narcotic analgesic possible without compromising ventilation.

Intravenous infusion. Routinely, narcotic analgesics should be administered in frequent intravenous doses or via titration of a continuous infusion. Maintaining blood serum concentrations at a stable level prevents the development of severe pain, which is more difficult to abate with drugs without producing drowsiness. Added advantages of the intravenous route are the assurance of accurate dosage and absorption, prompter action, and thus prompter relief.

There are few reliable indicators of analgesic requirements for the relief of postoperative pain. Narcotics often are prescribed on the basis of body weight, but weight does not seem to be a reliable predictor of analgesic need (Faherty & Grier, 1984; Keeri-Szanto & Heaman, 1972). Elderly patients and children often are undermedicated for postoperative pain because it is assumed that they tolerate pain better. This is not necessarily so (Burokas, 1985; Faherty & Grier, 1984).

Critically ill or injured patients should be assessed carefully for concomitant physical problems, such as decreased circulation or decreased kidney and liver function. These conditions could affect both uptake and clearance of analgesics and therefore could prolong the duration of action of these drugs.

Narcotics must be used judiciously for the postoperative patient with chronic obstructive pulmonary disease (COPD). Narcotics should be used in lower than normal doses, or, if the COPD is severe, they should be avoided completely. Meperidine may be preferred over morphine because it seems to be somewhat less of a respiratory depressant and acts as a bronchodilator. The opiates, such as codeine, are generally contraindicated because they severely depress the cough reflex, stimulate bronchospasm, and produce thickened secretions. Ancillary measures such as repositioning, splinting the incision site, reducing anxiety, using transcutaneous electrical nerve stimulation (TENS), or practicing relaxation exercises can reduce the need for narcotic drugs.

A history of myasthenia gravis should alert the nurse to rely less on narcotic pain relief. If the patient cannot tolerate narcotics, the nurse will have to rely on adjunctive nursing interventions for pain management. The myasthenia gravis patient often receives anticholinesterases; these drugs may potentiate morphine and other narcotics, so that doses should be reduced initially and increased only if required.

Nerve infusion. Narcotics, primarily morphine, or local anesthetics may be injected around nerves to block pain impulse conduction. These blocks are particularly useful for the relief of severe acute pain in the critically ill patient. The intercostal block, which provides complete relief of pain in the thoracic region, is particularly useful to treat unrelieved pain after thoracic surgery, for patients with chest tubes, and for multiple trauma patients with rib fractures and flail chest. A significant advantage of these central blocks in the postoperative patient is that pain relief is achieved without central depression; this means that no respiratory depression or interference with the patient's cough reflex will occur. The patient therefore can perform the ventilatory procedures necessary to cleanse the tracheobronchial tree after receiving anesthesia.

The intercostal block also may be used to provide pain relief after abdominal surgery and is particularly useful after splenectomy and cholecystectomy. A block to relieve pain in the lower abdominal regions may induce urinary retention, so that output should be monitored closely to avoid the problem of a distended bladder (Leib & Hurtig, 1985).

Analgesic Adjuncts

Analgesic adjuncts include drugs developed to alter a component of disease or injury that may contribute to the pain phenomenon or to relieve associated symptoms of pain. Retching and vomiting aggravate the effects of noxious stimuli, and alleviation of these symptoms may significantly reduce the postoperative pain experience. Often an antiemetic such as promethazine hydrochloride (Phenergan) or chlorpromazine (Compazine) may be given concurrently with an analgesic. Anxiety may be alleviated by the administration of a mild tranquilizer such as diazepam (Valium). Drugs administered to promote sleep, to relax muscles, or to reduce inflammatory processes also are useful in augmenting pain relief from the narcotics. An advantage of the concurrent administration of these drugs is the potentiation of the narcotic, but the nurse must be alert for an exaggeration of respiratory depression when these drugs are administered during the postanesthesia period.

Noninvasive Interventions

The complexity of postoperative pain in the critically ill patient compels the nurse to design and implement multidimensional, combination approaches to prevent pain and as interventions for its relief. Combinations have been shown to be far more powerful than singular interventions. A number of adjunct pain relief measures may be added to the administration of analgesics to ensure adequate pain management for the postoperative patient.

Stimulation

Stimulation techniques include the application of heat or cold, pressure, massage, vibration, and TENS. These techniques are not used as often as they might be and can be quite useful in augmenting narcotic analgesia for the postoperative patient.

Warmth or heat provides relief from pain by improving circulation and promoting muscle relaxation. Cold applications are particularly useful to relieve pain after orthopedic procedures and to relieve incisional pain. Cold applications reduce edema and thus relieve pressure.

Controlled studies have demonstrated that TENS is effective for the alleviation of postoperative pain (Bakker, Wong, Wong, & Jenkins, 1980; Christoph, 1985; Miller-Jones, Phillips, Pitchford, and Smallpiece, 1980; Neary, 1981; Solomon, Viernstein, & Long, 1980). It is not satisfactory as the sole modality for pain relief in the critically ill postoperative patient but provides significant augmentation of narcotic analgesia. Because there are no deleterious side effects with TENS, it is an excellent adjunct for pain relief in the critical care unit. It is particularly effective for relieving the incisional pain associated with large thoracic and abdominal incisions. It may also be effective for relieving pain associated with chest tubes and sternal pain after open heart surgery.

Recent evidence indicates that it is safe to use TENS with patients with internal or external pacemakers (Shade, 1985). Nevertheless, TENS should be used with caution and the patient observed closely for any adverse effects. TENS may interfere with electrical monitoring equipment. The method has not been tested with patients who are taking anticoagulant medications, who are pregnant, or who have a diagnosis of myasthenia gravis and should be used with caution because its effects are unknown.

Relaxation

Relaxation may be induced through the use of back rubs, massage, light stroking, heat, reassurance, personal attention, or learned relaxation techniques. Relaxation usually is not sufficient as the only pain relief modality but can significantly augment the effect of narcotic analgesia for the postoperative patient. Relaxation is effective in increasing tolerance to pain and in reducing the amount of narcotic analgesia necessary to control pain (Wells, 1982).

Behavioral Techniques

Behavioral techniques that may be used to augment pain relief for the postoperative patient include biofeedback, hypnosis, distraction, diversion, imagery, and music therapy. For the most part, these techniques are only useful in the critical care unit if the patient has previously been taught how to use them or has previous experience with them. A patient's preference for one technique over another will have a substantial influence on its effectiveness. Behavioral techniques for pain control can be powerful and are particularly desirable for use in the critically ill patient because they are safe and have few, if any, demonstrated side effects. Some of the behavioral techniques require concentrated and active thought processes. The clouding of sensorium by residual anesthesia may preclude the use of behavioral techniques in the immediate postoperative period. Intense pain will adversely affect concentration and preclude successful use of these measures. In addition, the use of behavioral techniques for pain relief may be fatiguing, so that the nurse must plan accordingly.

CONCLUSION

In the face of maintaining the airways and providing circulatory support, postoperative pain relief may be given a low priority in the critical care unit. Given the deleterious effects that postoperative pain may have on the critically ill or injured patient, pain relief must be given a high priority and multidimensional measures taken to provide adequate relief.

REFERENCES

Bakker, S.B.C., Wong, C.C., Wong, P.C., & Jenkins, L.C. (1980). Transcutaneous electrostimulation in the management of postoperative pain: Initial report. *Canadian Anaesthesia Society Journal, 27*, 150–155.

Benedetti, C., Bonica, J., & Bellucci, G. (1984). Pathophysiology and therapy of postoperative pain: A review. *Advances in Pain Research and Therapy, 7*, 373–407.

Burokas, L. (1985). Factors affecting nurses' decision to medicate pediatric patients after surgery. *Heart & Lung, 14*, 373–379.

Christoph, S.B. (1985). A comparison of patient-controlled transcutaneous electrical stimulation with traditional analgesics for postoperative pain relief. Unpublished doctoral dissertation, Catholic University of America, Washington, DC.

Christoph, S.B. (1988). Pain. In M.R. Kinney, D.R. Packa, & S.B. Dunbar (Eds.), *American Association of Critical Care Nurse's clinical reference for critical care nurses* (2nd ed., pp. 372–398). New York: McGraw-Hill.

Drain, C.B., & Christoph, S.B. (1987). *The recovery room: A critical care approach to post anesthesia nursing* (2nd ed.). Philadelphia: Saunders.

Faherty, B.S., & Grier, M.R. (1984). Analgesic medication for elderly people post-surgery. *Nursing Research, 33*, 369–372.

Jaggard, R.S., Zager, L.L., & Wilkins, D.S. (1950). Clinical evaluation of analgesic drugs: A comparison of NU-2206 and morphine sulphate administered to postoperative patients. *Archives of Surgery, 61*, 1073.

Keats, A.S. (1956). Postoperative pain: Research and treatment. *Journal of Chronic Diseases, 4*, 72.

Keeri-Szanto, M., & Heaman, S. (1972). Postoperative demand analgesia. *Surgery, Gynecology, and Obstetrics, 134*, 647–661.

Leib, R.A., & Hurtig, J.B. (1985). Epidural and intrathecal narcotics for pain management. *Heart & Lung, 14*, 164–174.

Loan, W.B., & Dundee, J.W. (1967). The clinical assessment of pain. *Practitioner, 198*, 759.

McQualy, H.H., Carroll, D., & Morroe, R.A. (1988). Postoperative orthopaedic pain—The effect of opiate premedication and local anaesthetic blocks. *Pain, 33*, 291–295.

Miller-Jones, C.M., Phillips, D., Pitchford, E.A., & Smallpiece, C.J. (1980). Transcutaneous nerve stimulation in post-thoracotomy pain relief. *Anaesthesia, 35*, 1018.

Neary, J.M. (1981). Transcutaneous electrical nerve stimulation for the relief of post-incisional surgical pain. *American Association of Nurse Anesthetists Journal, 49*, 151–155.

Papper, R., Brodie, B.B., & Rovenstein, E.A. (1952). Postoperative pain: Its use in the comparative evaluation of analgesics. *Surgery, 32*, 107.

Porter, J., & Jick, H. (1980). Addiction rare in patients treated with narcotics. *New England Journal of Medicine, 302*, 123.

Shade, S.K. (1985). Use of transcutaneous electrical stimulation for a patient with a cardiac pacemaker. *Physical Therapy, 65*, 206–208.

Solomon, R.A., Viernstein, M.C., & Long, D.M. (1980). Reduction of postoperative pain and narcotic use by transcutaneous electrical stimulation. *Surgery, 87*, 142–146.

Wells, N. (1982). The effect of relaxation on postoperative muscle tension and pain. *Nursing Research, 31*, 236–238.

RECOMMENDED READING

Bach, S., Noreng, M.F., & Tjellden, N.U. (1988). Phantom limb pain in amputees during the first 12 months following limb amputation, after preoperative lumbar epidural blockade. *Pain, 33*, 297–311.

Beyer, J.E., DeGood, D.E., Ashley, L.C., & Russell, G.A. (1983). Patterns of postoperative analgesic use with adults and children following cardiac surgery. *Pain, 17*, 71–81.

Kaiko, R.F., Wallenstein, S., Rogers, A., Grabinski, P., & Houde, R. (1982). Narcotics in the elderly. *Medical Clinics of North America, 66*, 1079–1089.

Ketovuori, H. (1987). Nurses' and patients' conceptions of wound pain and the administration of analgesics. *Pain, 2*, 213–218.

Radwin, L.E. (1987). Autonomous nursing interventions for treating the patient in acute pain: A standard. *Heart & Lung, 16*, 258–266.

Scott, L.E., Clum, G.A., & Peoples, J.B. (1983). Preoperative predictors of postoperative pain. *Pain, 15*, 283–293.

Tan, S.-Y. (1982). Cognitive and cognitive-behavioral methods for pain control: A selective review. *Pain, 12*, 201–228.

Thompson, S.C. (1981). Will it hurt less if I can control it? A complex answer to a simple question. *Psychological Bulletin, 90*, 89–101.

Wall, P.D. (1988). The prevention of postoperative pain. *Pain, 33*, 289–290.

Chapter 14

The Patient with Cancer Pain in the Critical Care Environment

Diana J. Wilkie

In a recent international survey of 669 nurses, the overwhelming majority indicated that their nursing education included little or no training in cancer pain management (Pritchard, 1988). Given this dismal finding, the purpose of this chapter is to provide the critical care nurse with practical information about cancer pain management. More specifically, the aims are to identify characteristics of patients with cancer pain who may be admitted to critical care units and to discuss cancer pain assessment and management from a multidimensional perspective. A case study is utilized to demonstrate practical application of such a perspective for assessment and management of cancer pain.

FACTORS INFLUENCING ADMISSION TO CRITICAL CARE

Oncology is a medical and nursing specialty with a rapidly expanding knowledge base that is developed through experimental protocols. Given the rapidity with which technological and therapeutic advances are made in oncology, a number of environmental and health factors influence the type of patient who is likely to receive care from the critical care nurse. These factors are summarized in Table 14-1, but several warrant brief discussion.

Factors Related to the Environment

Institutional, governmental, and family factors are examples of environmental determinants of the type of patient admitted to the critical care unit with cancer and pain. Institutional factors are the most common because advances in oncology care are not implemented simultaneously in all health care institutions. In settings with well-developed oncology units, only very ill patients receive care in critical care

Table 14-1 Factors Influencing Admission to Critical Care

Factor	Patient Characteristics
Environmental	
Institutional	Quantity and type of research
	Teaching or nonteaching hospital
	Specified oncology unit(s)
	Hospital policies
	Philosophy of nursing care
	Staffing patterns
Governmental	Regulations
	Reimbursement patterns
Family-culture/	Awareness/acceptance of patient's status
religious beliefs	
Health	
Cancer related	Septic shock
	Disseminated intravascular coagulation
	Cerebral herniation
	Seizures
	Spinal subdural hematomas
	Severe thrombocytopenia
	Vascular erosion/hemorrhage
	Visceral perforation
	Acute mesenteric ischemia
Non–cancer related	Myasthenia gravis
	Rapidly progressive polyneuropathies
	Myocardial infarction
	Acute adult respiratory distress syndrome

units because innovations in oncology are implemented by highly skilled oncology nurses. In those institutions with limited oncologic nursing expertise, however, all but the general oncology patient may be admitted to the critical care unit for innovative therapies to be implemented. Hospital policy, staffing patterns, equipment availability, and physicians' treatment patterns may affect the types of patients admitted to critical care.

Governmental factors also influence the type of patient admitted to critical care. For example, phase 1 analgesic drug trials may necessitate critical care admission of patients who are not critically ill but who require frequent monitoring because of Food and Drug Administration specifications (Krames, Wilkie, & Gershow, 1986).

Family members, too, may be important environmental factors influencing a patient's admission to the critical care unit. When family members are not able to accept the terminal state of their loved one, they may insist on every possible life-saving procedure, including admission to critical care. In this and other situations, family members may provide meaningful information about the patient's pain and effective management strategies when the critical care nurse collaborates with the family in the patient's care. Additionally, such collaboration may help the family accept the patient's status.

Factors Related to Health

Individuals who have cancer may be admitted to critical care for various health reasons, both related and unrelated to the cancer (Griffin, 1985; Nealon, 1985). Life-threatening toxicities from cancer chemotherapy (Carlon & Goldiner, 1985), obstruction or erosion of vital organs by the neoplasm (Turnbull, 1985), myocardial infarction, or respiratory distress syndrome are examples of conditions that may necessitate critical care of a patient with cancer pain. These health factors contribute to the complexity of managing cancer pain.

Factors Related to the Person

Although the meaning of cancer to a patient is not a crucial factor affecting critical care admission, the personal meaning of the cancer experience influences patients' responses to cancer-related pain. Additionally, an individual's past experience with pain may influence responses to cancer pain.

MULTIDIMENSIONAL PERSPECTIVE OF CANCER PAIN

Like other types of pain, cancer pain is a complex, subjective experience (Ahles, Blanchard, & Ruckdeschel, 1983; McGuire, 1987b). A host of factors contributes to the unique nature of cancer pain, including biological, psychological, social, and cultural attributes (McGuire, 1987b). These attributes represent the multiple dimensions of pain previously identified in Chapter 4, that is the physiological, sensory, affective, cognitive, and behavioral dimensions (Ahles et al., 1983). When a person with cancer is considered a biological and behavioral being (Johnson, 1980; Wilkie, Lovejoy, Dodd, & Tesler, 1988), the physiological and sensory dimensions of pain are related to the biological system, and the affective, cognitive, and behavioral dimensions are related to the behavioral system. Each dimension is crucial to understanding the intricacies of cancer pain.

Biological System

Physiological Dimension of Cancer Pain

Physiologically, the presence of malignant cells affects a number of biological systems and may result in nociception and pain. An important factor in this process is the nature of cancer. Cancer is not a single disease but rather a complex of diseases differentiated by primary site and tumor histology. Pain associated with one primary malignancy is somewhat different from pain related to other primary tumors because the rate and pattern of tumor growth vary for different tumor types. Data suggest that the incidence, location, intensity, and quality of cancer pain may vary by the anatomical structures invaded or compressed by the tumor (Daut & Cleeland, 1982; Greenwald, Bonica, & Bergner, 1987). Summarized in Table 14-2 are specifics of tumor growth patterns and the characteristics of pain associated with four common primary malignancies.

Tumor growth is but one of three causes of the pain that may be experienced by individuals with cancer. In addition, patients with cancer may have pain related to the antitumor therapies as well as pain totally unrelated to the cancer (Foley, 1979). Studies indicate that tumor progression accounts for nearly 78% of all pain experienced by patients with cancer, whereas therapy-related pain accounts for approximately 25% of the pain seen in patients with cancer (Daut & Cleeland, 1982; Foley, 1979; Twycross & Fairfield, 1982). Up to 45% of inpatients and 10% of outpatients with cancer experience pain unrelated to the cancer, such as migraine headaches, arthritis, and musculoskeletal pain (Foley, 1979; Kanner & Foley, 1981; Twycross & Fairfield, 1982). Therefore, pain

---

Table 14-2 Physiological Patterns of Cancer Pain

Primary Neoplasm	Typical Growth Rate[a]	Usual Distant Metastatic Sites[a]	Pain[b]	
			Incidence	Severity
Lung	Variable-Rapid	Brain Bone Viscera	40-80%	Moderate-Severe
Breast	Variable	Bone Lung Brain	56-94%	Moderate-Severe
Prostate	Slow	Bone	55-80%	Moderate-Severe
Colon/Rectum	Slow	Liver Lung	32-63%	Moderate-Severe

[a]*Source:* From *Cancer: Principles and Practice of Oncology*, 2nd ed., by V.T. De Vita, S. Hellman, and S.A. Rosenberg (Eds.), 1989, Philadelphia, PA: J.B. Lippincott.
[b]*Source:* From "Treatment of Cancer Pain: Current Status and Future Needs" by J.J. Bonica, 1985, *Advances in Pain Research and Therapy, 9,* pp. 589–616.

experienced by the patient with cancer may be related to the cancer or cancer therapy or may be unrelated to the cancer. Distinction among these three types of pain is crucial to appropriate application of pain therapy for the patient with cancer.

Pain related to cancer. Tumor proliferation may cause pain by encroaching on somatic, visceral, and neuronal structures. Soft tissue, skin, and bone are common somatic structures penetrated by primary and metastatic tumors. Bone pain is the most common type of cancer pain (Coyle & Foley, 1987) and may be present before objective evidence of bony disease (Kanner, Martini, & Foley, 1982; Low, 1981). Visceral pain may occur when tumor invades thoracic, abdominal, or pelvic viscera (e.g., lung pleura, liver, pancreas, or bladder). Peripheral and central nervous system structures, such as the brachial plexus, nerve root, or spinal cord, also may be invaded or compressed by proliferating tumor and result in severe pain.

Pain from tumor extension may represent an acute or chronic situation; this is defined by the temporal pattern and depends on the location and/or growth rate of the tumor (Foley, 1984). Acute pain has a well-defined temporal pattern, is a major symptom prompting patients to seek medical attention, and, with appropriate diagnosis and therapy, is usually relieved. Acute tumor-related pain frequently is a symptom of advanced disease, however. Abdominal pain caused by compression and obstruction of the bowel is an example of acute, tumor-related pain.

Tumors located close to vital structures or those with rapid growth rates may produce an oncological emergency, with pain often being the first symptom that the patient notes and reports. For example, in one study 90% of patients with epidural spinal cord compression (an oncological emergency) presented with back pain that was present for days to weeks before the development of weakness, sensory changes, or bowel or bladder dysfunction (Posner, 1985). With rapidly growing tumors, neurological signs and symptoms may occur sooner. Conversely, chronic radicular pain indicative of nerve root involvement may never progress to epidural cord compression if the tumor is slow growing (e.g., thyroid carcinoma).

When a neoplasm has a slow growth rate or is not responsive to anticancer therapies, tumor-related pain may persist and may be considered chronic cancer pain. Such pain often is difficult to control even when aggressive analgesic therapies are combined with psychological and behavioral therapies aimed at the "suffering" component of the experience (Foley, 1984).

Therapy-related cancer pain may be related to the acute and chronic effects of antitumor interventions: surgery, chemotherapy, immunotherapy, or radiation therapy. Acute, therapy-related cancer pain is easily diagnosed, predictable, self-limiting, and endured to achieve a cancer cure (Coyle & Foley, 1987). Stomatitis after whole-body radiation for bone marrow transplantation is a prime example of acute, therapy-related cancer pain.

Additionally, antitumor therapies may cause chronic pain. Specific pain syndromes are associated with the major antitumor therapies, including postmastectomy pain, phantom limb pain, peripheral neuropathy, and radiation fibrosis. Because removal of the cause of these pain syndromes is not possible, they are challenging to manage (Foley, 1984).

Pain unrelated to cancer. Adequate diagnosis and management of pain experienced by the patient with cancer is contingent upon differentiating cancer-related from non–cancer-related pain. Patients with cancer are as likely to have acute or chronic conditions associated with pain as the general population. Flu symptoms, angina, migraine headaches, and arthritis are examples of pain that may be experienced by individuals with cancer, but these pains are unrelated to the cancer. Commonly, patients and clinicians assume that any new pain is evidence of recurrent or metastatic disease; this assumption is premature, however, until the pain is proven to be related to the cancer. Presence of acute or chronic nonmalignant pain may amplify the cancer pain and create a pain syndrome that is difficult to treat (Foley, 1984; Kanner, 1988).

Summary. To summarize, the physiological dimension of cancer pain is complex because of the varied characteristics of neoplasms, including the primary site, preferred treatment modality, metastatic pattern, and trajectory of a particular tumor. Numerous somatic, visceral, and neuronal structures may be invaded or activated by tumor growth or affected by antitumor therapies. Additionally, patients with cancer may have pain that is not at all related to their cancer diagnosis. Because of the complexity of pain in the patient with cancer, careful assessment is warranted.

Sensory Dimension of Cancer Pain

The sensory dimension includes the location, intensity, quality, onset, and duration of the pain (Ahles et al., 1983). Each of these components is crucial to assessment and management of cancer pain.

Location. A number of studies have demonstrated that patients with cancer pain have pain in more than one location (i.e., Twycross & Fairfield, 1982; Wilkie et al., 1988). It is not unusual for patients to have at least two painful areas, with an occasional patient reporting up to 14 different pain locations (Wilkie et al., 1988). Of course, not all painful areas are related to tumor progression. Thorough assessment of each pain reported by the patient is crucial to distinguish tumor pain from therapy- and non–tumor-related pain.

Intensity. Cancer pain is assumed to be more intense than other pain syndromes (Levin, Cleeland, & Dar, 1985). A recent review of research that used one measure of pain intensity, the McGill Pain Questionnaire (MPQ), found that cancer pain is similar to other pain syndromes, including acute, chronic, and experimentally induced pain (Wilkie, Savedra, Holzemer, Tesler, & Paul, 1990). Depending on a number of factors, cancer pain intensity ranges from minimal to most severe and changes with effective therapy (Krames et al., 1985). Therefore, pain intensity is a vital parameter for initial and follow-up assessment of cancer pain.

Quality. A number of studies have demonstrated that patients with cancer pain describe their pain with similar words (Graham, Bond, Gerkovitch, & Cook, 1980; McGuire, 1984; Zimmerman, Duncan, Pozehl, & Schmitz, 1987). These words show some similarities and dissimilarities with words used by patients with other pain syndromes. Eighteen of the 78 words from the MPQ (Melzack, 1975) are commonly selected by patients with cancer pain (Wilkie et al., 1990; Table 14-3). It is hypothesized that these words represent a domain of language from which descriptors could be drawn for presentation to a patient with cancer pain who is unable to complete the entire MPQ, such as a critically ill patient. Research is necessary to test this hypothesis. Additionally, research is needed to determine whether pain language varies by variables related to the primary neoplasm because pain quality has not been investigated adequately when important oncological variables have been controlled.

Onset and duration. The temporal component of cancer pain is a crucial assessment parameter. Cancer pain may be constant, intermittent, or transient. Additionally, the patterns associated with the temporal component of cancer pain may be predictable or unpredictable. Because bone pain is common, often cancer pain occurs when the patient moves. The patient may be pain free at rest but

---

Table 14-3 Common Language of Cancer Pain: Pain Quality Descriptors from the MPQ

Sensory Words	Affective Words	Evaluative Words	Miscellaneous Words
Shooting	Exhausting	Unbearable	Nagging
Heavy	Sickening	Intense	Torturing
Sharp	Terrifying		Tight
Gnawing	Tiring		
Burning			
Throbbing			
Stabbing			
Tender			
Aching			

Source: Wilkie, D.J., Savedra, M., Holzemer, W.L., Tesler, M., & Paul, S. (1990). Use of the McGill Pain Questionnaire to measure pain: A meta-analysis. *Nursing Research, 39,* 36–41.

experience excruciating pain when making the simplest movement, such as raising or lowering the head of the bed or turning from side to side. Intermittent or transient pain may be problematic for the patient because most pharmacological analgesics exert action beyond the painful period and result in unacceptable side effects, such as sedation. Pain with a constant temporal pattern is more likely to be controlled effectively with pharmacological analgesics with fewer side effects.

Summary. To summarize, assessing the sensory dimension is crucial to adequate management of cancer pain. Critical care clinicians must remember that patients with cancer pain may have multiple pain sites that may vary in intensity, quality, and temporal pattern. Careful assessment and reassessment are necessary to evaluate fully the impact of therapy on these various components of cancer pain.

Biological Therapies for Cancer Pain

Physiological and sensorial complexities prove challenging to cancer pain management. Hence a number of therapies have been used, including antitumor, pharmacological, neurostimulatory, and neuroablative procedures. Although it is beyond the scope of this chapter to review fully all these cancer pain management modalities, several warrant brief discussion.

Antitumor therapies. When cancer pain occurs as a result of tumor progression, elimination of the tumor is the preferred pain-management therapy. Antitumor therapies, however, require time to reduce tumor bulk and to relieve the associated pain. Therefore, other analgesic therapies are needed while antitumor therapies are being used to eliminate tumor and when these therapies are ineffective.

Pharmacological therapies. Cancer pain pharmacological therapies are numerous. They include opiate and nonopiate drugs, which may be administered by systemic or spinal routes. Recently, the World Health Organization (WHO) published cancer pain-relief guidelines to promote systematic use of drugs in a model known as the Analgesic Ladder (WHO, 1986). The Analgesic Ladder provides for stepwise use of nonnarcotic drugs, weak narcotic drugs, and strong narcotic drugs with the addition of adjuvant drugs at any of the three steps (Fig. 14-1).

When the Analgesic Ladder was used, nearly 11% of 871 patients with advanced cancer pain were adequately treated with aspirin or acetaminophen (choice Step 1 drugs) until their deaths (Ventafridda, Tamburini, Caraceni, De Conno, & Naldi, 1987). Another 24% of the patients were maintained until death on weak narcotics (Step 2), and 61% required strong narcotics (Step 3) to control their pain. Although most of the patients were advanced to Step 3 drugs, 35% obtained adequate pain control at Steps 1 or 2, suggesting that systematic use of pharmacological therapies should include nonnarcotic drugs with progression to weak and strong narcotic drugs as necessary.

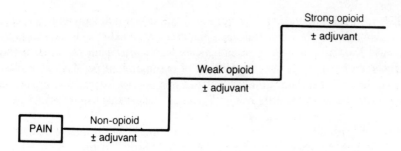

Figure 14-1 The analgesic ladder. *Source:* From *Cancer Pain Relief*, 1986, Geneva: World Health Organization. Copyright 1986 by World Health Organization. Reprinted by permission.

Oral morphine is the drug of choice at step 3 (WHO, 1986). Data, however, are accumulating regarding the efficacy of oral methadone as a Step 3 drug. Like morphine, methadone is a μ receptor opiate agonist, but methadone is more lipophilic and has a lower hepatic-extraction ratio than morphine, meaning that methadone has a long half-life (15 to 22 hours) and good bioavailability (average, 80% to 90%; Inturrisi, Colburn, Kaiko, Houde, & Foley, 1987). The average analgesic duration of methadone, however, is 4 to 5 hours. This means that methadone steady-state blood levels may not be achieved for 2 to 9 days and that there is a high risk of side effects, especially sedation, until steady state is achieved.

Until recently, these data were cited as a rationale against the use of methadone in chronic cancer pain management (Ettinger, Vitale, & Trump, 1979). Ventafridda, Ripamonti, Bianchi, Sbanotto, and De Conno (1986) evaluated this assumption when they randomized 54 patients with cancer pain to treatment with either oral morphine or methadone and similar adjuvant drugs. Although the patients were studied for only 14 days, analgesia and side effects were similar in the two groups. The patients on morphine escalated their dose 66% over the 2 weeks, whereas the patients on methadone maintained a stable dose, most probably because of the long half-life of methadone. These data provide initial evidence for the efficacy of methadone in cancer pain management. Nevertheless, longitudinal studies are needed to investigate fully the long-term use of this drug in cancer populations.

A common occurrence in cancer pain management is the necessity of large doses to control cancer pain. Whether increasing dose requirements are a function of disease progression or of the development of tolerance has not been established, but the reality of some patients' requiring huge doses is not disputed (Lo & Coleman, 1986). For example, the largest dose of continuously infused intravenous morphine reported in the literature to date has been 1,568 mg/hour (Miser, Moore, Green, Gracely, & Miser, 1986). Similarly, Coyle, Adelhardt, and Foley

(1987) reported that one patient required 35,000 mg of intramuscular morphine equivalents per day to achieve adequate analgesia. Such extreme doses, however, are rare. Data suggest that most outpatients with cancer pain can achieve and maintain analgesia with less than 600 mg of oral morphine per day (Twycross, 1988). The critical care clinician must remember, however, that analgesic response to the opiates is extremely variable and that patients require an analgesic therapy plan tailored to their individual needs.

When the patient with cancer pain requires critical care, health professionals must consider the patient's chronic opiate requirements. If the chronic pain is compounded by acute pain (e.g., surgical pain), additional opiates will be necessary. Additionally, if adjuvant drugs (e.g., tricyclic antidepressants, stimulants, and nonsteroidal anti-inflammatory agents) are not continued in the critically ill patient with cancer pain, increased amounts of opiate drugs will be required to maintain previous analgesic levels. The critical care nurse may be unfamiliar with administering the huge doses that are seen commonly in oncology practice. Therefore, use of equianalgesic conversion charts is essential to adequate management of the cancer pain as well as the additional acute pain experienced by the patient in the critical care setting (Table 14-4).

In addition to equianalgesic conversion charts, technical advances are becoming available to assist critical care nurses with dose conversions. For example, Grossman, Sheidler, and Fox (1989) developed a computer program that allows for rational equianalgesic conversion from one opiate to another. Although the program provides the physician with an estimate of the appropriate dose to prescribe, the program does not include individual factors that should be considered when a nurse administers opiates.

Oral analgesics do not always provide adequate analgesia for cancer pain (Kanner, 1988). Current trends are to use alternative routes of opiate administration, such as patient-controlled analgesia devices (particularly for intermittent pain), continuous subcutaneous or intravenous infusions, and intraspinal or intraventricular boluses or infusions (McGuire, 1987a; Payne, 1987).

Use of totally implantable infusion devices is becoming more popular for intraspinal opiate administration (Krames et al, 1985; Penn, Paice, Gottschalk, & Ivankovich, 1984). Two types of implantable infusion devices are currently available: the Infusaid and the Medtronics pumps. The Infusaid pump has a set flow rate that may be influenced by the patient's body temperature. The critical care nurse must recognize that elevated body temperature may increase the pump-delivered amount of opiate (5% per 0.5 Celcius degree), or it may reduce the opiate dose in hypothermic conditions. If body temperature cannot be stabilized, the opiate concentration must be altered to maintain acceptable analgesic and side effect levels. The Medtronics pump infusion rate can be modified, and body temperature is not crucial to analgesic delivery. Both pumps must be refilled on schedule, usually at 2- to 4-week intervals. Intraspinal (epidural or intrathecal)

Table 14-4 An Equianalgesic Comparison of Common Analgesics Stepped According to the Analgesic Ladder (WHO, 1986)

Analgesic Ladder Step	Drug	Dose	Equivalent to	Peak Effect	Duration	Plasma Half-Life
Step 1, nonopiates	Acetaminophen (Tylenol, Tempra, etc.)	600 mg orally 600 mg rectally	Aspirin, 600 mg	2 hours	3–4 hours	1–4 hours
	Acetylsalicylic acid (aspirin)	600 mg orally 600 mg rectally	Morphine, 2 mg intramuscularly (IM)	2 hours Slower than oral	3–4 hours	15 minutes
Step 2, weak opiates	Codeine sulfate	30–60 mg orally 200 mg orally	Aspirin, 600 mg Morphine, 10 mg IM Codeine, 120 mg IM	2 hours	3–4 hours	2.5–3 hours
	Oxycodone (Roxicodone w/aspirin—Percodan w/acetaminophen—Percocet)	5 mg orally 30 mg orally	Codeine, 60 mg orally Morphine, 10 mg IM	1 hour	3–4 hours	2–3 hours
	Propoxyphene HCL (Darvon, Dolene)	65 mg orally	Aspirin, 600 mg	2 hours	3–4 hours	12 hours
	Propoxyphene napsylate (Darvon N w/acetaminophen—Darvocet N)	100 mg orally	Aspirin, 600 mg	2 hours	3–4 hours	12 hours

Table 14-4 continued

Analgesic Ladder Step	Drug	Dose	Equivalent to	Peak Effect	Duration	Plasma Half-Life
	Pentazocine HCL (Talwin); may cause abstinence reaction in patients physically dependent on narcotics	60 mg IM 30 mg orally 180 mg orally	Morphine, 10 mg IM Aspirin, 600 mg Morphine, 10 mg IM Pentazocine, 60 mg IM	1 hour 2 hours	3–4 hours 3–4 hours	2–3 hours 2–3 hours
Step 3, strong opiates	Morphine sulfate Immediate release (tablets, liquids, Roxanol)	30 mg orally[a] 30 mg rectally[a]	Morphine, 10 mg IM Morphine, 10 mg IM	2 hours	4–5 hours	2.5–3 hours
	Sustained release (MS Contin, Roxanol SR)	30 mg orally[a]	Morphine, 10 mg IM	3.5 hours	8–12 hours	4 hours
	Preserved or preservative free (Astramorph, Duramorph)	10 mg Im 5 mg intravenously (IV)		1 hour 15–30 minutes	4–5 hours 2–4 hours	
	Methadone HCL	20 mg orally 10 mg IM 5 mg IV	Morphine, 10 mg IM Methadone, 10 mg IM Morphine, 10 mg IM	2 hours 1 hour 15–30 minutes	4–5 hours 4–5 hours 3–4 hours	15–22 hours

Drug	Dose	Equianalgesic	Onset	Duration	Half-life
Hydromorphone HCL (Dilaudid)	7.5 mg orally 3 mg rectally	Morphine, 10 mg IM Hydromorphone, 1.5 mg IM	1 hour	3–4 hours	2–3 hours
	1.5 mg IM 1 mg IV	Morphine, 10 mg IM	30 minutes 15 minutes	3 hours 2–3 hours	2–3 hours
Meperidine HCL (Demerol, Pethadol); causes central nervous system excitation ranging from irritability to seizures	50 mg orally 300 mg orally	Aspirin, 600 mg Morphine, 10 mg IM Meperidine, 75 mg IM	2 hours	3–4 hours	3 hours
	75 mg IM 50 mg IV	Morphine, 10 mg IM	1 hour 5–15 minutes	2–4 hours 2–3 hours	
Oxymorphone HCL (Numorphan)	1 mg IM 0.5 mg IV 10 mg rectally	Morphine, 10 mg Morphine, 10 mg IM Oxymorphone, 1 mg IM	1 hour 15–30 minutes 2 hours	4–5 hours 3–4 hours 6 hours	Unknown
Levorphanol tartrate (LevoDromoran)	4 mg orally 2 mg IM 1 mg IV	Morphine, 10 mg IM Levorphanol, 2 mg IM Morphine, 10 mg IM	2 hours 1 hour 15–30 minutes	4–5 hours 4–5 hours 3–4 hours	15 hours
Butorphanol tartrate (Stadol); see pentazocine	2 mg IM 2 mg IV	Morphine, 10 mg IM	1 hour 30 minutes	3–4 hours 3–4 hours	2.7 hours
Nalbuphine HCL (Nubain); see pentazocine	10 mg IM 10 mg IV	Morphine, 10 mg IM Pentazocine, 60 mg IM	1 hour 30 minutes	4–5 hours 3–4 hours	5 hours

[a]Repeated dose conversion that is equivalent to 60 mg in single-dose conversion.

Source: From *Cancer Pain Management*, (pp. 151–201) by D.B. McGuire and C.H. Yarbro (Eds.), 1987, Orlando, FL: Grune and Stratton. Copyright 1987 by Grune and Stratton. Adapted by permission.

opiate requirements must be included when calculating the patient's opiate needs. Intrathecal morphine doses have been reported to be as high as 140 mg/day with no compromise of respiratory function (Krames & Wilkie, 1985).

Regardless of the route by which pharmacological interventions are provided to the patient with cancer pain, most patients require supplemental opiates for "breakthrough" pain or as a "rescue." Patients become highly skilled in titrating their medications to achieve a balance of analgesia and opiate-related side effects. In the critical care setting, the patient may not be able to fulfill this role but instead may have to depend on a nurse who may be unfamiliar with opiate titration. Careful assessment is the key to the nurse's successfully fulfilling this role for the critically ill patient.

Neurostimulatory and neuroablative procedures. Neurological procedures also are important therapy considerations for cancer pain. Ventafridda and associates (1987) found that neurolytic procedures were a necessary supplement to the WHO Analgesic Ladder for 29% of 1,229 patients with advanced cancer. Surgical, percutaneous, or chemical neurolytic procedures may be used, depending on the patient's condition and available medical expertise. Percutaneous cordotomy appears to offer benefit to patients with a life expectancy less than 1 year and unilateral, well-localized pain (Cleeland et al., 1986).

Summary

To summarize, numerous modalities are effective in controlling cancer pain. Experts in the field have developed guidelines (WHO, 1986) and an algorithm (Cleeland et al., 1986) to help clinicians make systematic decisions in the application of these biological modalities. These tools provide critical care clinicians with alternative therapies when a particular modality is not totally effective in controlling a patient's pain.

Behavioral System

Affective Dimension of Cancer Pain

In general, cancer may provoke feelings of fear, helplessness, and hopelessness as well as affective disturbances such as depression and anxiety (Bond, 1985; Bonica, 1985). Investigators have demonstrated positive correlations between pain and affective disturbances and that affective disturbances improve or resolve when cancer pain is adequately treated (Bond, 1985; Bond & Pearson, 1969; Cohen, Ferrer-Brechner, Pavlov, & Reading, 1985). Whereas low pain intensity levels are associated with positive mood or affect, high pain intensity levels correlate with negative mood or affect.

Ahles and associates (1983) investigated affective variables in a sample of 40 patients with cancer pain and 37 pain-free patients and found that the presence of pain was associated with increased levels of anxiety and depression. Furthermore, hospitalized patients were more anxious than patients at home. Depression and anxiety were higher for those patients who believed that their pain was a sign of disease progression than for those who had not considered that possibility.

Although Bond (1978) reported that depressed persons tend to perceive cancer pain as more severe than people with a cheerful disposition, investigators have not systematically examined the relationship between pain and positive affect (e.g., joy or laughter). Anecdotal evidence suggests that positive affect may decrease pain (Cousins, 1983).

Cognitive Dimension of Cancer Pain

Beliefs and attitudes about pain, pain therapy, illness, and one's resources and ability to cope with pain are cognitive variables that may influence perception of pain (Ahles et al., 1983; Beecher, 1959; Daut & Cleeland, 1982). The cognitive dimension, however, has been the focus of limited research in cancer.

Beecher's (1959) classic finding that World War II soldiers with massive wounds reported little or no pain was interpreted as an indicator of the powerful effect of the mind over the body and suggests that the meaning that the individual gives to pain may influence the amount of pain perceived and reported. The meaning given to pain by individuals with cancer has been briefly explored with three major questions: (1) whether they believe that the pain is an indicator of disease progression (Ahles et al., 1983), (2) what they think causes the pain (Daut & Cleeland, 1982), and (3) what the pain means to them (McGuire, 1986). Data suggest that 40% to 60% of patients with cancer pain believe that their pain is caused by their cancer. The relationship between this belief and other critical cancer pain variables, such as pain intensity or pain quality, has not been evaluated, however.

Levin et al. (1985) found in a telephone survey of 496 randomly selected people from the general population that most (48%) rated cancer pain as extremely painful more frequently than the pain of heart attack, migraine, kidney stones, arthritis, toothache, or high blood pressure. Cancer treatment was believed by 79% of the sample to be moderately to very painful. Cancer pain was believed to be so painful that a person would consider stopping treatment (72%) or committing suicide (69%). Additionally, about 50% of the respondents were concerned about taking narcotic analgesics for cancer pain because the drugs were associated with confusion, disorientation, addiction, tolerance, and other unwanted side effects. These data indicate that, in the general population, beliefs and attitudes about cancer pain are quite negative and may influence decisions about cancer and cancer pain therapy.

Behavioral Dimension of Cancer Pain

The behavioral dimension of pain has been defined in a number of ways. Early behavioral studies defined pain behavior as somatic interventions (e.g., analgesic-consuming behaviors or medical treatment–seeking behaviors), impaired functioning (e.g., reduction of range of movement, curtailment of activities of daily living and job performance, and alteration or impairment of interpersonal relationships), and pain complaints (e.g., verbalization of pain, gasping, moaning, and contorted facial expressions; Frederickson, Lynd, & Ross, 1978). Later studies used a slight variation that defined behaviors as well behaviors (e.g., activity and physical exercise) and pain behaviors (e.g., medication intake, guarded movements, and time spent in bed; Keefe, 1982).

In keeping with these definitions, Ahles and associates (1983) investigated the behavioral dimension of cancer pain, defining it as activity level or analgesic intake. They studied 40 patients with cancer pain and 37 pain-free patients with cancer. The pain group was found to spend significantly less time walking or standing than the pain-free group. Activity level correlated negatively with affective and cognitive scores but not with sensory scores. Pain, not cancer, was found to be an important contributor to behavioral dysfunction because the pain group spent significantly less time walking or standing. Medication intake correlated significantly with sensory, affective, and cognitive variables. Most of these subjects (77%) reported that they communicated their pain effectively to others in the environment by indices such as facial expression (49%), mood changes (21%), going to bed (8%), and verbal complaints (6%). Responses from others when these behaviors were used included expression of concern (72%), offers of aid (72%), and assumption of the patient's responsibilities (49%).

More recently, investigators have defined the behavioral dimension to include behaviors used to control pain. Findings indicate that pain may be reduced, increased, or not affected by a number of behaviors, including pressure manipulation (massage, rubbing, and applying pressure), distraction, positioning, immobilization, guarding, and use of heat, cold, or analgesics (Barbour, McGuire, & Kirchhoff, 1986; Bressler, Hange, & McGuire, 1986; Copp, 1974; Donovan & Dillon, 1987; Wilkie et al., 1988). Because it is difficult to predict the effect of a particular behavior in a given patient, additional research is needed to determine when behaviors are and are not effective in controlling cancer pain.

Overall, research findings suggest that the behavioral dimension of pain includes various behavioral responses to pain, such as verbal and nonverbal expressions of pain, behaviors that control the pain, and behaviors prevented by the pain. In cancer populations, the behaviors used to control pain have received initial description. Little systematic research, however, has been conducted to describe behaviors used to express cancer pain or specific behaviors with which pain interferes. Full characterization of all three types of behavior remains to be completed and is crucial to accurate initial and follow-up cancer pain assessment.

To summarize, affective, cognitive, and behavioral components are significant elements in the cancer pain experience and most probably continue to impact the critically ill patient. However, much research is needed to fully understand this impact. Emotional responses may increase or decrease cancer pain. Erroneous beliefs or attitudes may contribute to more intense cancer pain. Additionally, cancer pain may interfere with a number of activities of daily living. Yet, patients may engage in a number of behaviors to express their pain to others or to control their pain.

Behavioral Therapies for Cancer Pain

Behavioral therapies are effective in the management of cancer pain as a single modality or in combination with biological therapies. Music, hypnosis, relaxation, attention diversion, guided imagery, provision of a supportive environment, and behavior modification are types of behavioral therapies that have been used in cancer pain management (Beck, 1988; Bond, 1985; Foley, 1984; Kanner, 1988; Spiegel, 1985). Most important, the various behavioral therapies can augment pharmacological therapy and thereby reduce the narcotic dose required to manage cancer pain (Kanner, 1988). The suffering component of cancer pain appears to be particularly influenced by behavioral therapies (Foley, 1984; Kanner, 1988). Nursing interventions, such as preparatory information and relaxation techniques, may be important behavioral methods of controlling cancer pain in the critical care setting.

NURSING CARE: INTEGRATING THE BIOLOGICAL AND BEHAVIORAL SYSTEMS

Thus far the discussion has included separate delineation of the biological and behavioral dimensions of cancer pain. Holistic nursing care, however, requires integration of all dimensions of the cancer pain experience. The following case presentation focuses attention on the needs of one person who experienced cancer pain in the critical care setting.

S.B., a 37-year-old, single mother of a 14-year-old boy, was diagnosed with infiltrating ductal right breast cancer in late August 1984. Initially, the tumor was metastatic to regional lymph nodes and was treated with simple mastectomy, chemotherapy, and radiation therapy. One year later, malignancy in her left breast was treated with mastectomy. In 1986, metastatic lung cancer required additional chemotherapy for 1 year. In July 1987, bone metastases were found and treated until December with chemotherapy, when radiation therapy was given to the sacral spine. In January 1988, S.B. developed a flail neck and was admitted to an intensive care unit after cervical spine stabilization with a halo traction device.

S.B. had complained of lumbar spine pain since her initial cancer diagnosis and had subsequently developed right hip pain. Before her admission for the flail neck, S.B. required 60 mg of Roxanol (liquid morphine sulphate, 20 mg/mL) every 3 hours to control her chronic back and hip pain (480 mg per 24 hours). During the 12 hours immediately after laminectomy, S.B. received 100 mg of intramuscular (IM) meperidine (Demerol), 50 mg of IM hydroxyzine (Vistaril), and 70 mg of intravenous (IV) morphine sulfate. Late in the morning of the first postoperative day, S.B. was transferred to the oncology unit. Analgesic requirements during the postoperative period are listed in Table 14-5.

Initial assessment of S.B.'s pain revealed the following: (1) Antitumor therapies had been exhausted; (2) the disease trajectory was in a late, terminal phase; (3) her chronic pain had been effectively controlled before hospital admission for an oncological emergency (cervical spine instability and possible section of the spinal cord); (4) her acute and chronic pains were inadequately managed in the immediate postoperative period; and (5) she was very anxious about the poor control of her pain.

The most obvious nursing diagnosis was alteration in comfort: pain due to insufficient narcotic therapy. Whereas S.B. required 160 mg of IM morphine sulfate equivalents to control her chronic tumor-related pain, she received only 183 mg of IM morphine sulfate equivalents during the first 24 hours after cervical laminectomy. Clearly, she did not receive an adequate dose to control her pain,

Table 14-5 Analgesic Requirements of One Critically Ill Patient Experiencing Cancer Pain

Time	Analgesic Dose (in IM Morphine Equivalents)	Patient's Response
Before admission	160 mg/24 hours (480 mg orally)	Comfortable
After laminectomy		
0–12 hours	83 mg (intensive care unit)	Sharp, stabbing neck incision pain; bone pain, hip/pelvic area
13–24 hours	100 mg (oncology unit)	
25–72 hours	210 mg/24 hours	Comfortable
4–5 days	214–330 mg/24 hours	Comfortable
6–7 days	634–876 mg/24 hours	Comfortable
8–14 days	600–970 mg/24 hours (mean, 766 mg/24 hours)	Agitation; increasing pain; comfort obtained with increased dose and psychological support
15–19 days	890–1,105 mg/24 hours (mean, 1,039 mg/24 hours)	Comfortable

considering her tolerance to morphine and the additional pain stimulus that she encountered (laminectomy). It is not uncommon for the first 24-hour postoperative analgesic requirements to be 60 mg of morphine sulfate IM equivalents (10 mg IM every 4 hours) for a person naive to opiates. Therefore, a reasonable, conservative dose for S.B.'s pain during the first 24 hours would have been 220 mg, 37 mg more than she received. This inadequate management of her pain intensified her anxiety, and 15 mg of IV morphine every 1 to 2 hours was required to restore adequate analgesia (100 mg per 12 hours). Although physicians ordered 5 to 15 mg of IV morphine, it was not until S.B. was transferred to the oncology unit that she was given a 15-mg dose. Such a scenario is unnecessary when critical care nurses understand opiate tolerance and the massive doses commonly required to control cancer pain.

As indicated in Table 14-5, S.B.'s pain was adequately controlled for 1 week, when she began to require escalating morphine doses to maintain analgesia. Just when her postoperative pain would be expected to decrease, her pain began to escalate. Careful assessment of physiological, sensory, affective, behavioral, and cognitive factors revealed that behavioral, not biological, factors were more relevant to this escalation. Although she was recovering from the laminectomy, she began to realize that she was dying and she had yet to make arrangements for her 14-year-old son. Here the nursing diagnosis was alteration in comfort: pain due to affective, cognitive, and behavioral factors.

Based on the nursing diagnosis, a simple nursing intervention was effective in reducing her agitation and in improving analgesia: the convening of a family conference to discuss the disposition of her son. Assurance from her priest and family that one person would assume responsibility for her son was adequate to allow the morphine dose again to control her pain effectively. Before the identification of this problem all dose escalations resulted in increased agitation, but resolution of the problem allowed S.B. to obtain adequate rest and then to have more than 1 week of peace and comfort until she died. Here, a behavioral factor was overwhelmingly the most significant reason that analgesia was inadequate, whereas the first episode was mostly related to the biological factor of an insufficient dose for the acute and chronic pain.

Together, these data emphasize the importance of multidimensional assessment and treatment of cancer pain. Armed with a solid knowledge base about cancer pain, the critical care nurse is more likely to assess and treat adequately the multiple components of the cancer pain experience. Many of the treatments for the behavioral factors related to cancer pain are totally within critical care nurses' scope of practice, yet both behavioral and biological factors can be addressed by critical care nurses through collaborative practice with other health professionals.

CONCLUSION

Cancer pain is a complex, multidimensional phenomenon and a challenging nursing problem. Numerous factors must be considered when assessing and managing pain in the critically ill patient with cancer. Physiological, sensory, affective, cognitive, and behavioral factors influence the incidence and severity of cancer pain but provide multiple areas in which to intervene and to relieve the pain. This holistic approach is consistent with nursing perspectives and provides the critical care nurse with sound intervention options.

REFERENCES

Ahles, T.A., Blanchard, E.B., & Ruckdeschel, J.C. (1983). The multidimensional nature of cancer-related pain. *Pain, 17*, 277–288.

Barbour, L., McGuire, D., & Kirchhoff, K. (1986). Nonanalgesic methods of pain control used by cancer patients. *Oncology Nursing Forum, 13*, 56–60.

Beck, S.L. (1988, March). *The effect of the therapeutic use of music on cancer-related pain.* Paper presented at Key Aspects of Comfort: Management of Pain, Fatigue, and Nausea, Chapel Hill, NC.

Beecher, H.K. (1959). *Measurement of subjective responses.* Oxford: Oxford University Press.

Bond, M.R. (1978). Psychological and psychiatric aspects of pain. *Anesthesia, 33*, 355–361.

Bond, M.R. (1985). Cancer pain: Psychological substrates and therapy. In H.L. Fields, R. Dubner & F. Cervero (Eds.), *Advances in pain research and therapy*, (Vol. 9, pp. 559–567). New York: Raven Press.

Bond, M.R., & Pearson, I.B. (1969). Physiological aspects of pain in women with advanced cancer of the cervix. *Journal of Psychosomatic Research, 13*, 13–19.

Bonica, J.J. (1985). Treatment of cancer pain: Current status and future needs. In H.L. Fields, R. Dubner & F. Cervero (Eds.), *Advances in pain research and therapy*, (Vol. 9, pp. 589–616). New York: Raven Press.

Bressler, L.R., Hange, P.A., & McGuire, D.B. (1986). Characterization of the pain experience in a sample of cancer outpatients. *Oncology Nursing Forum, 13*, 51–55.

Carlon, G.C., & Goldiner, P.L. (1985). Complications of cancer therapy. In W.S. Howland & G.C. Carlon (Eds.), *Critical care of the cancer patient* (pp. 9–24). Chicago: Year Book Medical.

Cleeland, C.S., Rotondi, A., Brechner, T., Levin, A., MacDonald, N., Portenoy, R., Schutta, H., & McEniry, M. (1986). A model for the treatment of cancer pain. *Journal of Pain and Symptom Management, 1*, 209–215.

Cohen, R.S., Ferrer-Brechner, T., Pavlov, A., & Reading, A.E. (1985). Prospective evaluation of treatment outcome in patients referred to a cancer pain center. In H.L. Fields, R. Dubner & F. Cervero (Eds.), *Advances in pain research and therapy*, (Vol. 9, pp. 655–662). New York: Raven Press.

Copp, L.A. (1974). The spectrum of suffering. *American Journal of Nursing, 74*, 491–495.

Cousins, N. (1983). *The healing heart.* New York: Norton.

Coyle, N., Adelhardt, J., & Foley, K.M. (1987). Changing patterns in pain, drug use, and routes of administration in the advanced cancer patient. *Pain, 4*(Suppl.), S339.

Coyle, N., & Foley, J. (1987). Prevalence and profile of pain syndromes in cancer patients. In D.B. McGuire & C.H. Yarbro (Eds.), *Cancer pain management* (pp. 21–46). Orlando: Grune & Stratton.

Daut, R.L., & Cleeland, C.S. (1982). The prevalence and severity of pain in cancer. *Cancer, 50*, 1913–1918.

De Vita, V.T., Hellman, S., & Rosenberg, S.A. (Eds.). (1985). *Cancer: Principles and practice of oncology* (2nd ed.). Philadelphia: Lippincott.

Donovan, M.I., & Dillon, P. (1987). Incidence and characteristics of pain in a sample of hospitalized cancer patients. *Cancer Nursing, 10*, 85–92.

Ettinger, D.S., Vitale, P.J., & Trump, D.L. (1979). Important clinical pharmacological considerations in the use of methadone in cancer patients. *Cancer Treatment Reports, 63*, 457–459.

Foley, K.M. (1979). Pain syndromes in patients with cancer. In J.J. Bonica & V. Ventafridda (Eds.), *Advances in pain research and therapy*, (Vol. 2, pp. 59–75). New York: Raven Press.

Foley, K.M. (1984). The treatment of pain in the patient with cancer. *CA—A Cancer Journal for Clinicians, 36*, 194–215.

Frederickson, L.W., Lynd, R.S., & Ross, J. (1978). Methodology on the measurement of pain. *Behavioral Therapy, 9*, 486–488.

Graham, C., Bond, S.S., Gerkovitch, M.M., & Cook, M.R. (1980). Use of the McGill Pain Questionnaire in the assessment of cancer pain: Replicability and consistency. *Pain, 3*, 377–387.

Greenwald, H.P., Bonica, J.J., & Bergner, M. (1987). The prevalence of pain in four cancers. *Cancer, 60*, 2563–2569.

Griffin, J. (1985). Nursing care of the critically ill cancer patient. In W.S. Howland & G.C. Carlon (Eds.), *Critical care of the cancer patient* (pp. 339–347). Chicago: Year Book Medical.

Grossman, S., Sheidler, V., & Fox, M. (1989). *The Johns Hopkins Oncology Center's narcotic conversion program user's manual*. Philadelphia: Lea & Febiger.

Inturrisi, C.E., Colburn, W.A., Kaiko, R.F., Houde, R.W., & Foley, K.M. (1987). Pharmacokinetics and pharmacodynamics of methadone in patients with chronic pain. *Clinical Pharmacology and Therapeutics, 41*, 392–401.

Johnson, D. (1980). The behavioral system model for nursing. In J. Riehl & C. Roy (Eds.), *Conceptual models for nursing practice* (pp. 205–216). New York: Appleton-Century-Crofts.

Kanner, R. (1988). *Diagnosis and management of pain in patients with cancer*. Basel: Karger.

Kanner, R.M., & Foley, K.M. (1981). Patterns of narcotic drug use in a cancer pain clinic. *Annals of the New York Academy of Sciences, 362*, 161–172.

Kanner, R.M., Martini, N., & Foley, K.M. (1982). Incidence of pain and other clinical manifestations of superior pulmonary sulcus (pancoast) tumors. In J.J. Bonica, V. Ventafridda, & C.A. Pagni (Eds.), *Advances in pain research and therapy*, (Vol. 4, pp. 27–39). New York: Raven Press.

Keefe, F.J. (1982). Behavioral assessment and treatment of chronic pain: Current status and future directions. *Journal of Consulting and Clinical Psychology, 50*, 896–911.

Krames, E., Gershow, J., Glassberg, A., Kenefick, T., Lyons, A., Taylor, P., & Wilkie, D. (1985). Continuous infusion of spinally administered narcotics for the relief of pain due to malignant disorders. *Cancer, 56*, 696–702.

Krames, E.S., & Wilkie, D.J. (1985, April). *Continuous infusion of spinally administered narcotics: Dosages and flow patterns*. Report presented to the Food and Drug Administration, Anesthesiology Section, Washington, DC.

Krames, E.S., Wilkie, D.J., & Gershow, J. (1986). Intrathecal D-Ala^2-D-Leu^5-enkephalin (DADL) restores analgesia in a patient analgetically tolerant to intrathecal morphine sulfate. *Pain, 24*, 205–209.

Levin, D.N., Cleeland, C.S., & Dar, R. (1985). Public attitudes toward cancer pain. *Cancer, 56*, 2337–2339.

Lo, S.L., & Coleman, R.R., (1986). Exceptionally high narcotic analgesic requirements in a terminally ill cancer patient. *Clinical Pharmacology, 5*, 828–832.

Low, J.C. (1981). The radionuclide scan in bone metastasis. In G. Weiss (Ed.), *Bone metastasis* (pp. 231–244). Boston: Hall.

McGuire, D.B. (1984). Assessment of pain in cancer inpatients using the McGill Pain Questionnaire. *Oncology Nursing Forum, 11*, 32–37.

McGuire, D.B. (1986). *Cancer-related pain: A multi-dimensional approach.* Unpublished doctoral dissertation, University of Illinois at Chicago, Chicago, IL.

McGuire, D.B. (1987a). Advances in control of cancer pain. *Nursing Clinics of North America, 22*, 677–690.

McGuire, D.B. (1987b). The multidimensional phenomenon of cancer pain. In D.B. McGuire & C.H. Yarbro (Eds.), *Cancer pain management* (pp. 1–20). Orlando: Grune & Stratton.

Melzack, R. (1975). The McGill Pain Questionnaire: Major properties and scoring methods. *Pain, 1*, 277–299.

Miser, A.W., Moore, L., Green, R., Gracely, R.H., & Miser, J.S. (1986). Prospective study of continuous intravenous and subcutaneous morphine infusion for therapy-related or cancer-related pain in children and young adults with cancer. *Clinical Journal of Pain, 2*, 101–106.

Nealon, N. (1985). Neurologic complications in the cancer patient. In W.S. Howland & G.C. Carlon (Eds.), *Critical care of the cancer patient* (pp. 25–35). Chicago: Year Book Medical.

Payne, R. (1987). Novel routes of opioid administration in the management of cancer pain. *Oncology, 1*(Suppl.), 10–18.

Penn, R.D., Paice, J.A., Gottschalk, W., & Ivankovich, A.D. (1984). Cancer pain relief using chronic morphine infusion. *Journal of Neurosurgery, 61*, 302–306.

Posner, J.B. (1985). Back pain and epidural spinal cord compression. In K. Foley (Course Director), *Management of pain: Syllabus of the postgraduate course* (pp. 51–63). New York: Memorial Sloan-Kettering Cancer Center.

Pritchard, A.P. (1988). Management of pain and nursing attitudes. *Cancer Nursing, 11*, 203–209.

Spiegel, D. (1985). The use of hypnosis in controlling cancer pain. *CA—A Journal for Clinicians, 35*, 221–231.

Turnbull, A.D. (1985). The surgical oncologist's role in the intensive care unit. In W.S. Howland & G.C. Carlon (Eds.), *Critical care of the cancer patient* (pp. 318–338). Chicago: Year Book Medical.

Twycross, R.G. (1988). The management of pain in cancer: A guide to drugs and dosages. *Oncology, 2*, 35–43.

Twycross, R.G., & Fairfield, S. (1982). Pain in far-advanced cancer. *Pain, 14*, 303–310.

Ventafridda, V., Ripamonti, C., Bianchi, M., Sbanotto, A., & De Conno, F. (1986). A randomized study on oral administration of morphine and methadone in the treatment of cancer pain. *Journal of Pain and Symptom Management, 1*, 203–207.

Ventafridda, V., Tamburini, M., Caraceni, A., De Conno, F., & Naldi, F. (1987). A validation study of the WHO method for cancer pain relief. *Cancer, 59*, 850–856.

Wilkie, D.J., Lovejoy, N., Dodd, M., & Tesler, M. (1988). Cancer pain control behaviors: Description and correlation with pain intensity. *Oncology Nursing Forum, 15*, 723–731.

Wilkie, D.J., Savedra, M., Holzemer, W.L., Tesler, M., & Paul, S. (1990). Use of the McGill Pain Questionnaire to measure pain: A meta-analysis. *Nursing Research, 39*, 36–41.

'World Health Organization. (1986). *Cancer pain relief.* Geneva: Author.

Zimmerman, L., Duncan, K., Pozehl, B., & Schmitz, R. (1987). Pain descriptors used by patients with cancer. *Oncology Nursing Forum. 14*, 67–71.

RECOMMENDED READING

Catalano, R. (1987). Pharmacological management in the treatment of cancer pain. In D.B. McGuire & C.H. Yarbro (Eds.), *Cancer pain management* (pp. 151–201). Orlando: Grune & Stratton.

Foley, K.M., & Arbit, E. (1989). Management of cancer pain. In V.T. De Vita, S. Hellman, & S.A. Rosenberg (Eds.), *Cancer: Principles and practice of oncology* (3rd ed., Vol. 2, pp. 2064–2087). Philadelphia: Lippincott.

Howland, W.S., & Carlon, G.C. (1985). *Critical care of the cancer patient*. Chicago: Year Book Medical.

McGuire, D.B., & Yarbro, C.H. (1987). *Cancer pain management*. Orlando: Grune & Stratton.

Index

A

A-delta fiber, 11, 13–14
Acetaminophen
   burn, 206
   infant, 145
Acute myocardial infarction. *See*
   Myocardial infarction
Acute myocardial ischemia. *See*
   Myocardial ischemia
Acute pain, chronic pain, compared, 177
Addiction, physical dependence,
   compared, 147–148
Adult vs. infant pain differences, 140–141
Affective dimension, pain assessment,
   52–53
Analgesia. *See also* Specific type
   burn, 200–202, 202–205, 206
   cancer pain, 230–236, 240
   endogenous, 17–22
   infant, 145–146
   myocardial ischemia, 187–188
   opioid, 18–19
   postoperative pain and, 216–218
Analgesic ladder, cancer pain, 230–236
Analog chromatic continuous scale, 51
Anchoring, 129

Anesthesia
   intravenous, 91
   local, infant, 144–145
   postoperative pain, 213–214
Angina
   Prinzmetal's, 177
   referred pain, 182
   stable, 175–176
   unstable, 176
Antihistamine, infant, 145
Anxiety, 33–35
   burn, 202–205, 206
   cancer pain, 237
   cross-cultural study, 67–68
   myocardial ischemia, 188
   pain assessment, 52–53
   postoperative, 218
   preprocedural information, 123–124
Anxiolytic, infant, 146–147
Assessment, 45–64
   analog chromatic continuous scale, 51
   anxiety, 52–53
   autonomic nervous system, 52
   barriers, 46–48
      environment, 47
      health professional, 47–48
      personal characteristics, 46–47